CHEKHOV'S LEADING LADY

CHEKHOV'S
LEADING LADY

A Portrait of the Actress
OLGA KNIPPER

HARVEY PITCHER

John Murray
LONDON

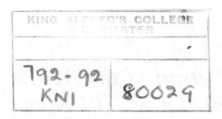
© Harvey Pitcher 1979

First published 1979
by John Murray (Publishers) Ltd
50 Albemarle Street, London WIX 4BD

Printed in Great Britain by
Latimer Trend & Company Ltd, Plymouth

British Library Cataloguing in Publication Data
Pitcher, Harvey John
Chekhov's leading lady.
1. Knipper, Ol'ga Leonardovna
2. Actors – Russia – Biography
I. Title
792'.028'0924   PN2728.K/
ISBN 0–7195–3681–2

Contents

		Introduction	I
PART I	1	Finding a Vocation	7
	2	Summer at Pushkino	18
	3	Fiasco	25
	4	Triumph	33
	5	The Other Women	43
	6	Dear Author . . . Dear Actress	54
	7	Anton Delays	66
	8	Winter 1900	78
	9	A Quiet Wedding	89
PART 2	10	Masha's Reactions	103
	11	Hopes and Disappointments	109
	12	The Lyubimovka Crisis	118
	13	Anton's Last Appearance	128
	14	Badenweiler	140
	15	Olga's Last Letters	150
	16	Verdicts	162
PART 3	17	First Revolution and First Tour	171
	18	Knipper the Actress	177
	19	Knipper in Chekhov	190
	20	Dear Temple	200
	21	Upheaval	213

Contents

22 The Years of Wandering   219

23 The White House   231

24 Knipper in America   236

25 The Difficult Years   251

26 Olga's Last Appearance   263

Notes and References   272

Bibliography of Source Material   280

Index   283

Illustrations

Between pages 136 and 137

1 Olga Knipper, 1899

2 Olga Knipper

3 Mariya Chekhova (Masha)

4 Anton Chekhov

5 Olga and Anton on honeymoon at Aksyonovo, 1901

6 Chekhov family group, 1902

7 Olga and Anton, 1902

8 Chekhov reading *The Seagull* to the actors and directors of the Moscow Art Theatre, 1898

9 Knipper as Irina in *Tsar Fyodor*, 1898

10 *The Seagull*, Act III: Knipper and Meierhold

11 *Three Sisters*, Act I: Knipper as Masha

12 Scene from *Uncle Vanya*, Act I

13 Cover of the first edition of *Three Sisters*, 1901

14 Knipper as Ranyevskaya in *The Cherry Orchard*

15 Scene from *The Cherry Orchard*, Act III

16 Card from Knipper to Gordon Craig, showing scene from *The Inspector General*

17 Photograph by Gordon Craig of a group of Art Theatre friends, May 1909

18 Knipper in America, 1923

19 Knipper as Ranyevskaya in *The Cherry Orchard*, 1948

Illustrations

20 Masha and Olga in the garden at Yalta

21 The Chekhov Museum at Yalta, 1948

IN TEXT

Postcard from Knipper to Gordon Craig, 1935   211

ACKNOWLEDGEMENTS

The author wishes to thank the following for the generous loan of illustrations in their possession: Dr Edward Braun, 10; Edward Craig, 16, 17 and the postcard on page 211, from the Edward Craig Collection; Patrick Miles, 4.

1, 3, 5, 6, 8, 9, 11, 12, 13, 15, 18, 19, 21, are by courtesy of the *Novosti Press Agency*; 2, 7, 14, 20 by courtesy of the *Society for Cultural Relations with the USSR*

Introduction

The year 1979 is the seventy-fifth anniversary of the death of Anton Chekhov. It is also the twentieth anniversary of the death of his wife, the actress Olga Knipper, who died in Moscow in 1959 in her ninety-first year.

The years with Chekhov occupied a relatively small part of Olga Knipper's life. She met him in 1898, married him in 1901 and became a widow three years later. Yet had she been asked what was the most important event in her long and chequered life, there can be no doubt that marrying Chekhov would have been the answer. From the outset, however, the marriage was the subject of a controversy that has never died down. Olga Knipper might be recognised as the Moscow Art Theatre's leading actress and interpreter of Chekhov's heroines (so well-known that when photographs of the pair appeared in the newspapers after their marriage, Chekhov's sister was prompted to enquire tartly: 'Which of you is the more famous?')[1]; but how had she succeeded in marrying Russia's most elusive literary bachelor when he was already past forty? Could she be anything but one of those predatory females often described by Chekhov himself in his fiction? And what sort of wife was it who for more than half the year continued to pursue her acting career in Moscow while her husband was confined for health reasons to the Crimean resort of Yalta, more than two days' journey from Moscow by train?

So far we have had only Chekhov's side of this story. His biographers have understandably been looking at the marriage more from his point of view than from Olga's. His numerous letters to her have long been familiar to English readers from the translations by Constance Garnett published in 1926. Not until the 1930s, however, was a project launched in the Soviet Union

1

Introduction

to publish *both* sides of the correspondence. Of the three volumes planned, two have become collectors' items; the third was never published. Olga's even more numerous letters to Chekhov, of which extensive use has been made here, have never previously been translated and are known to English readers only from occasional brief extracts quoted in connection with the contents of his letters to her.

In 1972, two important volumes appeared under the editorship of V. Ya. Vilenkin, the Moscow Art Theatre's official archivist-historian. These volumes filled the gap left by the missing third volume and also contained previously unpublished writings by Olga of great interest: a more detailed account than had appeared hitherto of the events leading up to and immediately after Chekhov's death, and a remarkable series of letters, published here for the first time in English, that she wrote to him *after* his death, in which she looks back very frankly and movingly on their all too brief married life.

In this book I have tried not to identify myself either with Olga or with Chekhov, but to enter equally into the feelings of both. I have also tried to appreciate the feelings of Chekhov's sister, Mariya Pavlovna (Masha), who was so closely involved in the situation, as Chekhov's devoted helper and as Olga's best friend, that she formed part of what I have called an emotional triangle, in a sense not broken even by Chekhov's death. The story that emerges is like the novel that Chekhov might have written but never did: subtle, full of fine shades of feeling, ambiguous, alternately charming and light-hearted, almost (but not quite) dramatic, and undeniably poignant. It gives little support to the unkind comments that have been consistently made about Olga Knipper as Chekhov's wife. And it offers a new perspective on Chekhov's elusive character by showing how he appeared to the one person who had the greatest need to try to understand him: his wife.

Vilenkin's volumes also contain a wealth of letters and memoir material spanning the whole of Olga Knipper's life. In 1924 Nemirovich-Danchenko, co-founder with Stanislavsky of the

Introduction

Moscow Art Theatre, wrote to her: 'There are times when I feel that I must be living my fifth or sixth life already.'[2] This sense of having lived several different lives was common to all those who had reached artistic maturity in Tsarist times, had lived through the period of social and cultural upheaval, and were then pursuing their careers under the Soviet regime. In Knipper's case, one can point to at least seven lives: growing up in Tsarist Russia as a well-bred young lady with too little to do; breaking away to become a drama student; the years with Chekhov; reaching maturity as an actress with the Moscow Art Theatre before the Revolution; three years of adventurous nomadic life from 1919 to 1922 touring in the south of Russia and Europe; earning a new reputation on the Art Theatre's tours of America in 1923 and 1924; surviving the years of Stalin's Terror and living on to experience Khrushchev's Thaw.

Only the third of these lives, the Chekhov years, has become known outside Russia. In this book all seven lives are presented, though inevitably it is the third life which claims by far the largest share of attention. Chekhov was to accompany her, of course, all the way through life. She was eighty when she last appeared in 1948 as Ranyevskaya in *The Cherry Orchard*—her most famous role apart from that of Masha in *Three Sisters*—reluctantly deciding not to attempt the whole play but confining herself to Act III.

In this Chekhov anniversary year, *Chekhov's Leading Lady* is dedicated to the memory of two people whom it would certainly have been a great pleasure to know, and not only for the opportunity of discovering some of the mistakes that one has made in assessing them.

*   *   *

My thanks are due to the following for their kindness and co-operation: Mrs Olga Rabeneck for writing to me about her husband's cousin, L. L. Rabeneck, and Kyril FitzLyon for sending me an offprint of Rabeneck's article, 'Chekhov's Last Minutes'; Dr Nicolas Zernov for telling me about his family's

3

links with the Moscow Art Theatre and allowing me to quote from the letter written by his sister, Sofiya Zernova, from Paris in 1937; H. E. Robert Craig, Surviving Administrator of the Edward Gordon Craig, C. H., Estate, for permission to quote from Gordon Craig's letter to Olga Knipper of January 11th, 1909, now in the Bibliothèque Nationale, Edward Craig for lending me Knipper's postcard to Craig of September 21st, 1935, and Professor Laurence Senelick, who enthusiastically passed on his expert knowledge of Gordon Craig and the Moscow Art Theatre; Neil Buxton of Cromer Public Library for obtaining so many obscure books on my behalf, Marianna Tax Choldin and Mary Stuart of the University Library, University of Illinois at Urbana-Champaign, for providing American references, and D. L. L. Howells of the Taylor Institution Library, University of Oxford, for assistance with photocopying; Dr Edward Braun, Edward Craig and Patrick Miles for the generous loan of illustrations; and Stella Adler, Harold Clurman, Cheryl Crawford and Professor Simon Karlinsky for kindly finding time to answer my letters.

My special thanks to Mrs Osyth Leeston and her colleagues for their encouragement and for taking such a helpful interest in the book at every stage.

Cromer, 1979   H.J.P.

PART ONE

❦

CHAPTER ONE

Finding a Vocation

Knipper. Olga Knipper. To Russian ears, as well as English ones, the name sounds odd and faintly comic.

Both her parents were of German origin. As a very young man, her father had left his small native town in Alsace and gone to seek his fortune in Russia, the land of great opportunity for enterprising young Europeans in the nineteenth century. At the time of Olga's birth, on September 9th, 1868,[1] he was in charge of a factory in the small provincial town of Glazov, in the north-east of European Russia. Olga already had an elder brother, Konstantin, otherwise known as Kostya, and later there would be a younger brother, Vladimir (Volodya). For the sake of furthering his career and because he genuinely loved the country, Olga's father appears to have wasted no time in acquiring Russian citizenship. He spelt his first name in the Russian manner as Leonard, not Leonhard, so that Olga acquired the patronymic Leonardovna. All his children were given good Russian names, sent to Russian schools and presumably encouraged to think of themselves as purely Russian. Later Chekhov would enjoy teasing Olga about her origins, calling her his 'little Lutheran' and his 'rosy-cheeked little German', but she always took this in good part and was clearly not sensitive on the subject.

Nothing more is known of her father's family, but on her mother's side Olga's relatives were numerous. She had an aunt, a great-aunt, three uncles and various cousins. They were descended from Russianised members of the German gentry living in the Baltic Provinces that formed part of the Russian Empire.[2]

Chekhov's Leading Lady

In 1870 the Knippers moved to Moscow, where they were able in time to rent a large detached house and lead the kind of very conventional, upper-middle-class life that Tolstoy was so fond of deriding in his fiction. Olga, the cherished only daughter of the family, was pampered and protected. It seemed to her on looking back that the sole purpose of her existence had been to make a good match. Not that she was ever discouraged from developing her obvious artistic abilities. After attending a private school for girls, she continued to take lessons at home in languages, music and singing. She was fluent in French, German and English, enjoyed translating French and German literature into Russian, showed considerable promise as a painter, had an excellent voice and could accompany herself on the piano. Acting also figured among these cultural pursuits, though no more prominently than it would have done in any such family at the time. Each year the Knipper children converted the largest room in the house into a theatre, where they put on vaudevilles in which Olga always wanted to play the funniest parts.

But to paint for one's own pleasure, to sing for the entertainment of a small group of social equals, perhaps even to take part occasionally in amateur theatricals for the sake of some charitable cause—all that was perfectly proper and acceptable; to engage in such activities professionally, as a career—that was a very different proposition. Anxious to conform to the social conventions of his adopted country, to become more Russian than the Russians, Olga's father was quite clear about this distinction. She has described him as 'a family man *par excellence*',[3] for whom a woman's place was in the home. That his daughter should even contemplate the thought of becoming a professional singer or actress was as unthinkable as allowing her out of the house at the first sign of darkness without a maidservant to accompany her. To Olga's suggestion that she might form a small amateur dramatic group, his reply was a kindly but very firm 'No'. And when a medical student friend of her elder brother's kindled her enthusiasm by describing the kind of emancipated life led by girls who had left home to follow one of the popular

8

Finding a Vocation

new 'higher courses for women', the young man soon found that his presence in the Knipper home was no longer welcome.

Nor was Olga able to find an ally in the one person from whom she might have expected support, her mother. Anna Ivanovna was an exceptionally gifted singer and pianist, and a woman of strong character. Married at a very early age, she had been obliged by social convention to give up all thoughts of studying at the conservatoire and pursuing a professional career. When Olga put it to her that her whole life had been made miserable by this sacrifice, Anna Ivanovna only replied: 'Yes, I did suffer and you'll have to suffer too ... and don't you so much as dare to think of going on the stage.'

Early in 1894, when Olga was twenty-five, her life underwent a complete change. Her father died suddenly. It turned out that in his anxiety to keep up appearances he had been living well beyond his means. All he left behind was debts, the large rented house and five servants. On Olga and her mother the effect was immediate and electrifying: their talents and energies, previously unused and undirected, now had to be exploited to the full if they were to cope with the new situation.

They made a start by dismissing all the servants except one cook-housekeeper, who was almost a member of the family. They gave up the large house and rented a smaller flat. Two of Olga's uncles, Uncle Karl and Uncle Sasha, were invited to move in and establish a commune. Rooms were also let to students. At forty-four, Anna Ivanovna was still a comparatively young woman. She began to give singing lessons and soon built up a reputation throughout Moscow. Kostya, Olga's elder brother, was already working in the Caucasus as an engineer; her younger brother, Volodya, a law student who later became a singer, began to help the family exchequer by going out as a private tutor in his free time.

Olga also went out daily to give music lessons.

'Poor Olechka!' her society friends chorused in sympathy. 'She used to have a French dressmaker and wear silk, and now she has to earn her own living.'

9

Chekhov's Leading Lady

Poor Olechka, nothing! In spite of her father's recent death and their financial insecurity, she later remembered the commune as the jolliest period in her life; never had the house been so full of jokes and laughter. According to one observer, everything in the Knipper household was 'simple, modest, not at all bourgeois, yet also free from the tiresomeness of pretentious bohemia'.[4] The family was cultured, talented, highly strung and noisy. While Anna Ivanovna's pupils were singing at the tops of their voices in one room, loud voices might be raised in the room next door as a furious family argument developed over art or literature. 'All the same,' Olga wrote later to Chekhov, 'I like the atmosphere in our home. There are no moaners, they may be excitable and quick-tempered, but they all sincerely love and help one another, and you are not conscious of any digs or undercurrents. They are all cheerful, even though none of them has a penny to his name.'[5] Her Uncle Karl was a doctor with a rural practice near Moscow which he covered on a bicycle. Because of his fiery nature, he was nicknamed 'The Cut-throat'. Uncle Sasha was a captain in the infantry, with a fondness for the bottle; everyone liked him, including Chekhov and Gorky. Once he was among Olga and Chekhov's guests at a small gathering in Moscow. Since Olga refused to offer him any wine, he soon slipped off to the kitchen, where the cook and maid were happy to keep filling up his glass while he settled himself in comfortably and regaled them with stories from his military campaigns. Realising that Uncle Sasha had disappeared, Chekhov quietly made his way towards the kitchen, opened the door very slightly and began to observe the scene, doubling up every so often with soundless laughter. Aware of Chekhov's absence, Olga and her sister-in-law left the room as well and amused themselves in turn watching Chekhov watching Uncle Sasha.[6]

But Sasha also suffered from bouts of alcoholic depression when he talked of suicide—'though there's nothing to worry about, of course,' Olga assured Chekhov. In 1905, soon after returning from the Russo-Japanese war, where he distinguished himself by his bravery but in which the Russians were so humiliatingly deflated, he put a revolver to his head while out driving in a sledge in Moscow and shot himself.[7]

Surrounded by the cheerful atmosphere of the commune, Olga no longer reflected gloomily on the purpose of her existence. She took the daily round of music lessons in her stride and soon obtained an official music teacher's diploma. Almost overnight, the *baryshnya*—the sheltered 'young lady of the house' and spoilt only daughter—changed into an independent young woman, well able to earn a living and stand on her own feet. Meeting two of her former friends several years later, she was appalled by the narrowness of their lives. They were both fine girls and by no means unintelligent, yet they were content to sit around idly at home frittering their lives away. 'And to think that I lived and grew up with them!'[8]

The dream of a career on the stage had not been forgotten. In the summer there was less demand for music lessons, since the well-to-do families all left Moscow for Europe or their country estates. Olga spent the summers of 1894 and 1895 with the Goncharovs, family friends of long standing, who were descended from the same aristocratic stock as Pushkin's wife, Natalya Goncharova. They had an estate near Kaluga, with a beautiful neglected park and an old ancestral home of fifty-two rooms, inhabited by a strange assortment of guests and hangers-on, who seemed to be forever eating and drinking in endless relays. When the Goncharovs gave their summer ball, carriage loads of officers arrived from Kaluga, a military band played near the house, the park was illuminated by Bengal lights, and the numerous guests spent the night sleeping on hay-mattresses distributed all over the house. And if that was not enough to remind the guests of the country ball in Pushkin's *Eugene Onegin*, Olga and Dmitri, the Goncharovs' eldest son, who were mildly in love, sang the famous duet between Tatyana and Onegin from Tchaikovsky's opera.

This Dmitri Goncharov was a young man of radical outlook, to be associated in later years with the first Soviet Commissar for Education Anatole Lunacharsky. He was friendly with the workers from the paper mill which formed part of the estate. For their benefit and with their participation, he began to organise regular dramatic performances. Rummaging in the family archives, the young people discovered an obscure link between Pushkin and one of the lodges on the estate, now used as a tavern. Notwithstanding the loss of income involved, the tavern was converted into a small theatre, where the young enthusiasts built their own stage, scrubbed the floors and painted their own scenery. On this stage, before audiences that consisted of workers from the local villages, Olga Knipper found herself gaining in self-confidence as an actress, and determined to take positive steps to realise her old dream.

At that time the most famous theatre in Russia was the Maly Theatre in Moscow, one of the Imperial Theatres supervised by the state; so what could be more natural than that Miss Knipper should seek admission to the Maly Theatre's equally famous drama school?

This decision, which must have been taken in the summer of 1895, was not communicated to her family. Even though the Knippers had come down in the world, Anna Ivanovna's attitude was unchanged: to act professionally was synonymous in her mind with a loss of social status. 'Of course, if your Olechka goes on the stage,' Dmitri's mother had taken Anna Ivanovna to one side and confided, 'it'll mean that she'll have to break off relations with our circle.'

Keeping up her social relations, however, no longer seemed important to Olga. She had not escaped from the gilded cage so lovingly built round her by her father only to become a music teacher waiting for a husband. Art, The Theatre, had fired her imagination and given her a sense of vocation. 'Whenever in my life I really wanted something,' she wrote later, 'and really believed in the possibility of achieving what I wanted and acted energetically, I always succeeded and never regretted going my own way.'[9] In this respect she may have been her father's daughter after all. If her volatile temperament, her artistic flair, come from the mother's side of her family, then her drive and ambition seem likely to owe more to him. Just as he had followed his own lights and set off to seek his fortune in Russia, so she too now saw clearly ahead of her the course that her life must follow.

A conspiratorial meeting was arranged in the Knippers' garden between Olga and a friend of friends—a pupil of the Maly Theatre's great actor-director, Alexander Lensky. For the truth of the matter was that Olga, though less inexperienced in the way of the world than she had been eighteen months earlier, still had no inkling of how to fill in a form or make an official application. She had been right, however, to aim high. Before long she had passed the entrance examination, impressing the board with her classical declamations in French and German, and in the autumn of 1895 she was officially enrolled as a pupil of the Maly Theatre's drama school.

Term was only a few weeks old and Olga was just beginning to make new friends, when the rumour went round that an important official would be arriving from St Petersburg to conduct a progress examination. At the end of the examination Olga was summoned to the inspector's room and told that her studies were to be terminated forthwith, though she would be entitled to enrol again in the following year. Well-bred Miss Knipper even forgot her good manners so far as to tell the inspector that in her opinion the whole examination had been a farce, and slammed the door behind her as she left.

It makes a good story: Olga Knipper dropped from drama school after one month's study! For Olga at the time it was no laughing matter. She went home and threw herself down on the bed, but she did not cry her eyes out; she felt too numb with grief. And here it was Anna Ivanovna who came to the rescue. She had still not withdrawn her opposition, even after Olga's acceptance by the Maly, and it needed this manifestation of profound grief to bring home to her at last that it was pointless trying to thwart her daughter's theatrical ambitions. Because of her reputation in the musical and artistic world, Anna Ivanovna was well-known to the directors of the Philharmonic School, where she later taught singing for a number of years, and although term was already well advanced, Olga received permission to enrol at the drama school there. Later it transpired that of the four girls admitted in that year to the Maly, Olga was the only one without an influential patron, and when a place had to be found belatedly for a relative of one of the leading actresses, it was Knipper who had to be sacrificed.

Olga was horrified by her first impression of the Philharmonic. Instead of the formal, decorous atmosphere that had reigned at the Maly, everything was in uproar. The girls seemed free to wear whatever they liked. The sight of one girl, dressed in a bright blue velvet skirt and wearing *make-up*, so shocked Miss Knipper that she was in two minds about parting with her hard-earned money for the enrolment fee.

Amid the generally chaotic atmosphere of the Philharmonic there was one haven of disciplined and concentrated effort; and fortunately for Olga, this was the drama course run by Vladimir Nemirovich-Danchenko.

A member of the gentry, Nemirovich had been educated at Moscow University and was the owner, through his wife, of a modest estate in the south of Russia. Then thirty-seven, he was well-known as a writer of novels and short stories, but had become famous as the author of two highly successful plays, produced in 1888 and 1890. In 1891 he accepted an invitation to teach dramatic art at the Philharmonic, even though he had no experience as an actor. The terms of his contract stated that he was to give four two-hour lessons each week, but Nemirovich was not the kind of person who could do things by halves. At first he trod gingerly; then he started to exercise his authority, making himself unpopular by excluding from his course all those whom he considered too frivolous; and before long he had become so absorbed in his teaching duties that instead of eight hours a week, he was 'working every day, ignoring the number of hours, in the mornings, the evenings and until late at night—and even then there wasn't enough time'.[10] Only the most dedicated students were likely to keep up with that kind of pace. Classes with Nemirovich went far beyond the basic techniques of acting.

There would be wide-ranging preliminary discussion of a play's content, careful analysis of the psychology of its characters, and a painstaking search for the most effective means of dramatic expression. Under supervision, students presented whole plays instead of the extracts usually performed in drama schools, and were encouraged to work on their own and to exercise their talents as producers.

When Olga Knipper first went to see her new teacher, he asked her if she fully appreciated what she was doing in committing herself to the life of an actress. Did she realise that if she were to marry, to have children, the theatre would simply 'gobble them all up without trace'? In 1895, unmarried, sure of her own vocation after so much uncertainty, Olga was unlikely to have been scared by this kind of warning, but she would have good cause to reflect upon it in years to come.

Nemirovich for his part did not form an entirely favourable impression of his new pupil. 'You may leave here with top marks,' he told her early on, 'but that won't make you an actress.' Olga was deeply hurt: 'For me it wasn't a question of marks, but of life or death.' When she reminded him of his comment some years later, he laughed and said: 'You seemed just like all the other young ladies from good homes—oh yes, they thought, the theatre's all right for the moment, but I'll soon pop off and get married.'[11] He might have revised his opinion, had he known that Miss Knipper was still having to spend her spare time giving music lessons in order to keep herself and pay her tuition fees. In any case, by the end of the teaching year his views were very different; already he was using superlatives about her in his report, referring to Knipper as 'the most pleasing girl in her year'.

It was an exceptionally strong year too. Olga was constantly being compared with another girl of her own age, Margarita Savitskaya, who had been teaching at a state school in Kazan before enrolling at the Philharmonic. Either I succeed in becoming an actress, Savitskaya had decided, or I shall enter a nunnery.

In Olga's second year, that of 1896–97, the class was left more

15

to its own devices, since Nemirovich was busy putting the finishing touches to his play, *The Worth of Life*, to be presented with great success at the Maly Theatre under the joint direction of Nemirovich and Alexander Lensky. Lensky's students at the Maly also found themselves bereft of a teacher, and mutual sympathy took the place of the usual friendly rivalry between the schools. It was fortunate that Nemirovich had always encouraged his pupils to work on their own, and fortunate that a new student appeared on the course in that year who so impressed Olga and the others by his seriousness and intelligence, by his maturity as an actor and producer, that he was quickly accepted as a natural leader and organiser. This was Vsevolod Meierhold, then only twenty-two, and later to become the outstanding figure of the Russian theatre after the Revolution.

In their final year students at the Philharmonic had to take part in the so-called 'graduation plays'. During the seven weeks of Lent, the Maly Theatre company gave no performances, since the theatre was still regarded by the Church and by Tsarist officialdom as a sinful pastime, and Lensky was in the habit of taking over the theatre in those weeks for private performances by his pupils. The enterprising Nemirovich insisted that his pupils should be given an equal opportunity to use the theatre, and although these performances were not strictly speaking open to the public, the graduation plays soon became a showcase for the school's work.

Olga Knipper was chosen to appear in four of the six plays. Her best part was in Goldoni's *The Innkeeper's Wife*, where she played the title role opposite Meierhold. Peeping through a hole in the curtain one afternoon before a pre-graduation performance of the play at the Philharmonic, she was taken aback to see among the audience the unmistakable figure of Konstantin Alekseyev, or, to give him his stage name, Konstantin Stanislavsky.

A few years younger than Nemirovich, Stanislavsky was then in his mid-thirties, son of a wealthy merchant who, like many Moscow merchants of the time, was also a great patron of the arts. His tall, loose-limbed, energetic figure was quite unlike that of the dapper, rather stockily built Nemirovich. In a well-known photograph of the pair standing on a flight of steps, Stanislavsky has tactfully placed himself one step below his colleague, but still has to bend. What made his appearance striking was not only his impressive build, but the startling combination of hair that was prematurely grey with a thick black moustache and black eyebrows. He was a director of the manufacturing and trading firm of Alekseyev & Co., and would remain so until 1917, but for the past fifteen years much of his time had been devoted to his activities as an actor and theatrical producer. He had built up an amateur company that enjoyed a considerable reputation in Moscow, giving regular performances of plays in which Stanislavsky invariably took the leading part.

'Kostya Alekseyev,' pronounced Fedotova, the doyen of Moscow actresses, 'now *there's* an enthusiast for you. He'll go far —if he doesn't go mad first . . .'[12]

CHAPTER TWO

✠

Summer at Pushkino

The historic conference between Nemirovich and Stanislavsky
had already taken place the previous summer. They had vied with
one another, as Nemirovich recalls, in firing poisoned arrows at
the existing Russian theatre, with its conservatism, bureaucracy
and vulgar commercialism. The decision had been taken: jointly
to found a new professional theatre, on new principles and with
new ideals; its acting personnel to be drawn primarily from the
best members of Stanislavsky's amateur group and the most
gifted of Nemirovich's pupils, and only in exceptional cases from
among established actors, already hopelessly corrupted by the
bad habits of the commercial theatre. In matters of literary content and interpretation, Stanislavsky would bow to the better
judgement of Nemirovich, the successful writer and playwright;
but Stanislavsky, the experienced stage director, would have the
last word on all questions of stage direction and artistic production.
Administration would be in the hands of Nemirovich; Stanislavsky was likely to be heavily involved as an actor, and still had
his commitments to Alekseyev & Co. to consider.

The principles had also been outlined on which the new
theatre would be based. It must be a team, a collective, united by
a common sense of dedication to the art of the theatre; and the
contribution made by such normally despised individuals as the
scene-painters and stagehands must be regarded as no less
essential to the success of the whole undertaking than that of the
actors and producers. Similarly, attention must be paid to the
excellence of *every* aspect of a theatrical performance: not only to

18

the words of the play, but to the sound effects, lighting, costumes, scenery, incidental music and even to such details as the type of programme and the colour of the curtain. The theatre itself must be made comfortable, for the actors as well as for the audience, who were to be treated with consideration but without any commercial servility. Lights would be dimmed in the foyer to encourage people to take up their seats before the raising of the curtain, and in years to come admission during the course of a performance would be forbidden entirely—perhaps the most provocative of all the innovations of the Moscow Art Theatre, given the notorious lack of time sense of the Russians.

In contrast to the existing theatre, plays were not to be prepared hastily and haphazardly, but with careful deliberation, even though this was bound to mean having a much smaller repertoire than was usual. Ample time must be allowed for lectures by experts and preliminary discussions, for numerous rehearsals and several dress rehearsals; the first dress rehearsal ever in Russia, of Nemirovich's own play, *Gold*, did not take place until 1894. Final responsibility for a play must always, however, rest squarely on the shoulders of the director, whose task it was to conceive of each production as an artistic whole, into which every detail fitted.

Most important and far-reaching of all, the theatre must be purged of all 'theatricality'. The star system was to be abolished: the new theatre would have nothing to do with plays written to show off the talents of star performers, with actors' benefit nights or individual curtain calls. It was the ensemble that mattered. The actor who played a leading role in one production might find himself with a walk-on part in the next, but to both he brought the same degree of artistic dedication. 'There are no small parts, there are only small actors': to quote one of those famous aphorisms which Stanislavsky, always a lover of writing things down, claims to have recorded in the minutes of the first conference. All scene-stealing and playing to the audience, all theatrical histrionics, all the cheap tricks of the trade, must be ruthlessly eliminated: 'one must love art and not oneself in art'.

Acting should be stage-centred, and the actor should *live* his part on stage as if the audience were not present. In the off-stage life of the theatre his behaviour must show the same self-discipline, unselfishness and loyalty to the ensemble, for 'all disobedience to the creative life of the theatre is a crime'.

In the winter of 1897–98 both Nemirovich and Stanislavsky were carefully weighing up which of the actors and actresses known to them should be invited to join the new company. While Nemirovich attended performances by Stanislavsky's amateur group, Stanislavsky paid visits to the Philharmonic. What he saw there amply reinforced his enthusiasm. It was unthinkable that at the end of the year this remarkable class of graduating students, several of whom were quite outstanding, should be quietly disbanded and its manifold talents allowed to spill over and be squandered on the provincial theatre.

During the winter Knipper, Meierhold and Savitskaya were told by Nemirovich in strict confidence that if the plans for a new theatre materialised, they would be invited to become members of the company. But weeks passed and they heard nothing final; Nemirovich and Stanislavsky were still trying to raise the necessary capital. Meanwhile the graduation plays were performed on the stage of that same Maly Theatre which not long ago had shown Miss Knipper the door. The girl whom Nemirovich had once regarded as too much of a dilettante graduated from the school with the gold medal. 'One of the most gifted pupils of recent years,' Nemirovich wrote in his report. 'Suitable in appearance, a fine voice, a natural, confident tone, acts with general refinement and intelligence. Yet quite free of the fault of imitativeness. Technically not a pupil at all—a finished actress. Mark for the year: five plus.' This was the highest mark that could be awarded and was also received by Meierhold.

At last the plans for the new theatre began to take shape. Capital was raised through individual shareholders. The Hermitage Theatre in Moscow was rented for the winter season; the new theatre would make its debut in the autumn of 1898. But the Hermitage was not available until September, and where in the meantime were they to make the elaborate preparations and hold the numerous rehearsals that were such an important part of their artistic programme?

The answer was found some twenty miles outside Moscow near Pushkino, 'a large village with numerous datchas and manufactories, situated on a small lake in a pine wood'.[1] In a tree-filled park on the estate of a theatrical friend of Stanislavsky's stood a large wooden hut, solidly built, with an iron roof and outbuildings. Inside the hut a stage had been constructed, with a small auditorium, and on a fine day in June Olga Knipper was one of those who foregathered in Pushkino, where they split up into groups to find sleeping accommodation in the village.

It is an amusing paradox of Stanislavsky's personality that this pioneering crusader against theatricality in the theatre was always liable to inject a strong dose of drama into the situations of real life. Gathering the troupe together on the first morning, he delivered his inaugural address. 'If we do not approach our task with hands unsullied,' he said,

> we shall besmirch and vulgarise it, and we shall be scattered to the far corners of Russia, some to return to prosaic, everyday occupations, others to profane art for the sake of a crust of bread in grubby provincial peepshows. Do not forget that if we have to disperse, the dishonour and ridicule will be fully deserved, for we have undertaken a task which is not of a simple, private character but one of social significance. Do not forget that we are striving to illuminate the dark life of the poor classes, to give them moments of aesthetic pleasure amid the darkness that engulfs them. We are striving to create the first rational, moral, universally accessible theatre, and to this lofty goal we are dedicating our lives.[2]

Olga Knipper was probably sitting next to Margarita Savitskaya and both were leaning forward eagerly to drink in every word uttered by Stanislavsky in a voice that Nemirovich has described as 'deep, always warm and somewhat hoarse'.[3] This was their first and surely unforgettable encounter with Stanislavsky the enthusiast, Stanislavsky the inspirer of others, Stanislavsky the driving force. They could not fail to respond to the high moral tone of Stanislavsky's speech, very characteristic of liberal reformers then in Russia; to his inspiring picture of the new theatre as a temple of art and a powerful force working for the good of society; and to his quasi-religious appeal for them to dedicate their lives to the service of these lofty ideals. For Knipper, too, art was always to remain Art.

Stanislavsky was living in relative luxury on his mother's estate at Lyubimovka, a few miles away, and driving over daily by carriage. At first they had no servants at Pushkino and had to appoint orderlies from among themselves to keep the hut clean and tidy. To Nemirovich, then holidaying in the south, Stanislavsky reported on the comradely atmosphere that had been established. 'If it hadn't been for the orderlies,' he wrote, 'everything would have been in complete chaos. The orderlies swept the rooms, put on the samovars, tidied the tables, and did everything efficiently, perhaps because I was the first orderly and carried out every task very thoroughly.'[4] In his memoirs some years later, Stanislavsky tells a different story. With that disarming readiness to find fault with himself after the event, he admits that his debut in the role of orderly 'was a failure at first, for I filled a samovar empty of water with charcoal, and the samovar melted, leaving us without tea. I had not yet learned to sweep a floor, to handle a refuse shovel, or to remove dust from chairs with any degree of rapidity.'[5] Such criticisms could not have been levelled at Olga Knipper, who was used to scrubbing floors from her summer seasons with the Goncharovs.

Each morning at eleven the click of the gate leading to the hut announced Stanislavsky's arrival from Lyubimovka. This was the signal for rehearsals to begin. The first rehearsal of the day lasted until five. The actors were then free to bathe in the nearby river, and to eat and rest, but by eight they had to return for the second rehearsal lasting until eleven.

A strenuous life but by all accounts a high-spirited and exhilarating one, in spite of the oppressively hot summer. Quite a stir was caused by the arrival of two newcomers, Roksanova and Vishnevsky. She was a pupil of Nemirovich who had graduated brilliantly from the Philharmonic a year before and had since been acting in the provinces; he was a still bigger name from the provincial theatre. How would he behave towards these unknown amateurs? He proved most anxious to fit in. Soon Nemirovich's ex-pupils and Stanislavsky's colleagues ceased to think of themselves as separate groups. Relations among the troupe became close and friendly, not only on stage; Nemirovich writes with casual exaggeration of 'something like a dozen marriages' that were arranged within the first half year.

Not all the actors, however, were able to live up to the high moral tone set by Stanislavsky in his inaugural address. One of them so far forgot himself as to heap abuse on a fellow actor during the course of a rehearsal. This was a serious matter. To allow it to pass unpunished would be to condone all the bad habits of the old theatre. Rehearsals were immediately cancelled and the whole company summoned to a special meeting. Nemirovich and Stanislavsky explained how seriously they viewed the matter and invited the actors themselves to pass judgement. Somewhat to the embarrassment of the directors, since it entailed much re-casting and re-rehearsing, the offending actor was told to leave and not return.

Early in August Nemirovich took up permanent residence in Lyubimovka, while Stanislavsky left with a small party on an expedition in search of authentic props for the historical drama, *Tsar Fyodor*, with which the Theatre was to make its debut. Rehearsals continued at Pushkino, where Nemirovich spent much of his time working with Moskvin, another former pupil who had been acting in the provinces and was to play the title role in *Tsar Fyodor*. By now the hut had acquired its own caretaker. Because of lack of space, Nemirovich took Moskvin through his role in the caretaker's shed, while the latter 'sat on a small bench just outside the open window and listened to us, understanding nothing but smiling'.[6]

On his return from the expedition, Stanislavsky retired for

several weeks to compose the *mise en scène* for Chekhov's *The Seagull*, another play being prepared for the repertoire. When he rejoined the company in September, they had already moved back to Moscow and taken possession of the Hermitage Theatre, a dirty, rat-infested building that no amount of effort could turn into the temple of art that they dreamed of. Rehearsals took place at the Hunting Club, and it was here, on September 9th, 1898, at a rehearsal of *The Seagull*, that Anton Chekhov first met Olga Knipper.

It was also Olga's thirtieth birthday. During the previous three years, ever since her decision in 1895 to become a professional actress, good fortune had seemed to guide her. How lucky it had been that a place had to be found at the Maly for that relative of one of the leading actresses and she was forced to transfer to the Philharmonic; how timely to have arrived there just when Nemirovich was at the height of his powers and enthusiasm as a teacher; and how fortunate that without any of the trial of provincial engagements, she was able to step straight from drama school into a metropolitan company! And what a company!

CHAPTER THREE

Fiasco

'To Mr A. Che-v, Drachevka Street. Not at all bad. We shall
publish. Our blessings on your future endeavours.'

From this brief announcement, which appeared on January
13th, 1880, in the 'Postbox' column of a comic weekly called
The Dragonfly,[1] Chekhov learned of his first modest triumph as a
writer. He was then a few days short of his twentieth birthday.
In the previous autumn he had enrolled as a medical student at
Moscow University, and for several years, at least until his
graduation in 1884, he led something of a double life. Few of his
university contemporaries bothered to find out that the apparently unremarkable medical student, A. P. Chekhov, was the
same person as 'Antosha Chekhonte', a popular contributor to
just the kind of weekly journals from whose corrupting influence
young Miss Knipper was being carefully protected.

The young Chekhov made no secret of his reasons for writing.
'I have family dependents and no private means,' he explained to
an editor in 1884. 'If I don't earn at least 150–180 roubles a month,
I shall go bankrupt.'[2] Chekhov's father, the son of a serf who had
bought his freedom, had run a small grocery business in Taganrog,
a port in the south of Russia, but when the business failed in
1876, the Chekhov family made a hurried departure for Moscow.
Anton, the third son, then sixteen, was left behind in Taganrog
to complete his studies at the High School, becoming a lodger in
what had once been the Chekhov family home. When he rejoined his family in 1879, he found that they had just moved to
their twelfth apartment—a damp basement in the worst part of

B   25

Moscow. His father's earnings were paltry, and Anton soon became established not only as the family decision-taker, but later, thanks to his writing activities, as chief breadwinner also. Such was his industry that in the peak years of 1885 and 1886, a story by him was being published, on average, almost once every three days.

How did he manage to write so much when he seems never to have found enough peace and quiet in that large and boisterous family even for his medical studies? He was tirelessly inventive and he was quick. In reply to the elderly writer, Grigorovich, who had written unexpectedly in 1886 urging him to 'respect his talent' and to publish less frequently, Chekhov said that he could 'not remember a *single* story' on which he had spent more than twenty-four hours.[3] Chekhov heeded Grigorovich's advice, and from 1888 onwards his annual output of stories scarcely ever reaches double figures. That was the year in which he officially arrived as a writer: in March his long story, *The Steppe*, was accepted by one of the so-called Thick Journals in which only the very best works were published, and in October he received the annual Pushkin Prize for literature.

Of course, the winner of the Pushkin Prize could no longer sign his work 'Antosha Chekhonte', nor could he go on producing the kind of knockabout stories in which Chekhonte had special-ised: satirical portraits of minor civil servants and even more commonly, facetious tales of thwarted romance. Chekhonte rings endless comic changes on the theme of finding a husband or wife: on broken engagements, abortive proposals (the hero ruins his chances by hiccupping at the opera) and mistaken intentions ('My angel! My happiness!' exclaims the young artist to the expectant heroine after no less than eight pages of build-up, 'will you ... will you be my—my model?'); on match-makers, dowries ('an iron, three chairs, a mousetrap, the feather-bed that Grannie died on last year ...') and the young lovers' fond farewell ('Darling! You haven't given me a receipt for those twenty-five roubles!'); and on the theme of marital relations: 'scandals' at the wedding breakfast, a husband's murky past (it turns out that he was a clown in the circus—and his wife is absolutely enchanted), faithless wives and faithless husbands. How did a fat, red-nosed old husband manage to keep his pretty young wife faithful? By spreading the rumour that she was sleeping with the dreaded local chief of police!

Yet although Antosha Chekhonte was formally banished, he did not disappear. He surfaces unexpectedly, for example, in the comic irrelevancies of the dialogue in Chekhov's mature plays. Nor was he ever far away in his letters and conversation. After his departure from the estate where he had been staying in the summer of 1902, Olga reported that all the young people had begun copying his style. By this she probably meant his laconic, off-beat sense of humour, with its flippant attitude to all 'affairs of the heart'. Romance was a subject that Chekhov, no less than Chekhonte, found it hard to take seriously.

Like the writer Trigorin, whom he portrays in *The Seagull*, Chekhov was already a literary celebrity in his thirties. The flood of composition might have slowed down to a trickle, but each new story was likely to be something of a literary event. Editions of his stories were being constantly reprinted throughout the 1890s. Of course, he had his critics and denigrators, as well as his fervent admirers, but this was inevitable in a country whose educated class had always taken its literature very seriously and felt a close sense of personal involvement with its authors. Many would have claimed that even though he had never tackled the traditional Russian literary form, the novel, his reputation was second only to that of Tolstoy among living Russian fiction writers.

As a playwright, however, Chekhov's reputation was very far from established when he first met Olga Knipper and the new company in 1898. He had written plenty of indifferent stories in his time, but these had simply disappeared from view and not been held against him, whereas failure in the theatre was more glaring and less quickly forgotten.

His first play to be performed, the four-act *Ivanov*, had its première in November 1887 at Korsh's Theatre in Moscow and was received with an extraordinary mixture of applause and hissing. 'In all his thirty-two years' experience, the prompter had never seen such excitement among the audience and off-stage,' Chekhov reported to his elder brother, Alexander.[4] There was almost a fight in the refreshment bar, and two students had to be thrown out of the gallery by the police. Called on to the stage three times at the end of Act III—while his one hand was being pumped by the leading man, the other was being pressed firmly to her bosom by the leading lady—and again repeatedly at the end of Act IV, Chekhov, to judge from his letters, seems to have thoroughly enjoyed being at the centre of this furore; but it was all rather too much for his younger sister, Masha, who nearly fainted.

In January 1889 a revised and better rehearsed production of *Ivanov* scored a more solid success at the Alexandrinsky, the Imperial Theatre in St Petersburg equivalent to the Maly in Moscow. Meanwhile, his one-act vaudeville, *The Bear*, had been a spectacular hit in Moscow the previous October and was soon followed by three more equally successful vaudevilles, all of them re-workings of earlier Chekhonte stories. Chekhov felt sure that his next full-length play would be a far greater triumph than *Ivanov*. But *The Wood Demon* was rejected outright by the selection committee at the Alexandrinsky, in spite of Chekhov's earlier success there; and worse was to come, for Alexander Lensky, a personal friend, not only rejected the play for his benefit performance at the Maly, but strongly advised Chekhov in a letter to give up writing for the stage altogether. Finally put on in December 1889 by a Moscow theatre on the verge of bankruptcy, the play ran for just three performances. The last had not been heard, however, of *The Wood Demon*. Perhaps in 1890, but more probably in the autumn of 1896, Chekhov quietly transformed it into *Uncle Vanya*, which was published in 1897 as one of his collected plays, though it had not previously been performed on the stage.

Chekhov took Lensky's advice to heart. Very little more is heard of Chekhov the dramatist until October 1895, when he was working on *The Seagull* at Melikhovo, the small country estate about two hours by train from Moscow, which the newly affluent author had bought in 1892 as a home for himself and his dependents. The play was written in a two-roomed cottage that had recently been built away from the main house. It was so small that Chekhov's desk and bed would not go into one room, and there were nights when the lamp in the cottage window was constantly going on and off, as he went through to the desk to add some new lines to his manuscript.

The links between *The Seagull* and Chekhov's own life are close and numerous. It is about the kind of people that he knew best. Arkadina is the middle-aged actress and Trigorin the middle-aged writer who are both highly successful, whereas Nina, the young actress, and Kostya, the young writer, are at the start of their careers. Chekhov explores what it means to be successful or unsuccessful in the world of art, highlighting the reactions to initial failure of the two young beginners. That this autobiographical play would figure so prominently in his own life; that he himself, outwardly resembling the successful Trigorin, was going to have to live through the same agonising experience of failure as his young characters; that the play was going to be associated with dramatic events in the history of the as yet unborn Moscow Art Theatre and that it would be the occasion of meeting his future wife: all this would have sounded to Chekhov like the ingredients for a highly fanciful story as he sat writing at the rough wooden desk in the cottage, more amused than worried by the thought that in his new play 'he was sinning terribly against the conventions of the stage'.[5]

Because of difficulties with the censor, the first night of *The Seagull* did not take place until October 17th, 1896, at the Alexandrinsky Theatre in St Petersburg. It was a failure. Not an ordinary failure, like that of *The Wood Demon*, not an excitingly mixed reception, like that of *Ivanov* in Moscow, but a spectacular, appalling fiasco. A mood of openly mocking hostility towards the play seemed to spread through the audience almost as soon as the curtain rose, and from it *The Seagull* never recovered.

Many reasons have been advanced for this failure. The production was insensitive and the play under-rehearsed: the first reading took place only nine days before the première. Yet this was after all the Imperial Theatre, neither director nor cast could be regarded as incompetent, and in Moscow *Ivanov* had scraped by on four rehearsals, two of which, according to Chekhov, consisted of slanging matches among the actors. Then it has been plausibly argued that the Muscovite Chekhov was a victim of jealousy on the part of the St Petersburg critics and journalists. They had been happy enough to praise *Ivanov* in 1889 when Chekhov was a promising young author, but now that he was a literary celebrity, they were only too eager to gloat over the spectacle of him apparently making a fool of himself, to join in the chorus of voices running down the play and its author after the first interval, and to dash off hostile reviews for publication in the next morning's papers. Yet unless Chekhov was the victim of a deliberate conspiracy (seriously suggested at the time),[6] these critics were not likely to have been those who guffawed in all the wrong places in Act I and turned their backs on the stage. Immediate responsibility for the fiasco seems to lie with a ludicrous piece of administrative mismanagement. To mark the twenty-fifth anniversary of her stage career, the play was taken as her benefit performance by 'the fat Levkeyeva', a comic actress with a funny voice and a large following, who may have been understandably misled by Chekhov's description of *The Seagull* as a 'comedy'. Levkeyeva did not herself appear in *The Seagull* but was to star as the postmaster's wife in the revival of a comic three-act play afterwards. Her fans did not take kindly to the prospect of sitting through four acts of pretentious drivel without so much as a glimpse of their heroine. That the rot set in among Levkeyeva's followers and spread to the rest of the audience, and then to the cast, seems to be confirmed by the fact that at subsequent performances *The Seagull* was acted and received quite respectably. By then, however, Chekhov had rushed off to Melikhovo, where he reacted sceptically to the telegrams informing him that the second performance had been a great success and that there had been calls for the author.

All this, however, like the more general argument that the play was 'ahead of its time', is to be wise after the event. Though the odds may have been against it, *The Seagull* was not *bound* to be a fiasco at its first performance. A freakish element of bad luck also seems to have been at work in the theatre on the night of October 17th, 1896.

The title of the three-act comedy that followed *The Seagull* was *This Happy Day*.

Chekhov was not there to see it. After sitting through two acts of *The Seagull* in the auditorium, he took refuge behind stage and at the end slipped out of the theatre unnoticed. 'There is a legend,' writes Nemirovich, 'that for hours on this windy autumnal night he wandered on the Embankment, that he caught cold, hastening the course of the malady which was to shorten his life';[7] while according to another legend, he was 'discovered later in the night on the railway track walking in the direction of Moscow'.[8] In fact, he returned to the house of Alexander Suvorin (editor of the important right-wing newspaper *New Times* and a good friend of Chekhov's, though twenty-six years his senior) at two in the morning, though not before his sister Masha had been driven almost frantic trying to trace his whereabouts. When Suvorin came to the guest suite to see how he was, Chekhov vowed that even if he lived for seven hundred years, he would never write anything more for the theatre. Early next morning, without even saying goodbye to his host and hostess, he left for Moscow on a slow stopping train. Such was his state of perturbation that he managed to leave his luggage behind in a third-class non-smoker of the train that took him on next day from Moscow to Melikhovo. Did Chekhov always travel third class? Or was he afraid of being recognised?

Once returned to Melikhovo, he set about putting as good a face on things as possible. He immediately sent off a letter of apology to Suvorin's wife, claiming that it had always been his firm intention to leave immediately after the first night, success or failure. This was not true; he had written earlier that he'd be returning 'about the 20th . . . if I'm delayed in Petersburg, it'll be until the 25th at the very latest'.[9] To Suvorin, who accused him of acting like an 'old woman', he justified his behaviour at greater length. Yes, he admitted, his pride had been wounded, but then he had never expected the play to be anything but a failure. He had reacted in a perfectly calm and rational way: had gone along to Romanov's for supper after the performance, slept soundly and departed the next morning without a murmur of complaint. To another acquaintance he even went so far as to write that his cool behaviour might serve as an object lesson for young people.[10]

None of this self-justification is convincing, though it is certainly of psychological interest. It is a curious irony of *The Seagull* that in his precipitate flight from St Petersburg after the première, Chekhov's behaviour falls far short of the standard set in the play by his heroine, Nina, who steels herself to stand firm in the face of ignominious failure. Only some weeks later did he admit to Suvorin how deeply he had been hurt. 'It wasn't the play that failed on October 17th, it was myself as an individual. Even during the first Act I was struck by a particular circumstance: all those people with whom I had been on terms of frank and friendly intimacy before that date had on their faces a strange expression, a terribly strange expression. I'm calm now, my mood is normal, but all the same I can't forget what happened, any more than I could forget, for example, if I'd been struck by someone.'[11] The last phrase comes as a surprise from Chekhov, who was not given to extreme emotional reactions. Even more than this, however, the elaborate lengths to which he was prepared to go in order to justify his behaviour in the eyes of other people and himself, bear witness to an unusually highly developed sense of *amour propre*.

Yet *The Seagull* still had its champions, in spite of the fiasco. There was Chekhov's lawyer friend, A. F. Koni, who wrote after seeing the second performance that in the play 'life seemed so close that there were times when you forgot you were sitting in the theatre and felt capable of taking part in the conversation going on in front of you'.[12] And most important of all, there was Vladimir Nemirovich-Danchenko.

CHAPTER FOUR

Triumph

Chekhov and Nemirovich had been on friendly terms since the 1880s. They knew and admired one another's writings. It was Nemirovich and his friend, Sumbatov-Yuzhin, actor-dramatist at the Maly Theatre, who persuaded Chekhov in 1895 to write another play. Chekhov sent the manuscript of *The Seagull* to Nemirovich for his advice and criticism, but the latter did not see the play performed, as he was away in the country during October 1896 finishing his own play.

'I heard the play wasn't a success or, more accurately, was a strange kind of failure,' he wrote to Chekhov on his return. 'I feel you're going to give up the theatre now, just as Turgenev and the others did.'[1] The big success of the 1896–97 season turned out to be Nemirovich's *The Worth of Life*. When the judges decided to award him the Griboyedov Prize for the season's best play, Nemirovich protested. Why not give the prize to *The Seagull*? That would be a superb glove to fling at the public and the traditional theatre; but the judges refused to be persuaded.

At the historic conference in June 1897, Chekhov's name was among those mentioned by Nemirovich as possible playwrights for the new theatre, but Stanislavsky, more interested then in the classics, showed no enthusiasm. Nevertheless, Nemirovich did not forget about *The Seagull*. He decided to put it on at the Philharmonic as one of the graduation plays to be performed by his brilliant final-year pupils. Day after day Olga Knipper and the others carried round with them the small yellow volume of Chekhov's stories and immersed themselves in his world. Then

33

they read and re-read *The Seagull*, puzzling over how this unusual play was to be acted, until finally they were 'infected' by the enthusiastic exposition of their teacher.

In the event, *The Seagull* was not put on by the Philharmonic, since Nemirovich understood that Sumbatov and Lensky were intending to produce it at the Maly, but in April 1898 Nemirovich sent a long letter to Chekhov, outlining the plans for the new theatre and asking permission to include *The Seagull* in their repertoire; the best of his pupils, he wrote, were already in love with the play. He could not promise Chekhov storms of applause, but that it would be a fresh, artistic production, free from routine—that much he would guarantee.

Chekhov refused. The reasons he gave, according to Nemirovich (the letter has not survived), were that he was over-sensitive, did not wish to be caused any more emotional upsets by the theatre, and was not much of a playwright in any case.

Never one to be easily deterred, Nemirovich immediately sent off a second letter.

'Your refusal,' he wrote, 'would be a great blow to me, as *The Seagull* is the only contemporary play which fires my imagination as a director, and you are the only contemporary writer who can be of great interest for a theatre with a model repertoire.'[2] Before rehearsals began, he would be willing to visit Chekhov in Melikhovo to discuss the production. Delighted by this prospect, Chekhov promptly forgot his earlier scruples. 'For the pleasure of your company and conversation,' he replied, 'I am ready to let you have all my plays.'[3]

Nemirovich still had to 'infect' Stanislavsky. This was done at Pushkino. 'He could talk of a play so well,' Stanislavsky writes somewhat ruefully, 'that one had to like it before he was through.'[4] Left alone with the script, however, Stanislavsky's enthusiasm quickly evaporated, but he retired to his brother's estate to prepare the *mise en scène*. To his surprise the work went easily, and even more to his surprise, it was favourably received by Nemirovich and the prospective cast.

A mood of nervous agitation and excitement swept over the

volatile Miss Knipper on September 8th, 1898, when she received Nemirovich's note saying that the author himself would be at rehearsal the following evening. What would he be like, this literary celebrity for whom they had come to share Nemirovich's feelings of love and admiration? And what was he going to think of a performance by unknown artists of a play that had already caused him such anguish?

On his arrival at the Hunting Club, Chekhov was quickly buttonholed by the actor, Alexander Vishnevsky, who introduced himself by reminding Chekhov that they had been pupils together at Taganrog High School: a connection that he was never slow to publicise in the years to come. Still talking animatedly to Vishnevsky, Chekhov entered the hall, where the rest of the cast was anxiously lined up waiting to be introduced.

They rehearsed the first act and part of the second, and Chekhov then made comments and suggestions to Nemirovich and the artists.

'They were very nervous,' Nemirovich reported to Stanislavsky. 'He said that there was a pleasant atmosphere at rehearsal, that the company was excellent and we were working splendidly.'[5] A conventional pat on the back? Chekhov's letters show that his words were quite sincere.

It was not at all, however, as Olga had expected. Her experience may have been like that of Nina in *The Seagull*, who discovers to her surprise that famous people do not behave like famous people at all, but 'cry, go fishing, play cards, laugh and get angry, just the way other people do'. They liked Chekhov and he seemed to like them, but far from expounding the content of his play or laying down the law about their acting, he seemed to be as much at a loss to know what to talk about as they were. According to Olga, he kept plucking nervously at his beard, jerking his pince-nez back into position, and gazing intently at the Etruscan vases being prepared for the production of *Antigone*. When one of the actresses asked him how Nina's monologue in Act I was to be regarded 'from the historical point of view', these vases came in for particularly close attention.[6] No doubt the artists did feel nervous, but it seems to have been Chekhov who was the more overawed by the earnestness of the young company.

Two days later, Chekhov was present at another rehearsal of *The Seagull*; various of his suggestions had been adopted, though Nemirovich did not give way on every point. His attendance on the evening of the 14th at a full dress rehearsal of *Tsar Fyodor*, in which Olga had been given the role of the Tsar's wife, Irina, was unscheduled and flattering to the company. It took place in the Hermitage Theatre, then being hastily renovated in time for the opening a month hence. The theatre was unheated and lit only by candles in bottles. 'How strange our own voices sounded in that damp, cold, dark cavern of a building,' Olga recalled, 'where you couldn't make out the walls or the ceiling, but only huge, mournful, creeping shadows.' It was pleasant to think of Chekhov sitting out there in the darkness following the performance.[7]

Two days later Chekhov travelled south to Yalta. Following the official diagnosis of T.B. at the time of his illness in the spring of 1897—an illness which the *Seagull* fiasco had helped to precipitate, according to his sister Masha—he had been advised to spend every autumn and winter in a relatively warm climate. In letters from Yalta he referred enthusiastically to the new theatre, urging his friends to support it, and on October 8th he told Suvorin of the agreeable impression that *Tsar Fyodor* had made upon him. 'An atmosphere of genuine art emanated from the stage, even though the performers were not outstanding talents. Irina, in my opinion, is magnificent. Her voice, nobility and sincerity were so good that they brought a lump to your throat. Had I stayed in Moscow, I'd have fallen in love with that Irina.'[8]

October 14th, 1898, was the day chosen with the help of a gypsy fortune-teller for the opening of the new theatre. Was this the day, Stanislavsky wondered, on which he would 'pass through the portals of art', or would he be condemned to a future of boring business lunches? As stage director, his own part in *Tsar Fyodor* was over, but he could not resist the temptation of going on stage to deliver final words of encouragement and inspiration. Pale-faced, his voice breaking, his breathing irregular, he was only half way through his speech when his words were suddenly drowned by the orchestra starting up the overture. What was he to do? He broke into a wild dance (to be referred to later as his *danse macabre*), singing to himself, gesticulating, shouting out encouraging sentences.

'Konstantin Sergeyevich!' came the voice of the actor in charge of final preparations. 'Leave the stage at once! Don't annoy the artists!' An act of some courage and obvious good sense, as Stanislavsky himself later acknowledged; but not before he had slunk off to his dressing-room with feelings ruffled, and locked the door.

In fact, the curtain did not go *up*. As part of the theatre's innovations, it went sideways, and it was not the usual red and gold variety, but a sober shade of greyish-green.

The first prophetic words of the Moscow Art Theatre and of *Tsar Fyodor* were spoken: 'I have high hopes of this new enterprise.'

The choice of *Tsar Fyodor* for the opening performance had been a tactical one. This was their 'battleship', thought Nemirovich, the heaviest gun in their armoury. Because Tsars did not approve of plays about their predecessors, even those of the seventeenth century, its performance had been banned for thirty years. It appealed to the prevalent taste for national historical drama. It offered the widest possible scope for Stanislavsky's talents as a stage director. The first-night audience was bowled over, as Chekhov had been, by the extraordinary visual impact of the play: by the historically convincing costumes and stage props (fruits of Stanislavsky's 'looting expeditions' in the summer to ancient Russian towns) and by the vivid re-creation of life in medieval Russia. And when they had recovered from these effects, there was the acting to be appreciated: of the unknown Moskvin—who awoke the following day to fame, according to Nemirovich—as the weak-willed Tsar, and of the unknown Olga Knipper as his wife, Irina.

On October 12th, Chekhov's father died at Melikhovo after a short illness. In the midst of all the excitement of the opening nights, Nemirovich found time to send a telegram of sympathy on behalf of the company. 'Judging by the papers,' Chekhov wrote in reply, 'your opening was a glorious success, and I am very, very glad, more so than you can possibly imagine. But why don't the papers say anything about Knipper as Irina? Has something gone wrong? I didn't like your Fyodor,' (an opinion that Chekhov seems to have been alone in holding) 'but Irina seemed exceptional.'[9]

During the next two months, *Tsar Fyodor* continued to play to full houses, but one battleship does not make a flotilla. Stanislavsky's production of *The Merchant of Venice*, in which he played Shylock with a Jewish accent, was a complete failure. Hauptmann's *Hannele*, on which high hopes had been pinned, was never even launched, as its production was forbidden at the last moment by the Metropolitan of Moscow. Of the money contributed by shareholders nothing remained, and Nemirovich was having to borrow to keep the theatre afloat. As they approached December 17th, the day set aside for the first performance of *The Seagull*, it was clear to all concerned that 'the first rational, moral, universally accessible theatre' was on the verge of sinking without trace.

Chekhov's play had never been thought of as a battleship. It carried no heavy guns of brilliant stage effects. It had already failed once within recent memory and at a reputable theatre. That it should quietly take up its place at the rear of the flotilla was the most that could be hoped for from this frail vessel.

There was some doubt as to whether the first performance would go ahead at all on the 17th. Nemirovich claims that Masha Chekhova, knowing how anxiously her brother awaited the performance, was in a state of great tension that communicated itself to the actors, and kept imploring him not to proceed unless he could be sure of success. Then on the day before the première, Stanislavsky demanded a postponement to give time for more rehearsals. Nemirovich refused, since in his view the production was ready. Stanislavsky does not mention his demand for postponement, but he too claims that on the eve of performance Masha came to them 'with tears in her eyes' and begged them not to go ahead.

Masha herself, however, was very indignant with Stanislavsky and especially Nemirovich for presenting her in this light in their memoirs, and categorically denied the story of her 'tears', 'nerves' and 'entreaties'. According to her, until she received complimentary tickets for a box at the first night of *The Seagull*, she did not know that Nemirovich was involved in the new theatre and had never met Stanislavsky or the others in her life. In December she did however attend a performance of *Tsar Fyodor*, on which she reported favourably to Chekhov in her letter of December 9th, assuring him that *The Seagull* would have a comparable success and that she would be attending the first night with friends. This, however, was only for Chekhov's benefit. Fearing a repetition of the St Petersburg fiasco, she decided not to attend the first night and gave the tickets to her brother Ivan and his family; though in the event, overcome by curiosity, she joined Ivan in his box while the performance was already in progress.

Who is to be believed? One is inclined to dismiss the story of Masha's 'last-minute plea' as another *Seagull* legend, and to agree with Masha that her very dear friends had been guilty of embroidering in order to dramatise the difficulties of the *Seagull* production. Like the brilliant defence counsel described by Chekhonte in one of his earliest comic stories, both Nemirovich and Stanislavsky in their memoirs 'tend to ignore the facts, concentrating more on the psychological aspect'.[10] But there is an embarrassing inconsistency in Masha's story also. In her letter of the 9th she had assured Chekhov that she would be attending the first night; yet on the 17th Chekhov wrote: 'A pity you weren't at the first performance.' There was probably a small grain of truth in the Nemirovich/Stanislavsky story after all.

And what of Chekhov himself? Was it true, as Stanislavsky claims, that 'his spiritual condition was such that if *The Seagull* should fail, the great poet would not be able to weather the blow'?

He was certainly far from well that autumn. On October 25th a report appeared in the St Petersburg *News* that his health had deteriorated. Though he strenuously denied this in letters to his family, he confessed to Suvorin at the end of November that he had been spitting blood for five days—'but this is between ourselves, don't mention it to anyone'.

Nor did he mention to anyone in the family what he was feeling about *The Seagull*. His letters are full of other matters, especially his house-building and property-buying activities in and around Yalta. Only on December 17th itself, towards the end of a long business letter to Masha, does he write: '*Uncle Vanya* is being played all over Russia. By the summer I should think a thousand roubles will have accumulated for me at the Society of Playwrights. As I write these lines, *The Seagull* is being played in Moscow. How did it go?' He had referred to the success of *Uncle Vanya* in the provinces on several occasions, perhaps using it as a psychological cushion against the possibility of another *Seagull* disappointment.

Chekhov's Yalta doctor, Altshuller, confirms, however, what one might have suspected: that Chekhov did care very much indeed. 'He was unable to conceal his agitation, which expressed itself in detailed stories about the play's failure at the Alexandrinsky Theatre.'[11]

Spiritual crisis or not in Chekhov's life, there can be no doubt that the first night of *The Seagull* was a crisis in the life of the Art Theatre, although Chekhov, relying on newspaper comments, had no inkling of this.

Even by his own high standards, Stanislavsky excelled himself in dramatising the situation:

'You must play well, you must play better than well; you must create not only success, but triumph, for you know that if you do not, the man and writer you love will die, killed by your hands.'

These inner whisperings did not aid our creative inspiration. The boards were becoming the floor of a gallows, and we actors the executioners.

The members of the cast had all taken valerian drops to steady their nerves. In the first act a bold experiment had been made: the spectators watching Kostya's play within the play sat with their backs to the auditorium. This was fortunate, as it enabled Stanislavsky, playing the part of Trigorin, to suppress an uncontrollable nervous twitching in his leg.

The curtain was drawn at the end of Act I. Complete silence. Was it a failure? Another shattering failure? According to Stanislavsky, Olga Knipper, playing the part of Arkadina, fainted on stage; another version has it that she fought desperately to control the hysterical sobs welling up inside her.

'Then suddenly,' writes Nemirovich, 'in the auditorium, something happened. It was as if a dam had burst, or a bomb had exploded—all at once there was a deafening crash of applause.'

The curtain was hastily opened, surprising the actors in various unsuitable postures.

At the end of Act III everyone stood up to applaud and there were repeated shouts of 'Author!'

Nemirovich came on stage and announced that Chekhov was not in the theatre.

'Then send him a telegram! A telegram for the author!'

Whatever else it may have distorted, the legend does not seem to have exaggerated the wild scenes of jubilation that accompanied the triumphant rehabilitation by the Art Theatre of Chekhov's *Seagull*.

Many reasons have been advanced for this triumph. It was the Theatre's first attempt to convey the reality of *contemporary* life in Russia, and they succeeded so remarkably, Masha wrote to her brother on the next day, 'that you really forgot you were in the theatre'. The play had been carefully prepared and thoroughly rehearsed, and in Nemirovich it had an interpreter who was sensitive to the psychological nuances of Chekhov's characterisation. Moreover, claims Olga, the cast was imbued with a burning love of Chekhov and of their new theatre, and these feelings could not help but communicate themselves to the audience.

And yet, and yet ... the theatre was far from full on that first night. Chekhov himself was highly critical of certain aspects of the production, especially the acting of Roksanova as Nina and of Stanislavsky as Trigorin, when a special performance was put on for his benefit in the following spring. Olga admits that their acting on the first night was not all that wonderful, which does not surprise one in view of the tension that they were under, while Nemirovich also writes that 'it was remarkable that even the indifferent execution of certain roles did nothing to hinder our triumph'.

Was there not also a freakish element of *good* luck at work in the theatre on the night of December 17th, 1898? If so, it was no more than poetic justice demanded.

The Art Theatre was saved, at least for the time being.

Congratulations poured into Yalta, leaving Chekhov in no doubt of his success. Nemirovich, to whom goes the credit for rescuing *The Seagull* more or less single-handed, cabled twice. 'I am happier than ever I was at productions of my own plays,' he concluded the second telegram. Then followed a long letter about the play's reception and the cast's performances, in which Knipper was placed at the top of his order of merit.

Before long, however, Chekhov was complaining, somewhat ungraciously, that bad luck had struck him once again in the theatre: no sooner did he have a success on his hands than one of the actresses was taken ill and performances had to be cancelled.

The actress concerned was Olga Knipper, who had played the first night with a high temperature, had taken to her bed the day after with bronchitis, and was so infuriated by her illness that for days she lay there in tears refusing to see anyone.

'I have such bad luck in the theatre,' Chekhov wrote to friends, 'such rotten luck, that if I were to marry an actress, I've no doubt I'd father an orang-outang or a porcupine.'[12]

CHAPTER FIVE

The Other Women

When Chekhov first met Olga Knipper in September 1898, he was thirty-eight. His Yalta doctor, Altshuller, also met him for the first time that autumn and has described the impression that Chekhov made on him.[1] Just under six feet tall, he already walked with a slight stoop but still cut a fairly handsome and cheerful figure. As he recounted stories about his past life, his manner became animated, he kept straightening his right moustache with his right index finger, his expressive eyes lit up cheerfully, and the story would be frequently punctuated by that infectious laughter which appealed to so many who knew him. That he was a sick man, however, was indicated by the wrinkles round his eyes and mouth, his slow measured walk and shortness of breath even on the slightest inclines, and most of all by his tell-tale cough. Altshuller soon learned that there were two things you did not do in Chekhov's company: you did not ask him about his writing and you did not enquire after his health. Although he had begun to spit blood as early as 1884 and his elder brother Nicholas had died of T.B. in 1889, he refused to acknowledge the implications of his own symptoms and received no treatment at all until 1897. Was he ignoring his symptoms quite deliberately, on the grounds that nothing could be done about the disease in any case? Or was it, as Altshuller thought, an obvious example of a doctor being blind to his own condition? Or some delicate balance between the two?

This is one of many puzzles that Chekhov has set his biographers. As Ronald Hingley warns us in *A New Life of Chekhov,* the character of Chekhov may be as tantalising as that of a Chekhov character.[2] But since he was that much older and more experienced than Olga, it is necessary to an understanding of their relationship that we should attempt to outline certain aspects of his personality and his relationships with other people before Olga entered his life—especially, of course, his relationships with women.

If Chekhov's biography is obscure, it is not for lack of information. His life is documented by a prodigious array of letters and memoirs. The trouble is that none of this material tells us what we would really like to know. It seems probable, for example, that in the years 1889–90 Chekhov went through some kind of psychological crisis, but whereas in the life of a Tolstoy, the nature of such a crisis would sooner or later have become public knowledge, in Chekhov's case we can only guess at the reasons, noting that in 1889 he published a literary work, the famous *Dreary Story*, of much greater depth than anything he had written previously, and that in 1890, to the puzzlement of those round him, he undertook a hazardous expedition right across European Russia and Siberia to the notorious convict island of Sakhalin.

Thus, an episode like that of his reaction to the *Seagull* fiasco of 1896 may be especially revealing, because there one sees him caught off his guard.

It might at first seem unfair to attribute to Chekhov, as we did in discussing his reaction to the fiasco, an unusually highly developed sense of *amour propre*, since he has always been rightly praised for the modesty with which he conducted himself as a famous writer and public figure. The two, however, are not incompatible. One of Chekhov's most perceptive memoirists, his fellow writer, Ivan Bunin, saw in him 'a very strong sense of his own worth and independence'.[3] This sense had been painstakingly cultivated in order to counteract the feelings of inferiority and subservience that were liable to beset a talented young man of humble origin making his way up the social ladder in Russia. To call anyone a 'lackey' is a most damning epithet in

Chekhov's fiction. It was something more in him than self-respect. Great joker though he was, one cannot imagine him taking kindly to jokes against himself. The sneering expressions on the faces of members of the *Seagull* audience were a blow to his *amour propre*, because these people with whom he had felt himself to be 'on terms of frank and friendly intimacy' appeared to be laughing not so much at the play but at his discomfiture.

It is clear too that the distress which he felt after giving way to impulse and fleeing from St Petersburg came about because of the high standards of behaviour that he set for himself and others. Chekhov was a very self-disciplined person, both in his attitude to writing and in the everyday things of life: was never known to appear sloppily dressed, had a fixed place for everything on his writing desk, filed and answered letters with great conscientiousness, and was scrupulously fair in all his financial dealings. He was always generous with help and advice. His record of good works is beyond reproach. At a time when Russian liberals were distinguished more by their words than their deeds, Chekhov was quietly fighting cholera epidemics, giving free medical treatment to the peasants, organising schools and sanatoria, and regularly sending off parcels of books—many of them signed copies procured from his friends—to fill the shelves of Taganrog Public Library. One is inclined to agree with the suggestion of another interesting memoirist, the writer Potapenko, that he did all this not because of a 'warm heart', but out of a sense of duty:[4] this was the only honourable course of action open to an educated man in Russia's backward society. Not that Chekhov had any illusions about the educated classes. In his fiction he specialised in exposing the particular areas of human selfishness, self-centredness and self-importance; of posing, affectation and emotional self-indulgence; of insincerity, hypocrisy and self-deceit.

Yet paradoxically, as his reaction to the fiasco also illustrates, his own behaviour was not without occasional traces of this last set of qualities. It was self-deceit, born of a wounded sense of *amour propre*, that prompted him to write so unconvincingly that his cool behaviour on that occasion might serve as an object lesson for young people. And when he tried to deceive himself that he was not really suffering from T.B., in spite of all the indications to the contrary, was it not for a similar reason: that his *amour propre* hated the idea of having to think of himself as anything but a perfectly normal, healthy individual?

In considering Chekhov's personal relationships, we are faced by another puzzling question: was Chekhov a lonely man?

In one sense, obviously not. Writers of fiction cannot afford to be unsociable. He enjoyed a convivial atmosphere and was constantly inviting guests to Melikhovo. Then he was always making, though often failing to carry out, elaborate travel plans, preferring not to remain in the same spot for a long time but to visit new places and discover new people. With a wide circle of friends he kept up a lively correspondence. Yet on one point his most perceptive memoirists—Bunin, Potapenko, Altshuller—all agree: with Chekhov there was a barrier beyond which you did not pass. 'Even those nearest to him,' wrote Bunin, 'never fully knew what was going on in the depths of his soul.'[5] Among that wide circle of friends there is not one who can be described as a close friend. Suvorin, for many years the closest of his correspondents, was twenty-six years his senior. Nor was there anyone in his family with whom he had an easy, intimate relationship. In his later years, the sense of being cut off from other people, of having to lead his own, self-contained life, may have been intensified by his illness. That was a battle that he alone could wage, not only against the disease itself, but also to prevent it from turning him into an invalid in the eyes of the outside world.

Chekhov's stories also suggest that he was very much aware of feelings of alienation, for there are few themes that he handles so convincingly as that of the plight of the lonely individual. 'Just as I shall lie alone in the grave,' he wrote in one of his notebooks, 'so, in effect, I also live alone.'[6] The remark may have been intended for one of his characters, but he may equally well have been thinking of himself.

The Other Women

Among Chekhov's circle of friends was a large number of women. He took pleasure in female company and portrayed female characters with great sensitivity. It is the women whom we remember best from his plays: Nina in *The Seagull*, the three sisters, Ranyevskaya in *The Cherry Orchard*.

From his fictional portrayal of unsympathetic females an idea emerges of the kind of women to whom he is unlikely to have been attracted in real life. There are the over-sexed, predatory females, like Ariadna in the story of that name, who exploit their sexual power over men (Astrov in *Uncle Vanya* sees Yelyena in this light, as 'a fluffy marten who needs victims'); the over-managing household tyrants, like the usurping Natasha of *Three Sisters*; and the over-domesticated, complacent nest-builders (the heroine of *A Teacher of Literature*), whose way of life is symbolised by cooking smells and dogs with wet noses. In contrast to these anti-heroines, Chekhov created his own brand of romantic heroine: a fragile, child-like creature, seen against a poetic background, who inspires in the male not so much sexual lust as a feeling of protective tenderness. There is no evidence, however, that Chekhov was attracted to such girls—if they existed—in real life. In general, what is striking about his love stories is their one-sidedness. The romance is presented in terms of the effect that it has upon the hero. There is no sense of psychological fusion; and, of course, there are never any happy marriages.

From this it would be rash to conclude that Chekhov did not believe in the possibility of happy marriages in real life. As Virginia Llewellyn Smith reminds us: 'Marriage makes the best copy when its difficulties are greatest.'[7] To his younger brother Michael, Chekhov wrote in October 1898, not long after meeting Olga: 'Marriage is worthwhile only if it's for love; to marry a girl just because you like her is the same as buying some useless object in the market just because it takes your fancy. What makes family life work is love, sexual attraction, being one flesh.'[8]

How capable, though, was Chekhov himself of being one flesh? How willing was he to share his life completely?

'All right, I'll get married if you like,' he wrote to Suvorin in March 1895.

> But these are my conditions. Everything must remain as before: she must live in Moscow, I'll live in the country, and I'll go to visit her. I can't stand happiness that goes on day after day, from one morning to the next. When a person keeps telling me the same thing every day, in exactly the same tone of voice, I begin to feel violent. That's how I feel, for example, when I'm with Sergeyenko. He's very much like a woman ('intelligent and responsive') and when we're together I can't help thinking that I might get a wife who was like that. I promise to be a splendid husband, but give me a wife like the moon, who won't appear in my sky every day; it doesn't follow that I'll write any better for being married.[9]

Though the tone of these remarks may be Chekhonte's, the preoccupations are Chekhov's. A girl that one likes, an intelligent, predictable wife-companion, has no appeal for him; his wife must be glamorous, different, never a bore. And why should he sacrifice to marriage his well-established independence? In November he told Suvorin that he could not see how the disorderliness of his life could be reconciled with the restrictions that marriage would impose.[10] By 'disorderliness' he probably had in mind not any lack of self-discipline, but the kind of unbalanced, obsessional life that Trigorin describes to Nina in Act II of *The Seagull*: 'Here I am talking to you and getting quite carried away, yet I can't forget for a moment that there's an unfinished story waiting for me.' At one period in his life Chekhov had been fond of saying that medicine was his legal wife and writing his mistress, but those days were long past. Writing had become his legal wife, and psychologically a very demanding one.

From fictional heroines and hypothetical wives let us turn to three real women in Chekhov's life before he met Olga: the three Lydias.

Lydia Avilova was a married woman with children, living in

St Petersburg. Significantly perhaps, she also wrote fiction. Though her meetings with Chekhov between 1889 and 1899 were few and far between, and scarcely ever in private, she claimed in a memoir published long after Chekhov's death that she had been the secret love of his life. Her account is riddled with flaws and inconsistencies, and Virginia Llewellyn Smith has plausibly (and charitably?) suggested that what Avilova in 1895 'took to be a sincere declaration of passion was simply Chekhov putting on a display of the facetious gallantry with which he was accustomed —as his letters constantly demonstrate—to treat pretty young women.'[11] There remains the faint possibility that Avilova's story may be both true *and* unreliable, but this we are unlikely ever to know.

Lydia Yavorskaya was an attractive young actress, already divorced, who came to Moscow in 1893. She was extremely ambitious and probably cultivated Chekhov's friendship for that reason. Too corrupted by the commercial theatre to be considered seriously later by the Art Theatre, Yavorskaya was celebrated for such parts as that of the heroine in *La Dame aux Camélias*, and when Chekhov in *The Seagull* depicted Arkadina as a star in the old tradition, this was the one part to which he made her refer. It seems almost certain that in January 1895 Yavorskaya and Chekhov spent at least one night together in Room 5 of Moscow's Grand Hotel, but Llewellyn Smith concludes that however great a degree of intimacy was involved, it is probable that the affair 'was entered into in a casual spirit, and broken up by the circumstances of her obligation to go on tour in the spring of 1895— and that it left neither of them with any cause for regret or recrimination.'[12]

The third Lydia, Lydia Mizinova, or Lika, was a friend of the Chekhov family, to whom she had been introduced in the late 1880s as an eighteen-year-old schoolteacher colleague of Masha Chekhova's. Though early tending towards plumpness, Lika was beautiful, and when she first visited the house, all the Chekhov boys craned over the banisters to catch a glimpse of her. She was also unpredictable, good company and good fun. Chekhov subjected her to a barrage of Chekhonte tomfoolery, epistolary and presumably also conversational, inventing for her numerous lovers of whom he was supposedly jealous. But Lika's feelings for Anton appear to have been very much stronger than his for her. Lika, it seems, was too much a member of the family; though he admired her good looks and pleasant singing voice, she could not inspire in him any special feelings; she was no more than 'a girl that one likes'. He may also have been put off by what Llewellyn Smith describes as the 'potential vulgarity' of Lika's behaviour.[13] Lika not only liked singing and dancing, she also liked smoking and drinking. 'Lika was drunk,' Olga Knipper wrote to Chekhov in December 1901, describing an Art Theatre party, 'and kept pestering me to drink Brüderschaft, but I wriggled out of it . . . I can't drink Brüderschaft just for the sake of it'; while at another party a few days later, 'Lika was drinking Brüderschaft again with someone.'[14] In August 1893, by which time she had given up hope of evoking any stronger feelings in Chekhov, Lika wrote to him: 'You need people for when there's a spell of bad weather, and the nights are drawing in, when there's nothing to do and it's too early to go to bed, so that you can have someone beside you to relieve your boredom, but as soon as the moment passes you don't give a thought to that person.'[15]

On the rebound from Chekhov, Lika took up with Chekhov's writer-friend Potapenko, who was already married, became pregnant and was then abandoned by him: a situation that Chekhov made use of in *The Seagull*, where Nina is abandoned by her writer-lover Trigorin. Does this suggest a callous and unscrupulous Chekhov? Or someone whose compulsion to write was so strong that he was able to deceive himself into thinking that these obvious parallels would not be noticed?

There can be no doubt that until he met Olga Knipper in 1898 the most important woman in Chekhov's life was his sister Masha.

Anton was the third child in the family. His elder brothers, Alexander and Nicholas, were creative but dissolute; his younger siblings—Ivan, Masha and Michael—hard-working but pedestrian. Anton was fortunate in combining the best qualities of both. Although she was only three and a half years his junior, Masha inevitably looked up to Anton, who had enabled her to receive a good education and become a schoolteacher. A cultured person, modestly gifted as an artist, not without a mind and sense of humour of her own but lacking Anton's originality, her real creative talents lay in practical directions. More and more she saw it as her task in life to act as her famous brother's 'right-hand man'. In the family she was later nicknamed the Master Builder, and when the move to Melikhovo took place in March 1892, she threw herself enthusiastically into the task of helping Anton to transform the run-down property into a thriving estate.

In the summer of 1893 Chekhov's elder brother Alexander visited Melikhovo—only to leave a few days later after a domestic quarrel. Alexander was the one person in the family who did not mind telling Anton a few home truths. Anton was stifling himself in Melikhovo, he wrote on his return; the sooner he threw up this way of life, the better. The Bohemian Alexander was no doubt appalled by the prospect of Anton turning into a complacent country squire. But he also criticised Anton's relationships with the other members of the household, not only with their parents, but more surprisingly, with Masha. It was a false relationship, he fulminated; one kind word from Anton and she was eating out of his hand; 'she's afraid of you and gazes at you with such humble and respectful eyes'.[16]

These last words carry a ring of truth. In later years Masha never made any secret of the unbounded respect and admiration that she had felt towards her brother. But what of Anton? Alexander seems to imply that the relationship was false because Anton, perhaps unwittingly, was encouraging this attitude of exaggerated devotion in Masha and exploiting it for his own ends. That Masha's feelings for Anton, like Lika's, were very much stronger than his for her, seems obvious. From the letters between them a certain fixed pattern emerges that was no doubt characteristic of their relationship as a whole. They are newsy, factual, business-like letters. They suggest two people who are close but not intimate. Anton does not tell his sister any secrets; he holds certain things back. He seems to take her quiet dependability and helpfulness very much for granted, is affectionate towards her but in a minor key, as one might be towards some familiar object round the house.

In the autumn of 1892, when she was twenty-nine, Masha received a proposal of marriage (her third, and an attractive one). The timing may be significant: just after the first exhilarating summer of communal enterprise at Melikhovo. According to Masha, she could not make up her mind, but decided to test Anton's reaction by telling him that she was planning to marry. The latter refused to comment. Interpreting this as a sign of disappointment, Masha went to her room, feeling 'lost and helpless', and had a long cry. During the next few days Anton never once referred to the proposal but did not seem to be his usual jocular self and was withdrawn towards her. Deciding that she could not upset her brother's customary way of life or deprive him of the creative environment that she had always sought to provide for him, Masha turned down her suitor, who sent her a sharp, reproachful letter in reply.

Against this must be set Chekhov's remarks in a letter at the time to Suvorin:

> My sister hasn't married, but the romance seems to be continuing by post. I don't understand it at all. People are guessing that she's refused this time too. She must be the only girl who genuinely doesn't want to marry. Now about myself. There's no one I could marry, even if I wanted to. To hell with it. I'd be bored having to bother with a wife. But falling in love would be a very different matter. Life's a bore if you're not deeply in love.[17]

Masha's version of what happened is contained in the memoir which she dictated in her nineties—more than sixty years, that is, after the events themselves.[18] At that remove of time, one is bound to suspect that Masha was creating her own legend, remembering things in the way that she wanted to, especially in such an intimate matter as this. We shall note later how her recollection of the 'harmonious and cheerful' summer that she spent in Yalta in 1901 with Anton and Olga is flatly contradicted by Olga's account, written much nearer the time. Masha may have been right in interpreting Anton's reaction as an expression of barely concealed disappointment at the thought of losing his devoted helper (though he always liked to think of himself as independent); but it seems more likely that *she* was the one who secretly wanted to make this self-sacrifice and interpreted Anton's reaction accordingly. In other words, if anyone's motives are hidden, it is hers and not his. Anton's letter reveals self-centredness, in that it would never have occurred to him to realise how important his active approval was to Masha, but it is the very offhandedness of his approach to the whole affair that seems convincing; for someone supposedly concealing his true feelings from himself, this seems much too good a performance.

The point need not detain us. Whether voluntarily or under hidden pressure from Anton, the sacrifice was made. Masha gave up the possibility of becoming a wife and mother in order to concern herself with her brother's future welfare. This we shall have to remember when she was no longer the most important woman in his life but part of an emotional triangle that included herself, Anton and Olga Knipper.

✣

CHAPTER SIX

Dear Author ... Dear Actress

Eight years younger than Chekhov and in good health, Olga was not so tall but often seemed taller, since she had a good figure and held herself very erect. In a photograph of her as a small child, her back is as straight as a ramrod, and so it remained until her ninety-first year. The adjective 'beautiful' was seldom applied to her, but she was repeatedly described as 'charming', 'attractive' and 'fascinating'. Her features were too irregular for beauty: her lips were noticeably thin and her very dark eyes rather small and deep-set. But the eyes shone with vitality, and the expressive smile ranged from the sad and reflective to the playful and roguish. Her musical voice was rather low-pitched. If Chekhov's laughter, like his voice, became increasingly toneless as he tried to save breath, Olga's laugh was deep and rumbustious. Like Chekhov she had a high forehead which she accentuated by brushing her very thick, dark brown hair back off her face in a kind of halo effect. The face itself has an elusive quality, appropriate to a character actress. Looking at the photographs of Olga Knipper in her prime, one is struck by the way in which no two photographs seem alike; it is impossible to pin down the 'real' Olga. After receiving two photographs from her in February 1900, Chekhov commented that in one 'there's a little demon lurking behind your modest expression of quiet sadness', while in the other 'you remind me a bit of a Jewess, a very musical individual who's studying at the conservatoire and at the same time hedging her bets by secretly taking a course in dentistry'. He is careful to stress that this is only a joke, for the smartly dressed Olga was undoubtedly very conscious of her personal appearance.[1]

Of the men in her life before she met Chekhov there is little to say. Dmitri Goncharov, with whom she was mildly in love and sang duets from *Eugene Onegin*, does not seem important. From casual references in her correspondence to former admirers, one may guess that the latter were quite numerous, while in her Chekhov memoir she refers, without going into detail, to some unhappy love affair in her youth which had strengthened her conviction that the theatre alone should fill every aspect of her life.[2]

That the young actress had appealed to the playwright at first sight is clear from his letters. Eight months passed before they met again, but during that time Masha Chekhova was helping to keep the memory of Olga alive in her brother's mind. After the first night of *The Seagull* she had written to him about the actress Knipper, 'who's very, very charming and amazingly talented—it's a sheer delight to watch and listen to her'. Once so apprehensive about the play, Masha was now unable to restrain her enthusiasm: why did Anton not name the new house that he was building in Yalta 'The Seagull'? Visiting the play for the third time in February, she was introduced by Vishnevsky to all the company. 'If only you could have seen how they welcomed me! Knipper started jumping up and down, I gave her your regards. I advise you to start paying your attentions to Knipper. In my opinion she's a very interesting person.' Soon Olga was being invited to the flat in Moscow where Masha and her mother were then staying.

It was a pleasant surprise, therefore—if not a complete surprise—when on April 18th, 1899, shortly after his arrival from Yalta, Chekhov presented himself on a formal visit to the Knipper family commune and invited Olga to accompany him to an exhibition of paintings by his friend, Levitan. On May 1st, long after the season was over, he watched her playing Arkadina in the performance of *The Seagull* put on specially for his benefit. Melikhovo, the estate on which he had lavished so much attention, was soon to be sold and the household transferred to Yalta, but during May Olga spent three days there as the guest of

Anton, Masha and their mother. Always prone to rhapsodise in retrospect, Olga later recalled the visit in the most ecstatic terms. Everything about Melikhovo had appealed to her: the cottage in the grounds where Chekhov had written *The Seagull*, the simple affectionate atmosphere of family jokes and conversations, her growing friendship with Masha, the quiet Russian humour of Chekhov's mother, and, of course, Anton Pavlovich himself, delighted to have this last opportunity of showing off his pond, his kitchen garden and his greenhouse to an attractive visitor.[3]

At the end of May Olga left Moscow for the Caucasus to stay with her elder brother, having arranged to meet Chekhov again in the Crimea, and on June 16th he wrote her his first letter:

What does this mean? Where are you? You're withholding news of yourself so stubbornly that we've been reduced to making all sorts of guesses and are already beginning to think you've forgotten us and got married in the Caucasus. If so, to whom? You haven't decided to give up the theatre?

The Author has been forgotten—oh, how terrible, how cruel, how perfidious!

Everyone sends greetings. There's no news. Not even any flies. Nothing at all. Even the calves aren't biting.

I did think of coming to see you off at the station but fortunately the rain prevented me.

Went to St Petersburg and had my photo taken twice. Almost froze to death there. I shan't be going to Yalta before the beginning of July.

Allow me to press your hand and to wish you all the best.

Yours, A. Chekhov

Though one senses a genuine anxiety that Olga may have forgotten him, this is the kind of letter of which Lika Mizinova and the others had received many examples. Amusing and informal, it is also defensive, for in establishing so swiftly at the outset a certain level of bantering intimacy, it seems to lay down the level of familiarity at which future correspondence is to be conducted.

In her reply Olga recalled chilly Melikhovo, which she still preferred to the exotic south. She had been in a vile mood for a fortnight, but his letter had arrived just as she was beginning to feel herself again, and she was so delighted that she had laughed out loud. Falling in line with his style, she writes: 'And I thought it was the Author Chekhov who had forgotten the Actress Knipper—so you do remember me from time to time?'[4]

After characteristic problems with his itinerary, Chekhov finally joined Olga at Novorossisk and they took the steamer across the Black Sea to Yalta. Here Olga spent a fortnight with family friends, while Chekhov stayed at a hotel on the front. They went on outings together and paid frequent visits to Upper Autka, overlooking the town, where the new house was now well advanced. To Masha Chekhov wrote: 'Knipper is in Yalta. She's in the dumps. She was with me yesterday and drank tea; just sat there and said nothing.'[5]

On August 2nd they left Yalta together for Moscow. They made a leisurely start by travelling fifty miles in a carriage through the mountains to the railway station at Bakhchisarai. 'a very attractive drive', according to Baedeker, lasting a full day.[6] After a winding ascent through fragrant pine woods, they found themselves with an unimpeded view of the coast and sea-line. Passing close to the highest point in the range, the 4000 ft. Ai-Petri, they then traversed a bleak plateau before starting the descent to the Tatar village of Kokkoz. Here, Baedeker prosaically informed his readers, bargaining was advisable at the plain inn by the bridge; but for Olga, sitting back in the comfortable carriage, now chatting and joking with Chekhov, now dozing off in the heat of the southern sun, 'the picturesque Kokkoz Valley was full of its own special kind of enchantment'.[7]

Moscow in high summer did not suit Chekhov. During his three weeks there he saw little of Olga, who was busy with rehearsals for the coming season. His departure for Yalta left her feeling very low, but the news that she had been chosen to play Anna in Hauptmann's *Lonely Lives* did much to restore her spirits.

C

Looking back, it is clear that the carriage drive across the mountains in August 1899 marks an important turning-point in the relationship between Olga and Chekhov. 'What a wonderful moonlit night, oh for the country and the open spaces, won't you come with me? It's nice now in the Kokkoz Valley!!!' Olga wrote skittishly soon after Chekhov's departure.[8] And in January, commenting on a spoof report via Masha that he is about to marry a priest's daughter, she writes: 'Congratulations, dear Author, so you didn't manage to hold out after all? Don't forget that you and I came to an agreement—remember the Kokkoz Valley?'[9]

Knowing Chekhov, it is impossible to attach great importance to this 'agreement'. Nevertheless, a quite new note can be detected in the letters that he wrote to Olga after returning to Yalta. His letter of September 3rd has been described as 'the first authentic love letter by Chekhov that we have'.[10] Yes, he assures her, he had drunk three glasses of tea and lemon several times a day, and consumed all the food that she had provided, but a little doubt had crossed his mind: in fussing with his picnic basket and rushing off for boiling water at wayside stations, had he not been undermining the prestige of the Art Theatre? Then he writes:

> Driving past Bakhchisarai I thought of you and remembered our journey. Dear, remarkable actress, wonderful woman, if only you knew how much pleasure your letter has given me. I bow low to you, low, so low that my forehead touches the bottom of my well, which has now reached a depth of fifty-six feet. I've become so used to you that now I feel lonely and simply can't reconcile myself to the thought of not seeing you again until the spring. I'm in a bad mood—in short, if Nadenka found out what was going on in my heart, there'd be trouble.

Nadenka, a Chekhonte creation, was Chekhov's bourgeois wife, a lady of jealous and suspicious temperament.

An intriguing sidelight on the course of the relationship is provided by Chekhov's famous short story, *Lady with a Little Dog*. It was begun soon after his return to Yalta and published in December. Olga read it over Christmas and told Chekhov that it

58

had 'set her thinking'. Starting in Yalta, the story moves to Moscow, and clearly expresses Chekhov's own longing to escape from his southern exile and return to the bustling north, to exchange those stately palms and cypresses for Moscow's homely lime trees and birches, white with autumn frost. When Gurov, the hero of the story, arrives back in Moscow, he warms to the familiar sound of church bells, just as Olga had described them to Chekhov in her letter of August 29th.

On the surface, however, there is little in common, except age, between Chekhov and Gurov, the cynical womaniser with an unloved wife, and even less, apart from their German surnames, between Olga and the inexperienced young Anna von Diederitz, married to a 'lackey' of a husband whom she despises. The scene in which Gurov and Anna drive out in the early hours to Oreanda, a beauty spot not far from Yalta, and sit gazing silently at the sea, is likely to have been inspired by a similar excursion that Chekhov and Olga made in July; and he may well have been thinking of his own memories of Olga when he writes of Gurov that his impressions of Anna did not fade as the weeks passed but increased in their power over him. It is characteristic of Chekhov that the emphasis throughout is on what Gurov feels, not Anna; in particular, on the way in which the consciousness of his love changes him as an individual.

What must have set Olga thinking, however, was the end of the story. Catching sight of himself in the mirror of the hotel bedroom where he has gone to meet Anna on one of her infrequent visits to Moscow, Gurov cannot understand why he should have grown so old and ugly in the last few years. 'And it was only now, when his hair had turned grey, that he had fallen in love properly, in the way that one should do—for the first time in his life.'

Was Chekhov thinking of his own situation vis-à-vis Olga Knipper, and regretting that for a man in his state of health, happiness had come too late?

Chekhov leaves the fates of Anna and Gurov undecided. They see no way of escaping from their unhappy marriages. That at least was not a problem for Chekhov and Olga, though physical separation was. From August until March they kept up a fairly regular correspondence, with frequent discussion as to who was writing more often and who had forgotten whom.

'Yesterday was exactly a year since we met,' Olga wrote on September 10th. 'What a state of nerves I was in when the notice came round saying that "the author himself" would be at evening rehearsal! Can you imagine? And now I'm sitting and writing to that same "author" not with fear and trembling but with a feeling of lightness and well-being in my soul.' She asks him for a photograph with a nice inscription—'the only one I have is that small one where you're looking down.' Chekhov, with conventional gallantry, sends her instead a box to keep her gold and diamond jewellery in. 'What a tease you are, Anton Pavlovich!' Olga replies.

> Fancy presenting a poor actress of the Art Theatre with a box to keep her 'gold and diamond jewellery' in! I suppose you think we're rolling in it? I shall use the box for keeping letters from a dear good person in Yalta. And when on earth am I going to have a photo of you with your eyes open?! Couldn't you have put a little surprise inside? Cruel man. I want to see you terribly. Isn't there *any* chance before the spring? I long for you to be sitting comfortably on my settee drinking coffee, which I take such a disgustingly long time to prepare, while I go chattering on about this and that.[11]

At last, on December 1st:

> Hurrah, hurrah!!! Now I've got the Author Chekhov with eyes! I've just this moment received it and felt I had to drop you a few lines before dashing off to rehearsal. Thank you, thank you, you're a good, sweet, wonderful man! I press both your hands and kiss you on both temples.
>
> The photo's splendid! Such a good expression! The Actress is absolutely delighted and will try to rehearse especially well today. Heavens, I'm late already, I'll have to run. Only why isn't there a single word on the photo? But you'll put that right for me in the spring, won't you?[12]

Olga's long and attractively breathless letters—she wrote fast and admitted to atrocious handwriting—contrast with the shorter, more studied, letters that reached her from Yalta; but as Chekhov ruefully explained, for him there was no season about to begin and he had nothing to look forward to except bad weather. 'I envy the rat,' he wrote, 'that lives under the floor-boards of your theatre.'[13]

The Art Theatre's second season began promisingly, with long queues at the box-office for advance bookings. They opened with A. K. Tolstoy's *The Death of Ivan the Terrible*. That same night a sleepless Olga wrote Chekhov what she herself later described as 'a desperate letter', headed 'Moscow, 4 a.m.', signed 'your despondent actress', and telling him that the first night had been a failure and that it was impossible to describe how miserable she felt;[14] but three days later she was writing that the press had been very decent, 'there are good reviews everywhere'. Chekhov gently reproved her for dramatising the situation, echoing the sentiments of *The Seagull* by reminding her that it was impossible to make progress in art without making mistakes, and that one bad performance was no reason to stay awake all night. If his own play, *Uncle Vanya*, were a failure, she was to go to bed and sleep soundly. He had not foreseen that his own sleep might be disturbed. Among the innovations in the new house at Yalta was a telephone. Congratulatory telegrams began to be phoned in late on the evening of October 27th, the day after the première.

On each occasion I woke up and ran to the telephone in the dark, barefoot, and got chilled through; then I'd scarcely dropped off when the bell rang a second time, then a third. Never before has my own fame kept me from sleeping. Next evening I put my slippers and dressing-gown in position, but there were no more telegrams. The telegrams were all about curtain-calls and a glorious success, but I seemed to detect in them something subtle and barely perceptible that made me think your general mood was not so cheerful after all.[15]

That Olga Knipper was very far from pleased with herself he
soon learned from her letter.

I ought not to be writing to you today, dear Anton Pavlovich.
There's such chaos and darkness in my soul, I can't describe it.
We played *Uncle Vanya* yesterday. It had a terrific success and
gripped the whole audience, there's no doubt of that. I didn't
sleep a wink and today I can't stop crying. I acted inconceivably
badly—for what reason? In my opinion what happened was
this: I was forced to forget about my image of Yelyena, which
the directors found boring. They depicted her to me in quite a
different light, claiming that this was essential for the play. I
resisted for a long time and remained unconvinced. At dress
rehearsals I was relaxed, so I may have given a calm and
even performance. But on the first night I was horribly worked
up, I was simply scared stiff—something that's never happened
to me before—and so it was difficult to play the image of
Yelyena imposed upon me. If I'd acted the part as I wanted to,
probably the first night wouldn't have thrown me out. Why
didn't I insist on doing it my way! I'm tearing my hair, I don't
know what to do with myself.

It's strange! After *The Seagull* I suffered physically, now
after *Uncle Vanya* I'm suffering morally. I can't tell you how
mortified I am at the thought of having given a bad performance in one of *your* plays![16]

To this letter Chekhov replied gently and reassuringly, while
stressing once again that it was time to stop being preoccupied
with success and failure.

By the time of the Theatre's short Christmas break Olga felt
exhausted. While Masha travelled south to spend a fortnight in
Yalta, Olga celebrated Christmas with her family. Uncle Karl,
the doctor, prepared an excellent punch which made them all
slightly tipsy, while Uncle Sasha, the company commander, gave
them a reading of comic stories by Chekhov. Sasha had only just
begun to sober up after a bout of heavy drinking that had started
in November. Visiting the Knippers in January for a musical

evening, Masha Chekhova was very taken aback when Uncle Sasha woke up around midnight and bawled out in a drunken bass the line from *The Seagull*: 'Bravo, Silva'; though not so horrified as Olga the night before, when he had done the same thing at a performance of the play at the Art Theatre.[17]

In January 1900 Chekhov added another property to his house at Yalta, and the cliff-side cottage that he had bought the previous autumn. This time it was about ten miles to the north-east of Yalta, at Gurzuf: a four-roomed cottage with its own little bay. Masha received the news enthusiastically, adding that 'her pleasure was shared by Knipper'.

On January 17th Chekhov celebrated his fortieth birthday. He had just been elected to honorary membership of the Academy of Sciences. But neither birthday nor honour gave him great pleasure, as he was ill on that day. The same evening in Moscow *Lonely Lives* had to be cancelled, and much to her delight Olga found herself instead playing Arkadina in *The Seagull*. Among the audience were Masha Chekhova and Lika Mizinova, who was seeing the play for the first time since the 1896 fiasco. Lika wept, Masha informed her brother, on being reminded of her past. After the performance Masha invited a few close friends back to her flat, including Lika and Olga, who had first met the previous August. Lika's gloom cannot have been lightened by the presence of one who was not only the star of Chekhov's play but now so obviously occupied a higher place in his affections.

Early in February Olga heard with alarm through Masha that Chekhov was threatening to spend the whole summer abroad, as she had taken it for granted that she would be visiting him in the south. It was her first but by no means last encounter with Chekhov's ability to forget about other people when making his own arrangements. 'Tell me at once it isn't true, that we'll be together in the summer', she wrote off with frantic haste, and Masha told Chekhov that 'certain people were in despair' over his plans.

It had been no more than a sudden impulse, a fit of pique, Chekhov as good as admitted: the winter was so long, he was unwell, no one had written to him—how else could he relieve his boredom except by thinking of the future? He felt better now; but at least if he complained occasionally of boredom he had more cause for doing so than Olga. 'You have something to work and hope for, you can drink and laugh when your uncle reads you stories—what more do you want? It's different for me. I've been uprooted, I can't lead a full life, I can't drink although I like drinking; I like excitement and here there isn't any, in a word, I'm like a tree that's been transplanted and can't make up its mind whether it's going to take or start withering away.'[18] To this Olga replied that she was glad that he had dropped his plan, adding rather too brightly that she was quite sure that the transplant had taken.

While Chekhov languished in Yalta, in Moscow the Knippers and the Chekhovs were becoming fast friends. 'I'm seeing a great deal of Knipper,' Masha wrote to her brother in November, 'I've dined with her family several times and become friendly with her Mama, i.e. your mother-in-law' (a joke that Masha would not have found so amusing later on). Of Olga Masha wrote: 'What a fine person she is, I become more and more convinced of that every day'; while Olga, writing to Chekhov in February, refers to Masha for the first time as Masha, not Mariya Pavlovna. 'Did you know that we had drunk Brüderschaft?' At Shrovetide there was an orgy of pancake-eating. Olga visited Masha's flat for a pancake party, on the next day she was eating pancakes at the home of Chekhov's younger brother Ivan, a Moscow schoolteacher, while on the day after that, it was Masha's turn to take pancakes with the Knippers, where 'our noisy family,' Olga wrote to Chekhov, 'must have made her head start spinning'.

Following this letter of February 20th, no more letters were exchanged for a month. When Olga next wrote, on March 22nd, she explained her silence by referring to the vile mood that she had been in: she had left three letters to him unfinished. Chekhov offered no explanation, but it seems likely that having known since the end of February that the Art Theatre company, including Olga, would be making a short tour of the Crimea in

April, he did not see the same point in writing. For Olga, however, always seeking reassurance about their relationship, such knowledge was not enough. 'I'm bored without letters from you. Do answer this one—it'll make things easier for me when I come to see you. Does that sound comic? You know, there are times when I feel you've lost touch with me, and I'll be like some kind of stranger coming to see you.'[19]

Chekhov did reply at once, predicting that her mood of black melancholy would vanish as soon as she was on the train south, and applauding the fact that she and Masha would be arriving a few days ahead of the main party.

❧

CHAPTER SEVEN

Anton Delays

It had been Chekhov's idea that the Art Theatre should make a tour of the Crimea. Fretting in his Yalta prison, he told Olga how wonderful it would be if they were all to come down in the spring for a combined tour and holiday. If he could only see *Uncle Vanya* in performance, he felt sure that it would give him the impetus to sit down and write a new play, and in November he asked Vishnevsky to put the idea of a tour to Nemirovich and Stanislavsky. The bait—a new play by Chekhov for the following season—was one they dared not refuse.

Masha and Olga arrived in Yalta at the beginning of April. Olga particularly enjoyed the first few days of her visit, when she was still a private individual, not an actress. Chekhov delighted in showing her the new house, pointing out every detail and indicating what improvements still had to be made, but it was the garden, with its astonishing variety of trees, bushes and flowers, already well established, in which he took special pride and pleasure.

Of Sevastopol, where the Theatre opened its tour on April 10th, Olga had nothing but vile memories: Chekhov had been taken ill with haemorrhoidal bleeding and should never have made the journey. Yalta, however, was one long noisy celebration. The young company was making its first guest tour. The heroes of Moscow, accompanied by fans, friends and families, were rapturously received. No longer could Chekhov complain of a lack of excitement, what with visitors to entertain during the day and performances to attend in the evening. Among the celebrities who converged on Yalta were the young writers, Bunin,

Gorky and Kuprin, and the rising young pianist-composer, Rachmaninov. Actors, writers and musicians met daily at Chekhov's house. Olga, staying with the family again on her return from Sevastopol, was kept hard at work helping Masha and her mother to provide a continuous relay of breakfasts, lunches and teas. Chekhov himself was in great form, and Masha later described the Art Theatre's visit as the happiest time he ever spent in Yalta.[1] His drooping spirits were revived by all the laughter, talk and serious discussions about art and literature, that seemed to fill every corner of his house and garden. Gorky, invited by Chekhov to Yalta to meet the Art Theatre for the first time, kept his listeners spellbound with tales of past adventures, and outlined to Stanislavsky the plot of what later became *The Lower Depths*. When the company returned to Moscow, they left behind the garden bench and swing that had been used in *Uncle Vanya*, and took with them the promise of new plays from both Chekhov and Gorky.

In the letters between Olga and Chekhov during the winter of 1899–1900 there are very few discordant notes. With his dislike of self-dramatization, Chekhov may have been less sympathetic to Olga's desperate letters after *Ivan the Terrible* and *Uncle Vanya* than he revealed, and when Olga threatened to send him 'another desperate letter but of a different kind', she seems to be accusing him of indifference towards her. In her gloomy letter of March 22nd, she complains that she is the one person who knows nothing about his new play, but Chekhov was quick to reply that this was all newspaper talk. In her much calmer letter of May 1st, however, Olga makes a more pertinent comment on Chekhov's character. 'In general, were you pleased with our visit?' she asks. 'Write me a good frank letter, only don't go palming me off with clever phrases, as you often like doing.'[2]

Chekhov did not reply, as he himself left for Moscow early in May; but it was still cold there, he developed a fever and returned to Yalta after only nine days. At the end of the month Olga and her mother left for a holiday in the Caucasus. 'Wonderful, magnificent South!' Olga rhapsodised to Anton. 'We're basking in southern sunshine, the air is full of intoxicating perfumes . . . Don't you believe it! The rain's coming down in buckets, we're simply dreading the thought of travelling along the Georgian Military Highway.'[3] Unknown to Olga, Chekhov had also been touring in the Caucasus with a party of friends, and they all met on the train from Tiflis to Batum, spending six hours together before Olga and her mother had to change to another line.

Early in July, Olga travelled alone to Yalta to spend her previously arranged holiday with the Chekhovs.

One short sentence is all that she devotes in her memoir to this decisive month at Yalta in the summer of 1900.[4] Part of the time was spent at Chekhov's recently purchased cottage at Gurzuf. In accordance with the social conventions of the day, Masha presumably kept them company there, and we know that she did a sketch which Olga took back to Moscow to hang on the wall of her room.[5] The Russian language, however, reveals what Olga and Anton would not have dreamed of proclaiming openly—that it was during this month that they became lovers: for in subsequent letters the formal second person plural is replaced by the intimate 'thou' form of address.

On August 5th Anton accompanied Olga to Sevastopol and saw her off on the night express to Moscow. 'It'll be strange arriving home,' she wrote from the train next morning, obviously thinking of her new intimacy with Anton, 'I shall feel like a stranger in my own family. I'm thinking back to Gurzuf and regretting a great deal. Now you'll go and tick me off for being a little German—right?'[6] And on the 16th she wrote: 'How I'd like to sit in the alcove in your study for a while, relax beside you absolutely quietly, then ruffle your feathers, start talking nonsense and playing the fool. Remember how you took me to the stairs and the staircase creaked so treacherously? I absolutely adored that. Heavens, I'm writing like a schoolgirl!'[7]

On August 9th Masha wrote to Olga in Moscow:

My dear Olya,
    I dreamed of you on the night of the 5th. Your eyes were

clouded over and you were swaying from side to side. I woke up in a foul mood. That day, the 6th, Anton didn't come back on the steamer but only the day after. You must have arrived in Moscow on the morning of the 8th.

I didn't think I'd feel so miserable without you! What kind of mood are you in? The uncertainty is making me terribly anxious. What was your reception like from the company and the director? Write and tell me as soon as possible, my dear, how you're feeling and what has been decided. Today Anton received the letter you wrote from the train, but *I* can't very well go and ask him about it! He's been coughing very badly all morning. Alekseyev [Stanislavsky] was here yesterday, stayed for hours and had loads to eat.

Dearest, do be frank with me as you have been up till now and write soon.[8]

Over half-a-century later Masha claimed that 'somehow I never gave any thought to what might be the outcome of the relationship between Olya and my brother, although sometimes at the back of my mind there was the idea that they might get married.'[9]

Her letter at the time, however, seems to make it clear that the one thought in the forefront of her mind was precisely whether Olga and her brother were going to marry. Did she suspect that they were already lovers? Olga referred later to the 'bewildered expression' on Masha's face during that month *à trois*. Be that as it may, Masha appears from her letter to be under the impression that Anton has already proposed, that Olga is making up her mind, and that the question of whether she will be able to combine marriage with her career is central to this decision: hence the reference to her reception from the company and the director (i.e. Nemirovich). That the subject was one on which she and Olga had already had some discussion is suggested by Masha's remark: 'Dearest, do be frank with me as you have been up till now.'

How did Masha herself, delicately placed between her much loved brother and her much loved friend, feel about the situation?

Towards Anton she appears characteristically deferential: it is not for her to ask him about Olga, nor to question the wisdom of his decisions. There was no such deference in her attitude towards Olga, whose confidence she feels that she has the right to expect. Masha's dream on the night of Olga's departure seems to hint at disturbed feelings, while her reference to Anton's bad cough might be seen as the discreet Masha's tactful way of reminding Olga that for anyone in Anton's state of health, marriage might not be a suitable step. On the face of it, however, what seems to worry her most is not the question of marriage as such, but that she should not be kept in the dark about their plans, should not be excluded from their confidences and made to feel an outsider. Olga reminded Anton some time later of the agonies that she had suffered during that month because of having to make pretend and play games of hide-and-seek. The bewildered Masha must have found this situation equally painful.

On the same day that Masha had written to her, Olga wrote to Masha from Moscow:

Greetings, tender Mashechka! How I'd love to see your funny face, to kiss and hug you and have a chat. I feel strange without you.

Here I am in Moscow. My nerves are in a state, I can't stop that idiotic nervous laughing. I'm not even capable of describing what kind of mood I'm in. I don't understand it. It's like living in a station waiting-room. I feel tired. I wake up as early as ever and wander round the rooms. Yesterday evening at rehearsal I had a row with Vladimir Ivanovich [Nemirovich] about my part, I feel ashamed even to recall it. I've never behaved like that before, I've never allowed myself to adopt such a tone in my work. I went and apologised.

Anton and I had a wonderful journey, our farewell was very tender and affectionate. He was deeply moved, so was I. When the train pulled out, I burst into tears, peering into the dark night. It was frightening to be left alone after all I'd experienced in the past month. And the future is so terrifying and

unknown. Mashechka, Mashechka, how terrifying life is! I feel
I want to bury my head in your shoulder this very moment and
start crying. There, I've gone and begun howling already.[10]

Replying on the 13th to Masha's letter, Olga is feeling even
more anxious and desperate. She has still not received a letter
from Anton, and 'the most terrible thoughts keep coming into
my head. If there's no letter tomorrow, I shan't know what to
think. You ask me what decision your brother and I have come
to. That's a strange question. Can one ever come to a decision
with him? I don't know anything myself and I'm suffering
deeply.'[11]

Writing to Stanislavsky on August 14th, Nemirovich also
referred to his little quarrel with Olga Knipper, and how he had
told her afterwards that she would have to work harder that year,
if they were not to lose a good actress. 'By the way, I ought to
pass on to you a little secret. She told me that her marriage to
Anton Pavlovich is *quite settled* . . . Oh oh oh! Maybe it isn't a
secret, I didn't ask. But what she said to me was: "You're the
first person I've told after Mama." '[12] To Anton, who had heard
that Nemirovich might be visiting Yalta, Olga wrote on the 23rd:
'If he speaks to you, don't go and disown me in your usual way
and put me in an awkward position, as he knows I spoke to him
with your knowledge—right?'[13]

So clearly there *had* been a definite understanding between
them about marriage; but what tormented Olga, making her so
depressed and irritable, was Anton's failure to let her know
exactly where she stood, to commit himself to any specific details
of time and place. Hence the heartfelt cry to Masha: 'Can one
ever come to a decision with him?' As each day passed without a
letter from Yalta, so the chances of such a formal commitment
receded.

In looking at the situation from Olga's point of view, one must
remember that she was still the highly respectable Miss Knipper.
She might be an actress, but her standards were not those of the
loose-living actress, Arkadina, whom she portrayed in *The*

Seagull. As Nemirovich writes in his memoirs: 'It was clear that a transient affair with her would have been impossible.'[14] In some ways her life remained surprisingly sheltered. Unlike Masha who had her own flat, she was still living in the family commune. Though Olga was almost thirty-two, her mother still trembled at the thought of what might happen to her daughter if the Art Theatre went on tour to St Petersburg;[15] and when Olga arrived in Sevastopol from Yalta to join the main Art Theatre company, it was the first time in her life that she had spent a night in a hotel.[16] Not to be able to proclaim boldly to the world that she was Chekhov's fiancée, while knowing herself to be his mistress, must have been very disturbing for Olga. Uppermost among the 'terrible thoughts' that crossed her mind may have been the fear that the ever-joking Anton had not been entirely serious about marrying her, and was expecting her to remain his mistress instead.

As for Anton, he was obviously unaware of the stir that he had caused. After saying goodbye to Olga at Sevastopol on the evening of the 5th, he spent a leisurely day in Balaclava, returned to Yalta on the 7th, and on the 8th was monopolised by Stanislavsky, who extracted from him a conditional promise to finish his new play by the end of the month. Only on the 9th, on receiving Olga's letter from the train, did he write her a pleasant, fairly intimate letter—'I keep thinking the door's going to open and you'll come in to the room'—but without any reference to the future, let alone to marriage. It was enough that he loved Olga and had agreed to marry her; the details were unimportant and might be worked out later; in the meantime he must devote all his attention to the new play.

In her letters to him, Olga did not reveal the full extent of her feelings as she had done to Masha, but on the 10th she wrote: 'People in Moscow won't leave me alone. Many of them are certain that we're married already. Everyone's congratulating my relatives but they just shrug their shoulders, since they know nothing about it. It's all very amusing, isn't it? Are you smiling?'[17]

Anton Delays

One doubts whether Anton found it amusing, any more than Olga did herself; but she had made her point and did not press it. Her immediate concern was to find out when he intended coming to Moscow. Anton could not say. 'Would you believe it, I'm writing a play at the moment.' Soon, however, came bitter complaints that visitors were interrupting his work, though he still hoped to finish by the first week in September. Olga is at a loss to understand why he cannot protect himself, as she does when preparing a part, against unwanted visitors. 'I'm unable to refuse to see people,' Anton replied, 'it's not within my power.' Among his visitors, he teased her, was a rich young heiress. Olga casually retorted in a postscript that she was thinking of marrying Vishnevsky, and what would Anton advise?

At the end of August, Anton wrote that he had been 'slightly unwell', but had resumed work on the play, though progress was slow. On September 8th he is having trouble with one of his heroines, but will be leaving for Moscow on the 20th. As if to strengthen his resolve—Anton having written previously that he had not seen grass for two years—Olga sent him a lyrical description of a family excursion to the Sparrow Hills outside Moscow:

> In the woods the maples and birches are already golden, the aspens are turning red, but the oaks are still green. The earth was damp and smelt of mushrooms. Some of those favourite little flowers of mine still lingered on, and there were spiders' webs in the air—in a word, it was all so beautiful that you couldn't tear yourself away. A gentle, thoughtful sun, and the same softness in the shapes of the clouds. We stood for a long time admiring 'mother Moscow with her golden domes'; the city was covered in haze, and the sun seemed to light it up in patches. I've loved that view ever since I was a child.

'I want to see you terribly,' she goes on, 'but what if the weather's cold by the time you arrive?'[18]

Her description had moved him deeply, Anton replied, but he was in low spirits. He had been ill for almost a week and done no

73

work on the play. 'So you advise me not to come to Moscow? Mother is leaving for Moscow at the beginning of October, I shall have to stay behind to see her off, so it looks as if I shan't be coming to you.'[19]

Provoked and disappointed, Olga wrote back at once. 'I don't want you to come to Moscow? *I* don't want you? When I've been so upset and annoyed that the weather's still warm and you're not here? I *must* see you before the winter sets in. For heaven's sake, don't keep anything to yourself, tell me everything.'[20]

It was their first misunderstanding. Technically, Olga was in the right. Her remark—'but what if the weather's cold by the time you arrive?'—was intended to hasten Anton's departure from Yalta, not to deter him from coming; and in the context of her letter as a whole, it is hard to see how anyone in normal health could have taken it otherwise. But Anton's health was not normal, he was only just beginning to recover from a week's illness, and he seized on Olga's careless phrase as an excuse for not visiting Moscow and going straight abroad.

By the 20th his spirits were sufficiently recovered for him to send Olga the following telegram:

SATURDAY MOTHER LEAVES MOSCOW PLAY NOT READY COMING LATER GREETINGS KISS HAND   ANTONIUS

But Olga by this time was thoroughly worked up:

I'm terribly hurt that you won't tell me anything. You write so vaguely—I'm coming later. What does that mean? It's been warm and pleasant here, you could have lived and worked here splendidly, we could have loved one another and been close. Then it would have been easier for us to endure several months apart. I shan't be able to live through this winter unless I see you. You have such a tender, loving heart—why do you harden it?

Anton, my dear, my darling, do come. Don't you want to know me any more, or is it that you can't bear the thought of uniting your fate with mine? Write and tell me all this frankly, everything must be clear and open between us.[21]

74

Anton Delays

Anton replied (September 27th):

> Olya my darling, my wonderful little actress, why this tone, this plaintive, bitter mood? Am I really so guilty? I've not got away to Moscow yet, because I've been ill, there are no other reasons, I assure you, my dear, on my word of honour. . . .
>
> You write: 'You have such a tender, loving heart—why do you harden it?' When have I hardened it? My heart has always loved you and been tender to you, and I have never hidden that from you, never, never.
>
> Judging from your letter as a whole, you want and expect some kind of explanation, some kind of long conversation—with serious faces and serious consequences; and I don't know what to say to you, except the one thing that I've already said to you ten thousand times and shall probably go on saying for a long time to come—i.e. that I love you—and there's nothing more that I can say. If we're not together now, it's not my fault or yours, but that of the devil who implanted the bacilli in me and the love of art in you.

That the healthy Olga, bursting with vitality and so eager for him to come to Moscow, had not yet grasped the full significance of those bacilli, Anton must have been painfully aware; and he himself was liable to encourage such an attitude by playing down the seriousness of his complaints and informing her that he had been 'slightly unwell'. But health was not the only consideration that had kept him in Yalta. There was also the new play, to which he doggedly returned as soon as his health permitted. Writing it was 'very difficult', he told Masha, 'more difficult than my previous plays'.[22] He was under considerable pressure to have the play ready in time for production by the Art Theatre in the 1900–1 season. Visitors might plague him in Yalta, but he may have been even more apprehensive about the chances of doing serious work in Moscow, where Olga herself, of course, would be the chief distraction. Here too, in her eagerness to see him again, Olga was failing to enter fully into Anton's situation.

Yet there is an egocentric element in his attitude also. *He* had never doubted his feeling of love for her during those weeks of separation, and that, it seems, should have been good enough for Olga. In moments of illness and depression he had told her, repeatedly and sincerely, how much he longed to see her, and now he had spelled out his love in unmistakable terms; so what more could Olga want? The phrase about the bacilli and the love of art was neatly turned, but it would have been understandable if Olga had felt that it was one of those clever remarks that Anton was wont to hide behind. For it masks an essential difference between them at this stage: that whereas she could not contemplate the idea that they might not meet again before the winter, he obviously could. 'I shall be in Yalta until October 10th, working,' he wrote at the start of his letter on the 27th, 'then I shall leave for Moscow or, depending on my health, for abroad.'

Nor did he pay any attention to her question about 'uniting your fate with mine'. Was this because, as has been suggested, 'circumstances compelled him to dwell more on death than on marriage'?[23] Had his recent ill health made him have second thoughts? Given Chekhov's determination to see himself as a normal person, it seems more likely that he was stubbornly refusing to make of marriage an *issue*, 'with serious faces and serious consequences'. What difference, after all, did being married or not married make to their feelings for one another? He had yet to grasp that for Olga, more conventional in her moral and social attitudes, it did make a difference.

At the end of September Anton was taken ill again with influenza, and did no writing for ten days. Olga apologised for having sent him 'two crazy letters', was solicitous about his health, and promised that when they met, she would not subject him to any serious conversations, but again she could not help regretting that 'these beautiful autumn months have gone by in vain'.

Ironically, however, it was neither Anton's health, nor his play, that caused the final postponement, but his garden. 'The weather in Yalta is marvellous,' he wrote to Masha on October 6th, 'just like summer. There are some planting jobs I want to do, so I've put off my departure for a few days.' A perfectly rational decision; but had Olga seen this letter, it would have grieved her to think that after ten weeks in which he was constantly being reminded of how much she longed to see him, he had postponed his departure for such a trivial reason.

At last, on the 16th, Anton finished his draft, and on October 21st he took the step that Olga must have begun to think was never going to be accomplished: he left Yalta for Moscow.

🎰

CHAPTER EIGHT

Winter 1900

The play that Chekhov took with him to Moscow, *Three Sisters*, was his first since meeting Olga Knipper and the Moscow Art Theatre, and had been written with the particular actors and actresses of the company very much in mind. 'What a part I've got for you in *Three Sisters*,' he wrote to Olga. 'Give me ten roubles and you can have it, otherwise I'll give it to another actress.'[1]

Olga's part was that of Masha, one of the four grown-up children of the late General Prozorov. The theme of the play reflected Chekhov's own frustration at being cut off in Yalta, for the Prozorovs all long to escape from the backward provincial capital where their father's death has stranded them, and to return to their native Moscow. Andrei Prozorov, like Chekhov, dreams of sitting in a Moscow restaurant, 'where you don't know anyone and no one knows you, yet you don't have the sense of not belonging.' The cry 'To Moscow! To Moscow!' is cheerful at first but becomes more and more desperate as the dream of Moscow fades. Like her brother and two sisters, Masha is in her twenties when the play opens, but unlike them she is married: to Kulygin, her former classics teacher, who once seemed to her the cleverest man in the world, but for whom she now feels no more than a residual affection. During the play Masha falls in love with Colonel Vershinin, who is also married. They have to take their happiness 'in snatches', and the romance comes to an end when Vershinin and his regiment are posted abroad.

Masha is the most original and talented of the three sisters. To portray a young woman of culture and refinement, who speaks French, German and English, and is a first-class pianist, posed no problems for Olga Knipper, who was all those things herself. It was in February 1900, when he already had his subject of three sisters, that Chekhov commented about one of Olga's photos that there was 'a little demon lurking behind your modest expression of quiet sadness'. This would have been an apt description of Masha, in whom such 'little demon' qualities as outspokenness, shortness of temper and boisterous high spirits are to be found alongside a capacity for great depth of feeling. Chekhov may well have been aware of a similar combination in Olga. Olga did not hesitate to speak her mind freely about anything or anyone that she disliked, just as Masha is openly critical of Natasha, the bourgeois wife whom Andrei acquires and who purposefully ousts the sisters from their own home. Of Olga, Chekhov later remarked that she was the most splendid wife but had one defect: 'You're quick-tempered, and when you're in a bad mood, it's dangerous to get too close to you';[2] just as in the play, after Vershinin has received a note telling him that his wife has tried to poison herself, Masha loses her temper and is rude to all those round her. Olga's boisterous high spirits, like Masha's at the party in Act I when she bangs her fork on the table and calls for wine, are revealed in frequent remarks like the one about wanting to ruffle Anton's feathers, 'start talking nonsense and playing the fool'. But Chekhov would also have observed that Olga, like Masha, lived very much in the realm of her own moods and feelings, and was liable to fall into moods of black depression. 'Knipper is in Yalta. She's in the dumps. She was with me yesterday and drank tea; just sat there and said nothing.' This description of Olga in the summer of 1899 is very reminiscent of Masha as she appears in the opening scene of *Three Sisters*.

A. B. Derman, the Soviet editor of the first two volumes of the Chekhov-Knipper correspondence, draws attention to the paradox that although Chekhov complained bitterly about unwanted visitors, there were frequent occasions when he apparently went out of his way to invite almost complete strangers to his house. The reason, Derman suggests, was the writer's constant need to observe and study people, to enrich himself with impressions.[3] In Yalta Chekhov found himself short of this kind of raw material. Olga's letters provided one kind of substitute. On September 8th he had written to her in great alarm that following a visit to the barber's, all his hair was coming out and he would probably be bald within a week. 'Take half a bottle of spirit,' advised Olga, 'add two drams of naphthalene and rub it in to your scalp. Will you do that? I don't want you turning up in Moscow bald—people will think I've been tearing your hair out.' A few days later she sends an urgent correction: not two drams, half a dram.[4] Chekhov put this formula (the wrong one) straight into his play. When he first comes on stage, the old army doctor, Chebutykin, reads it out from his newspaper and jots it down in his notebook: a comic and unexpected entrance which immediately fixes him in the audience's mind.

In August, after returning from Yalta, Olga wrote that Uncle Sasha had given up the bottle for the time being and was on milk. Later she described how one evening, sitting by a table on which stood sausage and a plate of gooseberries from which she helped herself, she listened in silence to Uncle Sasha's confession—'his dissatisfaction, consciousness of having lived his life absurdly, tales of wild parties and drinking bouts, the painful search for at least something pure and human in himself, his remorse, the desire to put everything right—and all of this uttered in a monotonous hollow voice by the light of a single candle.'[5]

The scene, nicely captured by Olga, is Chekhovian, in the sense that it reveals clearly, without any powerful explosion of passion, a psychological drama being played out in a person's life. Chebutykin in *Three Sisters* has a similar problem with the bottle. 'Mind you don't have anything to drink today,' Masha says to him sternly in Act I. 'Do you hear? It's no good to you.' One can easily imagine the forthright Olga speaking thus to Uncle Sasha in Chekhov's presence. It seems very likely that her account of his confession also gave Chekhov the idea for the scene in Act III where the doctor, who has been drinking heavily, soliloquizes with painful intensity about his past life and present situation: realising that he has forgotten all his medical knowledge and let a woman die, and wondering whether he is really alive at all or only pretending to be.

Anton's response to Olga's letter about her uncle might also have been spoken by one of his own characters. 'Find him a wife,' he wrote tersely.[6]

Anton had told Olga that he would be staying in Moscow for about five days.[7] In the event, he remained there seven weeks, basing himself during the day on Masha's flat and only spending the night in his room at the Dresden Hotel. On arrival he was immediately caught up in the Art Theatre whirl. Accompanied by Gorky, he attended performances of *Uncle Vanya* and *The Seagull*, and had to undergo the ordeal of being presented with a laurel wreath. On evenings when he was not attending a performance, he was most likely to be found pottering about somewhere backstage. Once he had finished writing out a fair copy, it was arranged that a reading of his eagerly awaited new play should be held in the Theatre foyer, attended by the two directors and all the company. Their reaction was one of perplexity, for the play contained even less external dramatic action than its predecessors, and its characters seemed to be no more than hinted at, not sharply delineated; while Chekhov for his part was filled with apprehension as to how the play would be interpreted. Nevertheless, he undertook to make final revisions, Stanislavsky began work on the *mise en scène*, and the play had already gone into rehearsal before Chekhov left Moscow.

Busy at the Art Theatre in the evenings, Chekhov during the day was constantly visiting or being visited. 'It's just like hard labour,' he wrote. 'They're tearing me to shreds.'[8] In his usual obliging way, he tried to fit everyone in, but his health soon began to suffer. At the first sign of illness, he should have sought out a warmer climate straight away, but instead he hung on, complaining of headache, cold and cough, and later influenza, while at the same time saying how very, very much Moscow appealed to him.

Was Olga the reason why he dragged his feet? They cannot have seen as much of one another as they would have liked during those seven weeks. Although Olga dropped all her other friends while Anton was in Moscow, performances and rehearsals still made heavy demands on her time, and they were probably lucky to be able to enjoy an occasional meal or carriage drive together. That they contrived, however, to meet in more intimate circumstances, is apparent from subsequent letters. 'Remember the Dresden Hotel?' asks Olga, while Anton, on arriving in Vienna, writes that he is 'looking with lust at the two beds in my hotel room'.[9]

From Vienna Anton travelled to Nice, where he spent seven weeks at the *Pension Russe*. Letters now flew rapidly between Nice and Moscow, but not all of them were swift in reaching their destination. From the outset the relationship had been at the mercy of the postal services. Three days was the minimum time for letters to travel between Yalta and Moscow, but when they took five days or six, this provoked bitter reproaches from both parties of being idle, indifferent, or downright callous. Seldom had Olga been so insulted, however, as when Anton wrote from Nice on December 17th, saying that he had not heard a word and adjuring her not to be lazy; nor was the situation greatly helped when in answer to her telegram pointing out that she had already sent him *ten* letters, he simply cabled back: *Salue, ma belle.* Then, on the 28th, an elderly Russian turned up at the *Pension Russe*. His name was Chertkov (not the friend of Tolstoy) and he had been receiving all Chekhov's letters.

It is not Olga's letters, however, but Anton's that are now the more arresting. In intensity of feeling they seem for the first time to match, and sometimes even to surpass, those of Olga. He can still exclaim: 'I am yours! Take me and devour me—with vinegar and Provence butter';[10] but this familiar Chekhonte banter has become rare. 'I dream of you frequently,' he writes, 'and when I close my eyes, I can see you as if you were really there.'[11] After Olga's fears that her love for Anton might be greater than his for her, it is Anton who now seems the more fearful. 'Don't be unfaithful to me,' he pleads, 'even in your thoughts.'[12] ('I've no time to fall for anyone else, even if I wanted to,' Olga replied rather crossly to one such accusation.)[13] 'I love you but then you don't understand that . . .'; 'I'd like your love to last for a good long time, say fifteen years or so. What do you think, can there be a love like that? For me, yes, but not for you. All the same, I embrace you.'[14] Olga did not know quite how to respond to such remarks. Not understand his love? 'I am convinced that no one has ever loved me, and no one ever will love me, as much as you do.'[15] And could Anton be so sure of his own feelings during the next fifteen years? 'Aren't you ashamed of bothering yourself with such questions, Great Writer of the Russian land? Carrying on with actresses like this?'[16]

Not long after Anton's departure, Olga was taken ill with influenza. Anton was alarmed to receive two letters scrawled in pencil, feared that it might be something serious and later wrote: 'My sweetheart, it's impossible not to be ill, of course, but it's better not to be. When you're far away, all sorts of dreadful thoughts come into my head and scare me.'[17] Because of her illness, Olga missed several rehearsals of *Three Sisters*. Anton kept urging her to give him a detailed account of how things were going. 'You've said nothing yet about the play, absolutely nothing,' he wrote on January 11th, 'except that today we had a rehearsal, or today we didn't have a rehearsal.' Alarmed by reports of how Stanislavsky was interpreting *Three Sisters*, Chekhov had made up his mind in advance that the play was bound to be a failure. Olga did her best to reassure him, pointing out with some justification that if she had written little, this was because she was still in the process of assimilating her role—'and after all, *you* never like to talk about anything while you're working on it.'[18]

By the time of the first night, on January 31st, 1901, Chekhov was no longer at the *Pension Russe* but in Italy. Rather than wait nervously for news of the play, he probably preferred to let the news catch up with him. Not until he reached Yalta on February 15th did he receive any detailed reports. He was inclined to think that it must have been a failure: Masha's letters, he commented unkindly, were so full of praise. Initial reaction to the play had indeed been muted. Like the directors and company at the first reading, the first-night audience seems to have been baffled by *Three Sisters*. Nevertheless, all seven performances were completely sold out in spite of increased prices, and on February 5th Olga wrote that Moscow was 'talking of nothing else'. That Olga Knipper had scored a personal triumph as Masha seems never to have been in doubt. The critics singled her out for praise, admirers came to the flat with photographs for her to sign, and after the final performance, which also concluded the Theatre's Moscow season, she was mobbed at the stage door and borne aloft through the theatre in triumph. 'What with the heat and the unpleasant sensation, I thought I'd go out of my mind,' she wrote to Anton. If only he could have been there to share the triumph! 'How I enjoy playing Masha! And she's been helpful to me as well, you know. I seem to have understood what kind of actress I am, I've explained myself to myself. All thanks to you, Chekhov! Bravo!!!'[19]

Triumph in Moscow, however, was followed by rebuffs in St Petersburg, where the Art Theatre began a four-week tour in February. Though audiences were highly enthusiastic, the critics were cool. Olga was described as 'a very bad actress' for her performance as Yelyena in *Uncle Vanya*, though the same critic raved about her Masha. Anton had predicted failure in St Petersburg and adopted an attitude of 'I told you so', but he was sufficiently annoyed by the critics to threaten to give up writing for the theatre altogether.

In St Petersburg Olga led a very busy social life. She met for the first time, and took an instant dislike to, Lydia Yavorskaya, whose flattering attentions so nauseated her that she felt obliged to give instructions that Yavorskaya was not to be admitted to her dressing-room in between acts—'otherwise I'll say something rude to her'. She also received a letter from another Lydia— Lydia Avilova; but came to the conclusion that Avilova was less interested in renewing their youthful acquaintance than in obtaining a ticket for *Three Sisters*.[20] Then there were two grand dinners given in honour of the Art Theatre by the writers of St Petersburg, which she described in great detail to Anton and at which she was undoubtedly a centre of attention.

As spring approached and the St Petersburg tour neared its end, Olga and Anton began to think more and more urgently about where they were next going to meet. For Olga this question was linked with another question, that of *how* they were going to meet: whether as an engaged couple, as lovers, or as good friends.

The marriage situation seems not to have changed since the previous summer: that is to say, there was an understanding on both sides that they would marry, but when and where still had to be decided—questions that seemed more urgent and important to Olga than to Anton. Anton's remark in a letter to Suvorin— 'Have you heard I'm getting married? It's not true. I'm off to Africa, to see the crocodiles.'[21]—was typical Chekhonte banter. Such rumours had been current for some time, and Chekhonte would have delighted in issuing facetious denials. In letters to Olga, he continues to see himself as her future husband. 'What you need is a husband, or rather a spouse, with side whiskers and a badge of office, but what am I? Not much of a catch.'[22] Of a proposed summer visit to Sweden and Norway he writes that it will be something for them to remember in their old age; and on March 7th, complaining once more of unwanted Yalta visitors, he tells Olga that he has decided either 'to go away or get married, so that my wife can chase them, the visitors, away. I'll get a divorce in the Yekaterinoslav District [Olga had passed on a Chekhonte-like rumour that he had married a provincial girl four days after meeting her] and marry again. Allow me to make you a proposal.'

Since nothing had happened after all in August, Masha may have concluded that the whole question of marriage between Olga and her brother had been shelved. To Olga she wrote on December 27th: 'I'm attached to you and have become extremely fond of you—and I'll be none the worse off for that. May the New Year bring us inner calm and peace: let us hope so. And let us wish our loved one a complete recovery.'[23] That Anton's health is of paramount importance to them both; that they are equal and united in their devotion to him, Olga ministering to his emotional needs as Masha does to his practical ones; and that the present situation *à trois* should continue unchanged: all this might be read into Masha's diplomatic greeting.

During the separation of 1900–1 Olga referred to the question of marriage only once in her letters to Anton. On January 20th he had written that he would be in Moscow in April and they would then go off somewhere together, and she replied: 'So you're coming in April? We'll get married very quietly and live together. Without any fuss. Agreed?'[24] It may be significant that she wrote this just a few days before the première of *Three Sisters*, when she was in a very highly strung condition. Though there is no doubt that marriage is still Olga's final objective, her letters dwell more on their feelings for one another and future life together, rather than making of marriage itself an issue.

On February 12th she told him that she might be free over Holy Week and Easter, and asked where they could meet, but made it clear that she did not want to come to Yalta, for reasons that she hoped Anton would understand.

The problem did not arise, however, for Anton replied: 'You ask when we shall see one another. At Easter. Where? In Moscow. Where shall we go? I don't know. We'll talk it over.' Then on the 26th, after being ill for several days, he suggested an alternative. 'Why don't you and Masha come down to Yalta in Holy Week and then we could go back to Moscow together?'

Olga, however, remained adamant: she would not be coming to Yalta and failed to understand how anyone of Anton's sensitivity could expect her to. On March 9th she spelled out her reasons more fully.

What would my position be? Having to make pretend again and see your mother suffer, playing games of hide-and-seek— believe me, I really do find this hard to bear. You don't seem to understand this point, or don't want to. And it's difficult for

me to talk about it. Surely you remember how agonising and
intolerable things were last summer. How much longer are we
going to be secretive? And what's the point? What people will
think? People will soon keep quiet and leave us in peace, once
they see it's an accomplished fact. And it'll be easier for us too.
I can't bear these ambiguities, why complicate life so? Well,
do you understand me, do you agree?'[25]

This was fair comment. Anton had already explained his
feelings, however, in a letter that crossed with hers. 'If you don't
want to come to Yalta, darling, that's up to you. Only I'm terribly
reluctant to leave Yalta! I don't fancy railway compartments and
hotels. Still, those are trifles, I'll be coming to Moscow—and
that's that.' And on receiving her letter, he wrote: 'I shall
definitely be coming to Moscow but whether I shall be going to
Sweden this year, I don't know. I'm fed up with traipsing about
and my health appears to be getting like an old man's—so that it
won't be a spouse you'll be getting in me, by the way, but a
grandfather.'[26]

Olga was now placed in a difficult position. Anton had agreed
to come to Moscow but was clearly not doing so from choice.
Was she making an unreasonable demand of someone in his state
of health? She may have recalled that in the previous year, Anton
had not come to Moscow until May, only to find it too cold for
him even then.

'I would come to you,' she wrote, 'but after all we can't live
now just as good friends, you must see that. I'm tired of this
concealment, believe me, I find it very hard to bear. To see your
mother's sufferings again and Masha's bewildered expression—
that's terrible! Don't you see I'm caught between two fires
staying with you? Do say what you feel about this. You never say
anything.' But she concludes on a more conciliatory note: 'Don't
you dare come to Moscow if you're not well enough. If not in
Yalta, we'll meet somewhere else in the south—I'll come down.'[27]

Next morning she received another letter from Anton. 'It's the
most wonderful spring they've had here for ages,' he wrote. 'I'd

be revelling in it, but alas, I've no one to enjoy it with, no one at all.'[28]

The appeal was irresistible. On no account was he to dream of coming to Moscow. Noting that it was exactly a year since she and Masha had gone down to Yalta in advance of the main Art Theatre company, she wrote that she would be leaving St Petersburg immediately, stopping briefly in Moscow to see the family, and then travelling straight on to Yalta.

CHAPTER NINE

A Quiet Wedding

Olga spent a fortnight with the Chekhovs, leaving on April 14th with Masha and Ivan Bunin, who accompanied them as far as Sevastopol. On the steamer Olga overheard an attractive lady saying how thrilled she had been to catch a glimpse of the writer Chekhov on Yalta pier. At Sevastopol Olga received treatment for toothache, but the journey to Moscow was a nightmare. Never before, she wrote to Anton, had she experienced such acute pain. Masha had been an angel, looking after her all the time and massaging her jaw. 'One thing is certain, if ever I'm ill, I shan't let anyone near me except Masha, she can work wonders with me.'[1]

In Moscow, however, another preoccupation soon filled her mind. 'I can't get away from the thought,' she wrote on arrival,

that there was no reason for us to part, in view of the fact that I'm not working. This is keeping up appearances, is it? What do you think? When I said that I was leaving with Masha, you didn't give the slightest indication that you'd like me to stay or that you didn't want to be parted from me. You kept quiet. I decided that you didn't want me in the house, once Masha had left. *Que dira le monde?!* . . . Was that the real reason? I don't think so. I've racked my brains, thinking of every possible explanation. Perhaps it's because I'm so clearly aware of everything that's going on inside you, that it was difficult for me to talk about what I kept wanting to. You remember what an odd mood I was in on the last day. You kept thinking I was angry with you. I'm feeling very wrought up now and there

D 89

are many things I want to say to you, I want to say everything that I feel, but so that you'll understand and not interpret it in your own way. What's your opinion? Is it better to keep quiet about what you want to say or the other way round? I know that you're an enemy of all 'serious' explanations, but I don't want to explain myself, I want to talk to you as someone close to me. Somehow it's extremely painful for me to think of my last stay in Yalta, even though we fooled about a lot. It's left an unpleasant kind of taste, an impression of something hazy, not out in the open. Perhaps you don't like me writing about this? Tell me frankly. I don't want to upset you in any way. I longed so much for the spring, longed so much for us to be together, to live at least a few months for one another, to become close, and now I've been 'entertained' at Yalta once more and gone away again. Don't you find all this odd? You yourself? I've gone and written all this, and already I'm regretting it, I feel that you too are perfectly aware of it all and understand. Answer this letter straight away, if you want to write frankly; write everything that you think, scold me if necessary, only don't keep quiet.

Now I'm going to give you a kiss, my darling—may I?

In a postscript she writes: 'Come at the beginning of May and we'll get married and live together. Will you do that, Antosha my darling? What are you doing now all day long? Tell me everything, every little trifle, and don't go making a joke of things as usual.'[2]

Anton replied promptly:

My darling, wonderful Knippschütz, I didn't try to detain you, because I hate being in Yalta and I had it in mind that I'd be seeing you soon in any case without other people around. Be that as it may, you've no reason to be angry, my sweetheart. I don't have any secret thoughts, I tell you everything that I think.

I'll come to Moscow at the beginning of May, in the first few days, and if it's possible, we'll get married and sail down the

Volga, or we'll sail down the Volga and then get married—
whichever's more convenient to you. . . . Then I'll spend the
whole or part of the winter with you in a flat in Moscow. Just
so long as I keep well and don't get poorly. My cough's taking
away all my energy, it's an effort to think about the future, and
I'm working without any enthusiasm. It's up to you to think
about the future and look after me, I'll do whatever you say,
otherwise we shan't live but sip life once an hour by the table-
spoon.

I'll send you a telegram, don't tell anyone and come to the
station alone. Understand? Au revoir, sweetheart, wonderful
girl. Don't mope and don't start imagining all kinds of things;
I give you my word of honour, there's nothing in my mind that
I'd wish to keep secret from you for a moment. Be a good girl,
don't be angry.

I give you a big kiss, doggie.　　　　Your Antoine[3]

It seems as if Olga, understandably disappointed that Anton
had not raised the subject of their future life together, had tried
to force him into action by announcing her intention of leaving
Yalta with Masha, but without result. In the previous September,
provoked by his seeming reluctance to come to Moscow to see
her, she had accused him of hardening his heart, and he had
replied that he did not know what to say to her, 'except the one
thing that I've already said to you ten thousand times and shall
probably go on saying for a long time to come—i.e. that I love
you': a rare occasion on which she had extracted from him a
'formal emotional declaration'. Now too her plain speaking had
produced the desired effect. The recurrent fears that she had
expressed in her letter of April 18th—that Anton had grown cold
towards her and did not love her as before, and that he only
needed her as an entertaining visitor, not an intimate companion
—had been set at rest: he had agreed to marry her in the immediate future and to live with her in Moscow.

Yet Olga may still have felt at the back of her mind that Anton's
reply was not entirely satisfying. There is no reason to doubt his

sincerity when he says that he has no secrets from her, but neither does he lay bare his soul to her in the way that she might have wished. Anxious to penetrate those bewildering silences of which this was not the first example, to feel that there were no inner recesses of his mind and heart that were closed to her, Olga had racked her brains to find some explanation of his silence in Yalta. The justification that he gives—that he knew that he would be seeing her soon in any case without other people around—is plausible and confirmed by his letters immediately after her departure; but why did he not say this to Olga at the time? Why could he not at least have mentioned marriage plans to her while she was on the spot in Yalta?

The explanation was not, as Olga obviously feared, that he had grown cool towards the idea of marriage. Perhaps the blame should be laid at Antosha Chekhonte's door. To treat the subject of love facetiously and to avoid all 'serious' explanations had become such a deeply ingrained habit that Anton found the greatest difficulty in breaking it. As Olga reproachfully pointed out, he had not once during the whole fortnight managed to call her by the affectionate name of Olya, although he did so in his letters.

In contrast to the prolonged delays of the previous autumn, Anton arrived in Moscow quite promptly on May 11th, in spite of previous illness. He had already laid down elaborate conditions on which he was prepared to go through with the wedding ceremony. Olga had to promise on her word of honour that not a soul in Moscow was to be told about it until after the event. 'For some reason,' he wrote, 'I'm terribly scared of the wedding and congratulations, and having to clutch a glass of champagne in your hand while you smile vaguely.' Chekhonte was obviously breathing down his neck again. The man in whose fiction a wedding breakfast is bound to turn into a hilarious (for the reader) disaster was afraid that he himself might become the object of ridicule: a risk that his highly developed sense of *amour propre* would not allow him to take. From the church they would drive straight to the railway station. 'Everything's in order with me,' he concluded this letter of April 26th, 'except for one trifling matter—my health.'[4] In Moscow he underwent a thorough medical examination. There had been further deterioration in both lungs, he reported on May 20th to Masha, now back in Yalta, and he had been ordered to travel immediately to the distant Ufa Province to take the koumiss cure, which consisted of drinking fermented mare's milk. The cure would last two months. 'Travelling alone is boring, the koumiss cure is boring, and to take somebody with me would be selfish and therefore unpleasant. I would get married, but I haven't got the documents, they're all in my desk in Yalta.'[5]

This reference to documents has puzzled Chekhov's biographers. Olga had reminded him about them earlier, and he had replied that he did not have any, apart from his passport. Whatever the documents were, they cannot have been vital, since the marriage went ahead smoothly only five days later. Was he still, at this eleventh hour, undecided about marriage in view of the unfavourable medical report, and casting around for some means of averting a decision, if only temporarily? To a friend he later claimed that the report had had the opposite effect: 'It threw me out a bit, so I got married quickly and went off on the cure.'[6] Or was it that he did not want Masha to realise that he had taken the decision to marry some time before and had kept it secret from her? By suggesting that his plans were still open— how much pleasanter if Olga could accompany him, but they would have to go as man and wife, it would be selfish to expect her to be just his travelling companion—he made it seem that Masha continued to enjoy his complete confidence, while preparing her for the shock of his forthcoming marriage.

If he had hoped, however, that the studied casualness with which he had slipped in the reference to getting married would forestall any complications in the relationship *à trois*, he was mistaken. Masha knew her brother's casual tone too well, and wasted no time in letting him have her opinion about his marriage.

To my mind, the whole business of weddings is appalling! And all that unnecessary fuss is no good to you either. If a person loves you, she's not going to leave you, there's no sacrifice on her part, nor the slightest selfishness on yours. How could that have occurred to you? What selfishness?! You can always get hitched later on. Tell that to your Knippschütz. It's your health that's most important. For heaven's sake, don't think I'm being selfish in this. You've always been the closest and dearest person to me and I wish only for your happiness. So long as you're well and happy, I need nothing more for myself. In any case, you must do as you think fit, perhaps I'm being partial in this instance. But it was you who brought me up to be without prejudices!

Coupled as it was with news of the deterioration in his health, Anton's evasive hint about marriage had stung the diplomatic Masha into addressing her brother in unusually forthright terms. But it is to Olga, rather than Anton, that her underlying criticism is directed: whatever had possessed her to want to subject him to the emotional ordeal of a wedding at such an unsuitable time?

'Heavens, how terrible it will be to spend two whole months without you,' Masha continued, 'and in Yalta too!' Anxious for news one way or the other, she adds in a postscript: 'If you don't answer this letter soon, I shall be ill.'[7] By the time that Anton received her letter, however, he was already on his honeymoon, as indeed he may have anticipated.

The marriage of Olga Knipper to Anton Chekhov took place on Friday, May 25th, 1901, at the Church of the Exultation of the Cross, in the Plyushchikha suburb of Moscow. Olga described the events of that day in a long letter to Masha, written while she and Anton were *en route* for the cure. She had not slept a wink the night before and got up with a foul headache. At 8.30, without breakfasting, she visited her dentist, and on her return packed her suitcases and did some last-minute shopping. There had already been a dramatic scene on the previous day with her mother, Anna Ivanovna, who was deeply offended at not having been consulted about the wedding arrangements, but as Olga pointed out, she herself had not known until the very last moment when the ceremony was going to take place. At 2 they had lunch, and afterwards Olga went to change into a white dress before going to join Anton. Zina, her maid, kept crying and making the sign of the cross over her, but Anna Ivanovna remained calm, since Olga had threatened to quit the house at the first hint of a maternal sob. At 5 Olga arrived at the church with Anton, who was wearing a frock-coat. The four witnesses, hastily recruited by Olga on the previous day, were already sitting on a bench in the churchyard. They consisted of Olga's Uncle Sasha, her younger brother Volodya, and two of Volodya's fellow students from the university. There was no one else to witness the ceremony.

> Because of my headache I could scarcely stay on my feet, and felt at one point that I was either going to burst out laughing or crying. You know, when the priest came up to me and Anton and led us both forward, the strangest feeling came over me, but afterwards I calmed down. We were married by the same priest who buried your father. It wasn't a long ceremony. I was terribly hurt that Ivan Pavlovich [Chekhov's younger brother] wasn't there, and don't understand why Anton let this happen. Ivan Pavlovich knew we were getting married, as he went with Anton to see the priest. The witnesses congratulated us, then we took our seats and drove off. Anton took me home, went off to collect his things and came back to us. My family were laughing about the wedding, but when I got back from the church, the servants just couldn't refrain from filing in to congratulate me, wailing and sobbing. At 8 we left for the station. All the family came to see us off, quietly and without fuss. [8]

So elaborate were the precautions taken by Anton to avoid publicity that all their other friends and relatives had been invited to a special dinner that evening in a distant area of Moscow—a dinner at which host and hostess never appeared. [9] As he and Olga settled down for the night in their sleeper, Anton may have congratulated himself that he had succeeded in having his quiet wedding. There had been a price to pay, however. The feelings of a number of people had been hurt: not least those of Anton's mother and sister in Yalta, who first heard the news of his wedding from the telegram which he sent on the day of the ceremony itself.

When Anton came to answer the letter in which Masha had expressed her disapproval of the idea of his marriage, he adduced three reasons why he had taken the step: that he was over forty, that Olga's family were highly respectable people, and that if it should be necessary for him and Olga to part (and he may have been thinking of the possibility of his own early death, rather than of divorce or separation), he could do so without hesitation, since Olga was independent and self-supporting.

Out of consideration for Olga's feelings, Masha forbade publication of this letter, which finally appeared in 1960 in the Chekhov Volume of *Literary Heritage*, where the editor refers to the 'half-joking' character of Anton's three reasons and comments that the reserved Chekhov 'remains silent about his deeper motives'.[10] Half-joking? No doubt those very practical considerations did weigh heavily with him. Nor is one surprised that he expressed himself to Masha in such unromantic terms. Masha had praised Olga's qualities often enough herself. To have reminded her of them at this juncture would have been superfluous as well as tactless.

What *were* the qualities in Olga that had appealed to Anton sufficiently for him to decide to make her his wife?

To consider first what Olga was not. She was not over-sexed, over-managing or over-domesticated, to quote the attributes of the unsympathetic females in Chekhov's fiction. Anton found her sexually attractive and admired her sense of style and elegance (it is hard to imagine him falling for a girl who was plain or dowdy), but she was not 'a fluffy marten who needs victims'. There were signs that she might try to organise him better on the domestic front, but such attention was not necessarily unwelcome; and in any case, she was far too involved in the theatre and the arts to be in danger of succumbing to a life of cooking smells and dogs with wet noses.

Nor did she bear the slightest resemblance to Chekhov's romantic heroines—those vulnerable girls of seventeen or eighteen with dreamy natures and sloping shoulders who never seem to be quite *there*. By the time that she came to know Chekhov, Olga was in her early thirties and quite unmistakably there: a robust, forthright young woman determined to succeed in the theatre, with large capable hands and a hearty appetite, perfectly willing to roll up her sleeves and sweep a floor, or to serve Anton's guests with food and drink in the garden at Yalta.

And yet she did have an undoubted romantic glamour in his eyes. It was the glamour of the highly talented actress. Chekhov always had a great admiration for talent of every kind; it was the quality obviously lacking in Lika Mizinova, for all her many other attractions. A particular glamour and excitement sur-rounded theatrical talent. As a schoolboy in Taganrog, disguised in false beard and dark glasses to avoid the watchful eye of the local school inspector, the young Anton had spent many an exciting evening in the gallery of the local theatre. Something of that youthful enthusiasm remains in the attitude of the mature Chekhov who loved being able to potter about backstage at the Art Theatre. Olga's talent, like his own, had not been given to her at birth, but was the product of much hard work and application. He had first been attracted to her when he saw her acting, admiring her not so much for her clever impersonation of his own character Arkadina in *The Seagull*, but as Irina in *Tsar Fyodor*— a role in which sincerity and nobility of character were combined with great femininity. That he did not have the opportunity of seeing her act sufficiently often for it to become routine helped to preserve this romantic image in his mind.

Unlike Lydia Yavorskaya, however, she did not carry over being 'the actress' into everyday life. There was never anything of the prima donna about her. In this respect she resembled Anton, who disliked people who played the role of 'the writer'. In her letters, apart from occasional questions on how to interpret the characters in his own plays, she never talks shop, rightly guessing that he would much prefer to hear the latest Art Theatre news and gossip. Her cultural interests, though wider than Anton's, were not highbrow; her comments on literature and the theatre, like his, show intelligence and discrimination, but are never weighty or abstract. There was no trace in her of that artificiality and affectation that Chekhov showed up so mercilessly in his stories and plays, and which he would certainly have detected in her had it been present.

Outstanding among her positive qualities was her zest for life. The future seemed empty to her unless she had something to look forward to. As in her acting, so in life she had the capacity for becoming intensely absorbed in whatever she was doing. One memoirist recalls her playing cards with her young nephews. The boys were playing with interest, Knipper with total absorption—'as if she were gambling away her fortune at the roulette table in Monte Carlo'.[11] Like Lika, she was an amusingly unpredictable companion, down in the dumps one day, the next day full of life and laughing her head off at anything that took her fancy. She shared Anton's sense of fun, his delight in observing the comic aspects of human behaviour, and his gifts as a story-teller. Nor did she treat *him* too reverentially, whereas Masha would probably have liked to wrap him up in cotton wool and cosset him as the Great Writer.

There seems little doubt that Olga's zest for life appealed to Anton the more he felt that zest ebbing away in himself. In Yalta he was not content to lead the quiet, contemplative life of the writer. 'I like excitement and here there isn't any,' he had written to Olga early on, and he never ceased to complain of Yalta's boredom. He wanted to borrow some of Olga's *joie de vivre* and to be swept along by it. 'It's up to you to think about the future and look after me, I'll do whatever you say, otherwise we shan't live but sip life once an hour by the table-spoon.' Subsequent events would show to what extent he was prepared to let his life be taken over in this way by Olga, or whether he had been used for so long to living on his inner resources and leading a life of his own that he had passed a point of psychological no return.

Is there any reason to suppose, as has been done, that an unsuspecting Anton was trapped into marriage by an unscrupulous Olga? In general, Anton does not strike one as either unsuspecting or incapable of putting his foot down. There was no coercion involved in August 1900 when they first agreed to marry. But then comes the long delay until May 1901. We have attributed this to Anton's dilatoriness ('Can one ever come to a decision with him?'), his resistance to all 'serious' scenes and explanations, and his fear of the actual ceremony, rather than to doubts about the wisdom of marriage itself. One cannot rule out the possibility, however, that Anton was keeping his options open and might have preferred the relationship to continue on the same informal footing. This was what Masha—surely not the world's greatest non-conformist or free-thinker—saw as the best solution for them, and she may well have been right. But as Anton pointed out to her, Olga's family, and Olga herself, were highly respectable people. Olga might not have been so shocked by the idea of a liaison, had Anton come out into the open and put it to her frankly, but what she could not tolerate was the thought of playing games of hide-and-seek indefinitely. Given her openness and lack of hypocrisy, this rejection of ambiguities strikes one as a genuine feeling and not as a means of pressurising Anton into marriage.

Had there been lingering doubts in his mind, he could certainly have used the adverse report on his health as an excuse for deferring a decision. That he chose to go ahead with marriage seems to make it clear beyond doubt that he was not dragged unwillingly to the altar.

PART TWO

CHAPTER TEN

🌿

Masha's Reactions

Masha had no sooner sent off her forthright letter to Anton advising him against marriage than his telegram arrived in Yalta: DEAR MAMA YOUR BLESSINGS AM GETTING MARRIED. EVERYTHING WILL REMAIN AS BEFORE. AM OFF TO KOUMISS CURE. ADDRESS: AKSYONOVO, SAMARO-ZLATOUSTOVSKY. HEALTH BETTER. ANTON.[1]

To mother and daughter this telegram came as a considerable shock. Old Mrs Chekhov sobbed loudly and appeared to be on the verge of a physical collapse, but within a day or two had fully recovered and was expressing the wish to see her new daughter-in-law as soon as possible. On Masha the effect of the telegram, though less dramatic, was more profound. 'I walk up and down thinking, thinking all the time,' she wrote to Anton on May 28th.

My thoughts keep jostling one another. I'm so appalled to think that all of a sudden you're married! Of course, I knew that sooner or later Olya would become your intimate friend, but the fact that you're married to her has somehow gone and shaken me to the very core, has made me think about you, myself and my future relations with Olya. I'm so afraid that they'll suddenly change for the worse . . . I'm feeling lonelier than ever. Don't think I'm angry or anything like that, no, I love you even more than before and wish you all the best from the bottom of my heart, and Olya likewise, although I don't know how things will be between us, and can't yet give myself an account of my feeling towards her. I'm a little angry with her for having said absolutely nothing to me about the wedding,

103

after all it couldn't have happened on the spur of the moment.
You know, Antosha, I'm feeling very sad and in a bad mood,
I can't eat anything and feel sick. All I want is to see you two
and no one else.

The garden is looking very lovely, she continues, detailing the
progress of the various plants; 'but Olya, of course, may not like
our house and won't be coming here after the cure, so you'll not
be coming either—how sad that will be!'[2]

Masha's sense of shock is understandable, since she was under
the impression that the whole question of marriage had been
shelved, perhaps indefinitely. One sympathises too over the *way*
in which the news had been broken to her: no word from Olga,
only Anton's evasive hint and the telegram to their mother. For
the mild Masha to admit to being 'a little angry' with Olga must
have meant that she was very angry indeed; well might she
suspect that Olga had been manoeuvring behind her back, since
she was not to know that all the secrecy had been imposed by
Anton. But her reactions clearly went deeper than that. The
feelings expressed are those of a jilted lover (her loneliness, loss
of appetite, almost a contrived pathos in her reference to Olga
not liking 'our' house and garden) but of a lover jilted not by one
person but two, by the two people in life closest to her, her dearly
loved brother and her best friend. Their joint failure to confide,
so dreaded by Masha in the previous August, made her fear that
they intended quietly to remove themselves from the centre of her
life, so leaving her without any *raison d'être*.

Masha realised that she had not been entirely forgotten when
she received a letter from Olga, hastily written on the day of the
wedding itself, deeply regretting that Masha had not been
present and stressing that 'you and I must always be together'.

'And so, my dear Olechka,' Masha replied on the 30th,

you alone succeeded in capturing my brother! How firm the
man stood, he wouldn't surrender, but his fate appeared and
that was that! There was simply no getting round you! Only
yesterday, when I received your letter, did I begin to calm

down a little. .... To me a wedding seemed such a shocking business—such a strain for Anton, who's a sick man after all— that I've asked myself more than once: why did you feel it was all necessary?

But if only you knew how much I've suffered, darling! What if our relations change for the worse—it all depends on you now. Supposing you suddenly become like Natasha in *Three Sisters*! If you do, I'll throttle you with my own hands. I shan't bite through your throat, I'll simply throttle you. You know that I love you and have become deeply attached to you during these two years. . . .

How is Antosha's health? Has he begun to drink the koumiss? If you are very happy, don't forget that I am suffering and completely on my own.

How strange to think that in a moment I'll have to write Mrs Chekhov on the envelope.[4]

During the journey to Aksyonovo, Anton sent two short letters to his sister, one a general progress report, the other with instructions on watering the plants. In a longer letter from Aksyonovo on June 2nd, he wrote:

That I have married, you already know. This action of mine will not, I think, in any way alter my way of life or the circumstances in which my life has been lived until now. Mother is no doubt saying all kinds of things, but tell her that there will be absolutely no changes, everything will remain as it was. I shall go on living in the way that I have done until now, and Mother likewise; and towards you my relations will remain as invariably good and warm as they have been until now.

This letter might indeed be called 'half-joking'. There is an amused condescension behind the mock-solemn, almost legalistic, style in which he informs Masha that everything will remain as it was. Its effect, none the less, was to ease Masha's state of mind considerably. Had he written it earlier, one wonders, would he not have saved his sister almost a fortnight of misery?

At this point Olga and Anton had still not received any of

Masha's letters. Then her letter of May 21st, advising him not to marry, finally reached Aksyonovo via Moscow. Anton did not show the letter to Olga, but sent Masha a sympathetic and more conciliatory reply (the 'suppressed' letter already referred to in the previous chapter), explaining his reasons carefully and stressing yet again that 'everything, absolutely everything, will remain as it was, and I shall go on living on my own in Yalta as before'.[5]

Masha's forthrightness on this occasion may have surprised Anton, who was used to exercising his authority over her, albeit unconsciously; the almost distraught tone of her letter of May 28th must have taken him aback still more. Olga too had heard at last from Masha—her somewhat calmer letter of May 30th—and it was she who now replied to both Masha's letters.

If only you knew, my dear Mashechka, what a burden your letter has lifted from my soul. After your letter to Anton I just didn't know what to think. I was completely at a loss. At first I was so worked up that I wanted to sit down there and then, and write you a good strong letter, but Anton stopped me, thank goodness. He himself was very upset by your letter and just couldn't make it out. I don't think you would have written a letter like that if you had known how it would grieve him. But enough of that.

Today's letter reassured us. And the thing was that we had just been talking a lot about you and considering what the best route would be for you to come here, so that we could all sail back down the Volga together. And then suddenly to receive a missive like that. What grieved me most was your unjust suspicion that I would persuade Anton not to go to Yalta. I should have been delighted to spend the whole summer in Yalta! And when we leave here, we shall go straight to you. Well, does that reassure you, my dear, anxious Mashechka?[6]

Masha was reassured, and chastened. It was the first time, she wrote to Anton, that she had expressed her feelings to him so openly, she was sorry to have upset them both, and promised that it would never, never happen again; but Olga herself had described how painfully she had reacted to her elder brother's marriage, so surely she should have understood how Masha was feeling and not scolded her?[7] Masha declined to join them on the Volga but revived an old plan for her and Olga to share a flat in Moscow for the winter—though actually, she adds in Chekhonte style, I've decided to get married myself, a suitor is already being sought for me.[8]

On the surface at least, the relationship *à trois* had survived this critical phase. Masha had undergone an emotional crisis. To Ivan Bunin, someone outside the triangle but well-known to all three, she wrote on June 6th of the deadly mood that she was in and of the feeling that her whole life was pointless.[9]

Instead of the two months prescribed, Olga and Anton remained in Aksyonovo only for the month of June, even though Anton drank four bottles of koumiss a day and put on weight. Olga rhapsodised later about the sunsets that they had watched together,[10] but Anton complained that living conditions were primitive and the people boring. On July 8th they reached Yalta, where Olga remained until August 20th. More than half-a-century later, Masha recalled the 'harmonious and cheerful' atmosphere of that summer together.[11] Time, however, had erased painful memories. The picture given by Olga, writing some three years after the event, is very different. Though one doubts the sincerity of the remark in her letter to Masha that she would have been delighted to spend the whole summer in Yalta, Olga arrived there with high hopes, for she and Anton had talked at length of how to make sure that Masha did not feel that she was being left out of things. From the very first day, however, nothing went right. Olga was careful to treat the Yalta house as Masha's home and strove not to resemble in any way the usurping Natasha of *Three Sisters*, but all to no avail: 'It was so painful for me to hear her say that now she had no home, no corner of her own, no garden. Oh, how I suffered during that month and a half in Yalta! And all those complications because of a church ceremony!'[12]

The situation was not helped by Anton's health. What progress he had made on the cure was quickly undone in Yalta. He was coughing badly and losing weight throughout July, writing no letters between the 9th and the 20th—an unusual event for such a conscientious correspondent; and during this time he made his will. Though Olga refrained from exercising authority in the house, she undoubtedly felt that she had every right to make sure that the invalid was looked after properly: a situation that was bound to breed tension between her, Masha and old Mrs Chekhov. Olga and Masha may have tried to conceal this tension from Anton, but early in August they took themselves off together for a while to the Gurzuf cottage, and there the tearful scenes and explanations went on unchecked.

And yet the bond of affection between them remained very strong. As Masha had written to Anton, had he married anyone else but Knippschütz, she would quite simply have hated his wife, and that would have been that.[13]

CHAPTER ELEVEN

Hopes and Disappointments

Olga left Yalta on August 20th to take part in preparations for the coming Art Theatre season, and Masha followed on September 1st, prior to the start of term at the private girls' school where she taught history and geography. Anton was sent a sketch plan of their flat. Very nice, he commented, but why had the room labelled 'Anton's study' been placed right next to the establishment? He was to join them for his customary autumn visit. 'Bring all your warm clothes,' Olga instructed, 'your Jaeger underwear, overcoat, galoshes, rug, umbrella, and two suits, please, so that you've got a change.'

He arrived on September 17th and was immediately busy with rehearsals of *Three Sisters*. They were joking in Moscow that now there were only two sisters, since Chekhov had married the third. At the end of the play's first performance of the season, he appeared on stage alone and was greeted with thunderous applause. On the 24th Stanislavsky's role as Colonel Vershinin was taken over by a talented newcomer, Kachalov, who in time came to personify the Moscow Art Theatre actor in the same way that Knipper personified the Art Theatre actress; but the only comment that he could elicit from Chekhov about his performance was that he saluted like a lieutenant, instead of a colonel.[1]

As usual, the excitement of Moscow life made Anton feel that his health was much better there than in Yalta, and as usual, it was not long before this excitement began to wear him out. By the end of October he was already back in his dreary Yalta rut, where a visit from the headmistress of the local girls' school was likely to be the highlight of his social activity. What did he care if it remained warm and sunny in Yalta? Give him the Moscow winter any day!

There now began a period of intensive correspondence between him and Olga that lasted until February 1902. In many respects the pattern of these letters is familiar. A day without a letter is already cause for anxiety or reproach; two blank days a whole drama. Anton argues that his letters only seem shorter because his handwriting is smaller. Each expresses the fear that his or her letters may have become boring to the other party, and each reassures the other that this is not so. The familiar anguished cry is heard repeatedly: when are we going to see one another again? 'How am I going to live through the winter?' wails Olga. 'I must get away from here,' groans Anton. For a time the letters are full of eager references to the possibility of a lightning visit by Olga over Christmas, but on the very day that Anton is complaining of intolerable boredom and passionately imploring her to come, Olga is writing that leave from the Theatre is out of the question at such a financially important time of year. The hope is briefly raised that the doctors may allow Anton to go to Moscow in January, while ambitious plans are periodically mooted for visits to foreign parts in the summer—but not Switzerland, Anton decides, there's no fishing there.

The new Mrs Chekhov now felt a more direct responsibility for her husband's welfare. From Moscow she sent the old Mrs Chekhov an elaborate diet sheet for Anton, but as he pointed out, his mother and the old cook were too set in their ways to be able to change, however good their intentions. Are you wearing warm clothes when you go out? asks Olga . . . Please don't let your hair grow too long . . . Tell me when you're taking castor oil . . . How are your bowels? I'd mention this each time I write but I know you don't like it. . . . If such subjects brought out a 'Germanic' strain in Olga, in Anton they were liable to provoke the spirit of Chekhonte. 'I'm using your toothpaste and think of you every time I brush my teeth . . . I'm behaving like a proper German husband, I'm even wearing long woollen pants.'

It is Olga's letters which are the longer and more interesting, because she had more to write about. Often they were written in the early hours of the morning, her only free time. 'You're always saying what the weather's like,' she snapped at him once, 'which I can find out from the newspapers': a thoroughly tactless remark for which she paid dearly. 'If I often wrote to you about the weather,' he replied with affected sadness, 'it was because I thought it would interest you, but forgive me, I shan't do so any more.' Two days later he writes blandly: 'There are some very interesting things I might say about the weather—what a pity that subject is taboo.' Eventually, Olga has to go down on bended knee and implore him to write whatever and whenever he likes about the weather. Her own life was so full of other things. Apart from performances and rehearsals, she took a lively part in the social activities surrounding the Theatre. Anton envied her the suppers and the parties: how marvellous to be able to drink and enjoy oneself without thinking all the time about the effects on one's health. 'Time was when I too, as the saying goes, could hold my liquor.'

Of the strength of feeling between them these letters leave no doubt. 'Whatever happens, even if you suddenly turned into an old woman,' wrote Anton, 'I should still love you—for your soul, for your disposition.'[2] Not that there is any doubt of the strong physical element in this love, even though the more explicit references have been cut out from the published letters: by Olga herself, and, for reasons less easy to appreciate, by subsequent Soviet editors.

Yet there are contrasting notes too in the pattern of the relationship during the early months of marriage. It was Masha who asked Olga in June why Anton kept on writing: '*I* shall be coming on such-and-such a day'—and not a word about his wife; did it mean that Olga was not coming to Yalta?[3] Amusingly, many months passed before he remembered to tell Olga that if she needed money, she could draw on the theatre royalties held for him by Nemirovich. As before, Olga wished that he would be more demonstrative about his love, sought reassurance, and feared that he loved her not for herself but only as a cheerful companion. She was confident that she could guess, from 'every little vein' on his face, exactly what he was feeling, but did she understand—and this was her chief source of anxiety—what was going on in his mind? 'How I want to know and understand you completely, completely,' she writes. Eager to probe, she refers to 'that quiet sadness which seems to be so deeply seated in your soul'.[4] It was the kind of sloppy phrase that Chekhov disliked people using about himself or his work. 'Rubbish, darling!' he replied. 'I do not feel the least sadness and never have done, I feel tolerably well and when you're with me, absolutely fine.'[5] This brightly reassuring tone did not help Olga. Was he withholding some part of himself from her? 'I'm interested only in you, in your soul, in your inner world, I want to know what's going on there—or am I speaking too boldly, and is entrance to that world forbidden?'[6] Anton did not reply.

What of the relations now between Olga and Masha? So long as the two of them were together in Moscow, all went well. In November they moved into a better flat, with electricity in three of the rooms. Masha took a lively interest in the Art Theatre, while Olga was delighted to be able to tell Anton that Masha had sold one of her paintings at an exhibition. They entertained and went out together, although Masha, unused to the hectic pace of Olga's life, complained that she saw little of her.[7] Just as soon, however, as Masha was alone in Yalta with Anton, Olga began to feel jealous. This had happened at the end of August, when Masha stayed on for a few days after Olga's departure. Olga complained bitterly to Anton that she was sure that her name was no longer mentioned in the house, and that she would always stand between him and Masha. Be patient, advised Anton, and say nothing, absolutely nothing: this was the golden rule for all newly married couples.[8] When Masha left to spend her Christmas holiday in Yalta, Olga's feelings were a mixture of sadness at her departure, satisfaction at knowing that Anton would be looked after properly, and jealousy. On Masha's return, Olga wrote to Anton that she was overjoyed, 'clung to her like a leech', and would have cried her eyes out, had not Ivan Chekhov and his family been invited to lunch. It was now after two in the morning, she and Masha had sat up talking for three hours, and Masha had told her everything, everything. Then abruptly the tone of her letter changes: 'I don't know what's going on in your head or what you're thinking about. You don't confide in me to the slightest degree. If you don't want to write, there's no need—just send postcards saying you're well. Either you've never been close to me, or you've grown apart from me, or else I'm only a woman to you, not a human being.'[9]

What had provoked this ill-humoured outburst? Olga's letter on the following day provides the explanation. 'From Masha's hints I realise that you've told her about the play you've thought up. You haven't given me even the slightest hint, though you must know how much it means to me. Very well, so be it, you've no faith in me. I shall never ask you about anything again, don't worry. I shan't interfere. Other people can tell me.'[10]

It was not the first time that she had accused him of not confiding in her about his work. On this occasion she felt touched at her two most sensitive points: her jealousy of Masha, and her fear that Anton was withholding some part of himself from her. It was not that he had no faith in *her*, Anton replied, but that he had no faith in the play. Had she been there, he could have talked to her about it, but to commit it to paper would risk killing the subject stone dead at the outset. As for her angry threats and ill humour: 'For me to be in low spirits is permissible, because I'm living in the wilderness, I've nothing to do, I don't see people, and I'm ill almost every week—but you? Your life is so much richer.'[11]

From the start of her marriage, Olga was acutely aware that her life was in fact split by conflicting loyalties: to Anton and to the Theatre. She discovered the truth of what Nemirovich had said to her at their very first interview: that if she wanted to marry, to have children, the theatre would simply 'gobble them all up without trace'. She had hoped that while he was in Yalta, Anton would remain in tolerably good health, that while she was

busy acting, he would be busy writing, and that he would be able
to spend at least part of the winter in Moscow. None of these
hopes was realised. Yet at the same time, Olga could not forget
that although it was the theatre that now separated them, it was
the theatre that had first brought them together. One can appreciate her feelings when she writes: 'There are times when I
absolutely hate the theatre, and other times when I love it madly.
After all it has given me life, it has given me much joy and much
sorrow, it has given me you, it has made me into a human being.
Before the theatre, I was half-dead, I had not made any kind of
life for myself. And I achieved everything alone, by myself, by
my own efforts.'[12]

When Anton had left Moscow in October, his wife, he wrote to
a friend, had been in tears, but he had ordered her not to give up
the theatre.[13] Writing to Olga on November 7th, his tone is more
equivocal: 'So you want to give up the theatre? Think it over
carefully, darling, very carefully, and only then come to a
decision.' But he goes on: 'Bear in mind that next year I shall be
spending the whole of the winter in Moscow.' Only four days
later he is writing that winter will soon pass and then they will
have spring and summer together. 'It's pointless to give up the
theatre for the kind of boredom there is in Yalta now.'

Early in December, however, when it became clear that they
were not going to meet over Christmas, Olga tormented herself
more and more with the thought that she ought to be living
permanently with her husband. Everyone seemed to be looking
at her with reproachful eyes, wondering how she could possibly
allow him to go on living miserably in Yalta by himself. She
appealed to him to make up her mind for her. 'If I've absolutely
nothing to do,' she feared, 'I shall bore you. I shall wander about
from corner to corner and find fault with everything. I'm completely unused to an idle life and I'm not so young that I can
demolish in one go everything that I've built up with such difficulty.'[14] When this letter arrived, Anton was ill in bed. A brief
note saying that Dr Altshuller had been to see him was the only
reply. Olga became more desperate. 'Living apart is still con-

ceivable, if I know that you're feeling well, but when this sort of thing happens, it's terrible! I feel capable of throwing everything up and rushing to be with you.'[15] And well might she have done so, had Anton given her the slightest prompting, even though it would have been a crushing blow to the Art Theatre to lose its least dispensable actress in mid-season; but Anton was soon on the mend, and though regretting her absence, said nothing to her about giving up the theatre.

There seems indeed to have been an underlying realisation by both of them that however much they longed for one another, living together permanently would not be the ideal answer. To have to give up the theatre and return to the idle life that she had renounced would have been a terrible wrench for Olga; but it was a sacrifice that she could have made, had she not feared that Anton would simply become bored and irritated by her constant presence. Anton is characteristically less forthcoming. To third parties he explained that no one should be idle in life and that he could never have allowed Olga to sacrifice her career.[16] But he too may have feared that an Olga with nothing to do would not be an easy companion over a long period. If she gave up the theatre, he would lose his life-line to Moscow; she would also lose her romantic glamour in his eyes and become just 'my wife'. Moreover— and this one might regard as the strongest consideration—his *amour propre* would have rejected absolutely the thought of Olga becoming no more than a glorified nurse-companion to him in Yalta.

The outcome of this situation might have been very different, however, had Olga produced the child for which they were both hoping. 'I'm terribly keen now for you to have a little half-German,' Anton wrote on November 2nd, 'who would amuse you and fill your life.' Alas, Olga replied on the 13th, 'there'll be no half-German this time; but what makes you think that he would fill my life, are you not able to do that for me?' Perhaps the unspoken thought in Anton's mind was that the child would still be there after he had gone. There are further references to 'Andryushka', 'Pamfil', and 'a certain little being'. Visiting the Kachalovs, Olga plays with their baby son in the nursery and longs desperately to have a child of her own.

At last, at the end of February, Olga and Anton were reunited in Yalta for five days. Olga had so often imagined the reunion. It must take place in Anton's study, not in public. 'Will you laugh when you see me? I don't suppose you'll give the least sign that you're glad—I know you.' Would they find after so much anticipation that when the moment itself arrived, they had nothing to say to one another? 'I like it when that happens.'

The five days passed far too quickly for Olga. As soon as she had gone, the Yalta ladies descended on Chekhov, headed by the headmistress of the local girls' school. 'All of them,' he told Olga, 'had exactly the same coy little smile on their faces: we didn't want to disturb you! As if you and I had done nothing during those five days except make love to one another.'[17]

From Yalta Olga was to travel direct to St Petersburg to join the company on their month's tour. The first part of the journey was by carriage through the mountains to Simferopol. It was very different from the delightful drive to Bakhchisarai that she and Anton had enjoyed in the summer of 1899. By the time she reached Simferopol it was pitch black and bitterly cold. To warm herself up she walked about for a long time. Sitting in the waiting-room before the train was due to leave, she suddenly felt very queer:

> I had a pain in the stomach, nausea, palpitations, and almost passed out. I was very scared, began pulling off my jacket, didn't know what to do with myself, tried to reach the door of the ladies' room to call someone but collapsed and couldn't get up, couldn't move my arms and legs properly, broke out in a cold sweat and didn't know what was happening. I thought I must have poisoned myself. It's never happened to me before. I thought I wouldn't be able to travel. I'm all right now.[18]

Olga's companion on the sleeper told her all the tragic details of her life story and asked if she liked the writer Chekhov. When Olga described her bad turn on the previous day, the lady 'promptly thought I must be "in an interesting condition". I thought so too, but it's unlikely.'

Hopes and Disappointments

In St Petersburg there were lilies from Stanislavsky and roses from Nemirovich, but for some days she felt tired and unwell. Though the St Petersburg critics, in contrast to the previous year, now universally recognised her as a major actress, acting gave her no pleasure. By March 13th, however, she was beginning to feel more like her usual self. On that date, to the accompaniment of elaborate security precautions, Tsar Nicholas II bestowed on the company the honour of attending a performance of *Three Sisters*, and gave every appearance of having thoroughly enjoyed himself. Olga was soon involved in those elaborate social functions which seemed an indispensable part of the St Petersburg tour. 'There really does seem to be something wrong with my insides,' she told Anton, who merely advised her to stop drinking so much champagne.

'Everything's in blossom here,' he informed her cheerfully. 'Your room with the piano is all ready. Not long now before you arrive. We'll spend a little time in Yalta, then go off to Moscow, then make for the Volga district.'[19] Olga had booked her seat, was longing to escape from noisy St Petersburg, and already imagined herself breathing in the spring air of the south as the train approached Sevastopol. She was due to leave on April 6th.

'This'll be my last letter,' Anton wrote on March 31st. 'My health is perfect. Nothing on earth is going to separate us now until September or October.'

On the very day before this letter was written, Olga suffered a miscarriage.

'It seems,' she wrote later from hospital, 'that I left Yalta with the hope of presenting Pamfil to you, but was not aware of it. All the time I was unwell but kept thinking it was my insides, and although I wanted to be pregnant, I didn't know I was.' While Olga shed bitter tears at the thought of the lost Pamfil, the ladies of the company fussed round, and Stanislavsky wandered aimlessly up and down the corridor. In the evening Olga was taken to hospital and operated on. She signed her letter to Anton, 'Your unsuccessful dog', adding in a postscript: 'What care I would have taken of myself had I known that I was pregnant.'[20]

CHAPTER TWELVE

The Lyubimovka Crisis

Anton's reference to perfect health has to be understood in a very relative sense. He had given a more sober assessment of his condition in February, when he told Olga that he needed to rest after pruning a single rose bush, and that his health had obviously got much worse that winter. The writer Korolenko, who had not seen him for several years, noted that Chekhov's features 'looked strained and somehow harder'.[1]

It was ironical, none the less, that Olga's crisis should occur just when Anton was feeling better and eagerly looking forward to the visit of his radiantly healthy young wife. She arrived from St Petersburg with a high temperature, very weak and in great pain, and had to be carried off the steamer on a stretcher. At the beginning of May she wrote to Stanislavsky that she was still very weak and not even enjoying convalescence, and that Anton had also been ill for some days, worrying about her.[2] Nevertheless, with Altshuller's permission, they both left for Moscow on May 25th. There seems little evidence to support the idea that Masha and her mother felt that Olga was to blame for the miscarriage and that this hastened Olga and Anton's departure;[3] it is more likely that Anton, who had been waiting so long for their trip down the Volga, was the one anxious to leave Yalta at the earliest opportunity.

The long train journey proved too much for Olga, however, and in Moscow she was ordered three weeks' complete rest. Then on June 1st, at ten in the evening, she suddenly began to experience acute pains in the stomach, which lasted until morning and were so agonising that in the course of one night, Anton told Masha, she had become considerably thinner and her cheeks quite hollow. No doctors were available, as they had all left for the country at the start of the Whitsun holiday. Fortunately, Vishnevsky arrived at midnight in answer to Anton's urgent note, but not until the morning did a doctor appear. The crisis passed, although Olga continued to look pale and very thin.

On June 11th there came another crisis. Olga lay awake all night with severe vomiting and stomach pains. Once more Vishnevsky hurried off at crack of dawn to summon doctors. A specialist was called in and Olga's illness now finally diagnosed as peritonitis, which had probably begun in Yalta or even St Petersburg. An operation was recommended, and Vishnevsky had already begun to make arrangements for moving Olga to hospital when suddenly she began to feel better, the vomiting ceased, her mood improved, and she felt able to sleep. The operation was postponed and soon became unnecessary. Within a day or two Olga was able to get up and take food, though she was so thin that for several weeks Anton continued to call her his 'little stick'.

All these crises did not help Anton's health. 'He's not looking very grand himself,' noted Stanislavsky, a frequent visitor.[4] Although Anton assured Masha on the 12th that he was feeling well in spite of not sleeping the previous night, to Gorky he admitted with characteristic understatement that he was 'a trifle exhausted'. There had been moments in those two anxious months when he had begun to fear for Olga's life, and he was badly in need of a rest and a change. Olga made such good progress that on the 17th Anton's place was taken by Olga's mother, and he felt free to leave for a short holiday in the distant Perm district on the estate of Savva Morozov, a millionaire industrialist who had taken the Art Theatre under his wing. If Olga was disappointed by his departure, she gave no indication. 'I'm so glad that he has gone and will at least get a change of air,' she wrote to Stanislavsky.[5]

Unfortunately, however, the air in the Perm district was

stiflingly hot, and the people were so dull, Anton informed Nemirovich, that to present them on stage would be intolerably boring.[6] A young student staying on the estate, A. N. Tikhonov, recalled how Chekhov wandered about aimlessly and kept asking the maid if there were any telegrams for him from Moscow. Tikhonov was sleeping in the room next to Chekhov's. One night, woken by a violent thunderstorm, he caught the sound of agonised groans coming from the other side of the wall. Rushing round to Chekhov's room, he flung open the door and called his name. Chekhov was leaning over the side of the bed, his whole body convulsed with coughing, and each time he coughed a stream of blood flowed out of his wide-open mouth into a blue enamel spittoon, 'like liquid from an upturned bottle'. Tikhonov called a second time, and Chekhov, looking up and speaking with difficulty, apologised to the young man for disturbing his sleep. Next morning he left for Moscow.[7]

On July 5th, still attended by the faithful Vishnevsky, Olga and Anton took up residence at Lyubimovka, where Stanislavsky had offered them the use of his summer datcha on his mother's estate. Although it was only forty minutes by train from Moscow, the estate was in the heart of the countryside. The Stanislavskys were on holiday in Switzerland, and had instructed two servants, Yegor and Dunyasha, to look after the visitors. 'We're eating and sleeping like bishops,' Anton reported.[8] After overcoming his disappointment at leaving behind two bottles of specially purchased beer on the train, he was in the best of moods, spending much of his time fishing in the nearby river. 'I can feel his soul relaxing here,' Olga informed the Stanislavskys, 'he's a completely different person.'[9] She too was making progress. Soon she was told that no further treatment would be necessary and that she could start rehearsals straight away, but she was not to travel by carriage or undertake the journey to Yalta.

Stanislavsky was one of a family of ten. Apart from his *maman*, who was half-French and lived in the big house next to the datcha, there were numerous relatives and their households, including a number of young people, living nearby. In contrast to dreary

Perm, the new environment and the new set of people at once gave Chekhov ideas for his play, the embryonic *Cherry Orchard*. He was fascinated by the noise of the train and wondered if it could be reproduced on stage. According to Stanislavsky, the Lyubimovka residents provided material for at least three of the play's future characters: the student Trofimov, the clerk Yepikhodov, whose basic features were derived from Chekhov's conversations with the servant Yegor, and the governess, Charlotte Ivanovna, whose prototype was a young English governess by the name of Lily Glassby, living with relatives of the Stanislavskys, the Smirnovs.[10] On meeting Chekhov out walking in the park, the inimitable Lily was in the habit of jumping up on to his shoulders and starting to doff his hat to the passers-by.[11] 'He's thought the play out fully in his mind, and any day now he'll probably start writing,' Olga reported triumphantly to Stanislavsky.[12]

It is tempting to see those six weeks at Lyubimovka as a bright interlude, perhaps the brightest interlude, in the Chekhovs' life together: a reward, as Anton expressed it to Stanislavsky, for the miserable months that had gone before. Olga had been 'blissfully happy' there, and when she revisited Lyubimovka in September, it brought back pleasant memories of Anton, fishing on the river bank, lying on the balcony reading a newspaper, sitting on a bench in the garden while a service was going on in the nearby church, or reclining on a sofa in the bedroom. Did Anton think that she was being sentimental? Her letter was splendid, he replied.

That this idyllic picture, though true so far as it went, did not tell the full story, is apparent from what happened after Anton had left for Yalta without Olga on August 14th.

Olga alone in the north, Anton and Masha together in Yalta: this situation had always spelled trouble. Anton took with him a letter, which has not survived, from Olga to Masha. When Anton handed it to Masha and she read it through, an uncomfortable silence followed. Next day Anton was given the letter to read. 'Why did you have to be so rude to Masha?' he wrote to Olga.

'Your letter is very, very unfair. I give you my word of honour, Mother and Masha invited both you and me, never once me alone, and they have always had warm and cordial feelings for you.'[13]

Anton's statement was not entirely truthful, since Masha had suggested on two occasions that he might come down to Yalta alone,[14] but she had also repeatedly proposed that Olga should come to Yalta to convalesce. 'Wouldn't it be better,' she wrote on June 6th, 'to bring Olya down to Yalta as soon as she is well enough? Or should I come to Moscow? Make sure *you* keep well, and, if possible, come down here for a fortnight's rest.' More than anyone else, Masha was conscious of the strain that Olga's illness was bound to place upon Anton, and it may have been a feeling of guilt that prompted Olga's wild accusations.

Olga defended herself, not very persuasively, against Anton's criticism; but why, she wanted to know, had Masha shown him the letter? When Masha had written such letters to *her*, Olga had always taken care to conceal them from Anton.

Contradicting himself, Anton replied that Masha had not given him the letter to read, he had found it in his mother's room, 'picked it up mechanically and read it through'. The phrase, 'picked it up mechanically', is unconvincing. Anton had been snooping but was unwilling to admit it. He repeats the charge that Olga's letter had been terribly rude and unfair. 'Where fairness is concerned, one must be absolutely beyond reproach. Forgive me, darling, for reading you these lectures, I'm scared of doing that kind of thing.'[15]

Anton had quickly sensed, however, that the real culprit was not Masha but himself. 'You're angry with me, and I simply can't understand why. Is it because I went away? But I'd been living with you ever since Easter, without a separation, not moving a step from your side, and I shouldn't have left you, had it not been for business to attend to and because I'd begun spitting blood. Don't be angry, dear.'[16]

On the face of it, there was little for Olga to be angry about. She had known for some time that Anton was planning to visit

Yalta in August. The business he referred to concerned a debt
that he was hoping to recover. This was a matter of some importance, since without the money he could not become a fully
paid-up shareholder in the newly constituted Art Theatre, and
his punctiliousness in such matters would not allow him to be
made a shareholder out of charity.[17] And he did stop spitting
blood in Yalta, although the move in general was a disaster for his
health. In any case, as his letters to other correspondents confirm,
he genuinely intended to spend only a short time in Yalta and to
rejoin Olga in Moscow for as long as his health permitted.[18]

Nevertheless, his conscience was not entirely clear. He sounds
too anxious to justify himself. When he claims that they had not
been separated, he glosses over his fortnight's absence in Perm.
And the two reasons that he gives could surely have been made
clear to Olga before rather than after his departure? Suddenly
fearful that he may have provoked a rift between them, he pleads
with her, half-humorously, not to leave him so soon, 'before we've
lived properly, before you've given me a little boy or a little girl.
And when you've done that, you're free to act as you please.'[19]

Olga's long letter of August 28th to Anton marks the most
critical point in their relationship, and is quoted here in full:

Today your two letters and postcard arrived, my dear! Thank
you for not forgetting me. So you don't want to come back
here? And I was foolish enough to dream that you might. Why
didn't you tell me at once that you were going away for good?
So my forebodings were justified. Why didn't you tell me
frankly that you were going away because you were spitting
blood? That would have been very simple and understandable.
So you concealed it from me. How painful it is to me that you
treat me like a stranger, or like a doll that mustn't be worried. I
should have been calmer and more controlled, had you been
frank with me. So you think that we've spent long enough
living together. It's time to part? Very well. There's something
I don't understand in all this. I just don't understand. Something must have happened. Your letters may be tender, but

why is it that a shudder passes through me when I read them several times.

How wonderfully we lived together here! If only you'd say just one word in your letters about the past month! I'd like that so much.

You're going to hate my letters. But I can't be silent. So now without any warning there's a long separation from you ahead, because it'll be quite out of the question for you to come to Moscow in the autumn. It would have made sense to spend September in Lyubimovka.

In general, we're making a mess of our lives. Heavens, if only I knew that you needed me, that I could help you to live, that you'd feel happy if I were with you all the time! If only you could give me that assurance! But you're able to live near me and say nothing. And there were times when I felt that I was in the way. I felt that you needed me only as an attractive woman, and that I myself, as a person, was a stranger to you and isolated. Tell me that I'm wrong, hit me if it isn't true. Don't think I'm talking nonsense, don't think I'm angry with you if I accuse you of anything. You are the only person in the world for me and if I cause you unpleasant moments, it's only unconsciously or when I'm feeling very confused. You mustn't blame me. You are strong but I am weak and completely worthless. You are able to endure everything in silence, you have no need to share things with other people. You lead your own special life and look upon everyday life with some indifference. How awful to think, Anton, that everything I'm writing may evoke no more than a smile from you, or that you may show my letter to Masha, as she did to you?

Forgive me, my darling, my dearest loved one, don't be angry with the tone of my letter. But try to understand it properly, that's all I ask. I feel terribly depressed and empty without you. I'm like a lost soul and simply can't imagine what life's going to be like in future. I know that you're not keen on letters of this kind. But tell me which is better: to write down everything as I have done, or to bottle everything up inside and write a nice superficial letter, leaving one's own feelings out of it? I'll do whichever you say. I give you a big kiss and embrace you and caress my beloved. Be happy.   Olya[20]

That Olga's loneliness and depression had affected her judgement is obvious from the confused, almost unbalanced, tone of this letter, with its self-abasement and its jealous dig at Anton and Masha. Though physically recovered, she had not yet fully regained her mental equilibrium. Anton had no choice but to answer her firmly. Who had said that he was leaving for good and not returning to Moscow? Had he not told her in plain Russian that he would be arriving in September and living with her until December? 'You accuse me of a lack of frankness, but you forget everything I say or write to you.' As for the shudder that passed through her on reading his letters, and her talk of separation, he could only conclude that some third person had been influencing her against him. And in answer to her charge that he never spoke of his love, that he needed her only as an attractive woman and that she was a stranger to him, he writes. 'You're my wife, don't you understand that? You're the person closest and dearest to me, my love for you was and still is boundless, yet you go on describing yourself as an "attractive" woman, a stranger to me and isolated . . . Well, that's up to you, have it your own way.'[21]

This letter at least helped to clear the air. Olga, now in Moscow and in a calmer frame of mind, apologised for all her 'strange' letters and strenuously denied that any third person had been talking to her; it was just that after his departure 'all sorts of crazy ideas' had come into her head.

Yet she could still not help asking herself *why* Anton had wanted to leave Lyubimovka. Did part of the blame lie with her? Had she scared him away because of the 'unpleasant moments' that she had caused him? 'There were plenty of them and I'm furious with myself for my lack of self-control.' At length, she looks the problem straight in the eye. 'I came to the conclusion,' she wrote on September 14th, 'that you had gone away, partly to have a rest from me.'

This was probably true. In June, eager for change after two anxious months as Olga's nurse-companion, Anton had taken himself off to Perm at the earliest opportunity—only to spend his time there looking out for telegrams from Moscow. In Lyubimovka Olga cannot always have been an easy companion, suffering as she was from the psychological after-effects of her illness. Anton may well have felt that a short period of separation might benefit them both before they met again in the autumn. To explain this to Olga would have been difficult; hence his belated, and somewhat conscience-stricken, attempt to find other reasons to justify his departure.

But what of Olga's more general reflections on Anton's character? 'You are able to endure everything in silence,' she had written, 'you have no need to share things with other people. You lead your own special life and look upon everyday life with some indifference.' In her letter on the following day, she developed her thought more fully: 'You're always so calm and even-tempered, and I sometimes feel that no separations, no feelings, no changes, have any effect on you. This isn't because you have a cold nature or are indifferent, but because there's something in you that won't allow you to attach importance to all the everyday happenings of life.'[22]

Olga knew that she was not that kind of person. She was volatile where he was calm. Separations *did* affect her, often profoundly. She was not a self-contained person and could not bottle everything up inside her. This last contrast puzzled her especially. Should one be silent or say what one felt? She had asked him this question before and would ask him again. If only he would act as her spiritual mentor, she would willingly follow his instruction, but this he refused, or was unable, to do.

When Olga writes—'This isn't because you have a cold nature or are indifferent, but because there's something in you that won't allow you to attach importance to all the everyday happenings of life'—she has taken her analysis of the elusive aspect of Anton's personality as far as she would ever do; further, indeed, than any of his other associates, none of whom had such good cause to ponder on his inner nature as his wife. Does this 'something' in him explain why he failed to anticipate how badly his wife would react to his departure from Lyubimovka, or how badly his sister would react to the news of his marriage? Was it, as Olga assumed, a *strength* in him, a by-product of that complex inner world of his to which she felt that she was denied access? Or was it a weakness? Was Anton quite capable, like lesser mortals, of turning an occasional blind eye to the implications of his behaviour for other people, and hoping that with some luck and ingenuity he would get away with it? Did that complex inner world of his in fact exist? Or was it only other people who assumed that it must do? 'You ask: what is life?' he wrote once to Olga. 'That's rather like asking: what is a carrot? A carrot is a carrot, and nothing more is known about it.'[23]

If the nature of that 'something' in Anton remains a matter for speculation, what does emerge clearly from the Lyubimovka crisis is a difference between him and Olga in their attitudes towards marriage. The more conventional Olga believes that marriage should represent an exclusive personal commitment. 'Heavens, if only I knew that you needed me, that I could help you to live, that you'd feel happy if I were with you all the time!' When Anton left Moscow for Perm, or Lyubimovka for Yalta, she felt that in some way he was 'walking out' on her, that had she 'meant more' to him, he would not have behaved like that. 'You are the only person in the world for me,' writes Olga. 'You're my wife,' Anton replies, 'don't you understand that? You're the person closest and dearest to me . . .'—words just as sincerely meant, but not precisely the same in implication, for they still seem to leave room for him to lead a life of his own.

CHAPTER THIRTEEN

Anton's Last Appearance

After their painful exchanges, it is a relief to find Olga and Anton in high spirits again. On September 22nd Anton is able to report that Altshuller has found a marked improvement in his health and given him permission to go to Moscow. Even Chekhonte makes a welcome reappearance. 'My jackets and trousers are threadbare. You'll be ashamed to be seen out walking with me in Moscow, so I'll just have to pretend you don't know me until we've bought new ones.'

Arriving on October 14th, Anton found the Theatre in a state of hectic preparation. After four years of renting accommodation, it was about to move into the permanent home where it has remained to this day. Anton approved of the comfort and lack of ostentation. Confined to the flat by autumn frosts, he received a stream of visitors, but it was the usual story: 'I've already begun coughing and don't feel well'; 'I've been ill, coughing all the time'; and on November 27th he returned south.

For Olga and Anton these had been six happy weeks none the less. Olga recalled later that 'he was joking non-stop'.[1] As always, she felt his departure very keenly: now there would be no one waiting to kiss her when she came home from the Theatre, no one to be given his daily dose of cod liver oil. And Anton wrote: 'On this visit you have become even more precious to me. My love for you is stronger than before.'

Five months passed before their next meeting: months in which Anton's health deteriorated rapidly. That he did not spit blood that winter and could proudly report that he had not had a single haemorrhoid, were only minor consolations. Apart from his persistent cough, he now suffered from shortness of breath and tired very easily, and his stomach was more or less permanently upset. When he was feeling unwell, he found it an almost intolerable strain having to make conversation, but forced himself to do so. Just before Christmas he fell ill with pleurisy, which had still not cleared up by March. Small wonder that when he did reappear in the town, the sympathetic words and glances that he received left him in no doubt that his appearance had changed very considerably that winter.

Dr Altshuller claimed that Chekhov had been ill ever since his return from Moscow, and that those six weeks had had a far worse effect on his lungs than any of his previous visits. Anton stubbornly disagreed: he knew better than Altshuller where he had, and had not, fallen ill, and he would visit Moscow whenever he chose. Certainly his letters to Olga during his first month in Yalta give no indication of ill health, though he was suffering from a bad attack of Yalta blues. His best eating apples, left to ripen by December, had all been used with the sour cabbage; the house was so cold that he felt more like lying down and biting his pillow than trying to write; his jacket was unbrushed and his teeth aching. Tell me everything that's going on, he instructed Olga, 'so that I can feel I belong to the north, not Yalta, and that this dismal, meaningless life has not yet swallowed me up'. Olga told him about Gorky's new play, *The Lower Depths*, in which she created one of her most famous roles, as the prostitute Nastya. Given its first performance on December 18th, 1902, it was received with wild scenes of enthusiasm, surpassed only by those which had greeted *The Seagull* almost exactly four years earlier.

Troubled already by Anton's Yalta blues, Olga's conscience was even more disturbed by news of his attack of pleurisy. Her preoccupations of the summer, temporarily submerged by their six weeks together and her hectic life at the Theatre, all come to the surface again in her letter of January 15th:

I suddenly felt so ashamed to think that I call myself your wife. What sort of wife am I to you? You're alone, you're bored and depressed . . . Oh, I know you don't like me talking about this subject. But there's so much that I need to say to you! I can't live bottling everything up inside me. I must express what I feel, even come out at times with a lot of stupid remarks and talk rubbish, because I feel better for it. Do you understand or not? You're so completely different. You never say or hint at what you feel, and there are times when I would so like you to talk intimately with me, more intimately than you've ever talked with anyone else. Then I'd feel really close to you. I'm writing this and I feel you don't understand what I'm talking about. Am I right? That's to say, you find it unnecessary.[2]

Much to Anton's annoyance, Dr Altshuller had also told Olga what he thought about her husband's visits to Moscow. The old question posed itself with fresh urgency: should she give up the theatre to live permanently at Yalta? Anton had already made his position clear. 'If you lived with me in Yalta all winter, your life would be spoiled and *I* should feel pangs of conscience, so that would hardly be an improvement. I knew perfectly well that I was marrying an actress, i.e. when I got married, I fully appreciated that you would be spending your winters in Moscow. I don't consider myself offended or cheated in the slightest degree, on the contrary, it seems to me that everything is going well, or as it ought to, so don't go upsetting me, darling, with your pangs of conscience.'[3]

Once again, the situation might have turned out differently, had Olga given birth to the child for which Anton was still longing. Olga was afraid that she might not be able to have children after her illness, but Dr Chekhov assured her that she need only recover her strength completely and then she would 'give birth to a son, who will smash your cups and saucers, and drag your dachshund round by the tail'.[4] Looking ahead to their plans for the winter of 1903-4, he wrote that 'if you were to become pregnant, I'd take you off with me in February to Yalta', and he even offered to shiver through the winter with her in Archangel, if only she became a mother.

Throughout the boredom and illness of those long months, Anton continually strove to boost his morale with thoughts of Olga and their reunion. There are times in Olga's letters when she seems to be having it both ways: grieving that she is not at his side, while going on to describe in detail how she has been living it up for the past two nights. Anton's loneliness and yearning are quite unequivocal. 'If I could spend just half a night with my nose tucked in to your shoulder, I'm sure that I should feel better,' he writes plaintively on December 25th. As usual, the thoughts of both become centred on their spring reunion and holiday. Olga insists that on no account is Vishnevsky to join the party this year. On January 17th, 1903, his forty-third birthday, Anton floats the idea of a summer visit to Switzerland, a scheme to which he returns with elaborate variations in letter after letter. 'You and I don't have long for seeing life, our youth will have gone within two or three years—if one can even call it youth—so we must make haste and exercise all our ingenuity.'

Early in March, however, there was a setback. Altshuller told Chekhov that he must not leave Yalta before mid-April at the earliest. Olga and Masha, meanwhile, were moving into a larger flat. Both omitted to send Anton their new address, and Olga made matters worse by claiming that she had sent the address and he must have lost it. Anton's ill-humour and constant harping on the subject seem out of proportion to the offence and out of character: yet another symptom of his failing health.

A friend who visited him on April 20th found Anton packing his bags for Moscow with all the glee of a schoolboy about to leave on his summer holidays.[5] He had been warned earlier that the flat was at the top of two flights of stairs, but had made light of it; now he found that the climb took him almost half-an-hour. On May 24th he was examined by the T.B. specialist, Professor Ostroumov, who had treated him in 1897. He reported the findings to Masha in Yalta. 'My right lung is in a very bad way, I've got swelling of the lungs (emphysema), catarrh of the intestines,

etc. etc.'⁶ He did not mention the most damning verdict of all:
'You're a cripple,' the Professor had told him.⁷ Apart from five
prescriptions there was also a startling piece of advice: so startling that when Altshuller heard about it, he concluded that
Ostroumov must have been drunk at the time (or so Anton told
Olga; Altshuller denies it).⁸ Anton was to stop spending the
winter in Yalta, and to live near Moscow instead; so why had it
been necessary for him to endure the last four winters in Yalta?
He and Olga, who must have been delighted by the news, were
already looking out for a house, Masha was told; and his two
smaller Crimean properties, at Gurzuf and Kuchukoi, would
have to be sold.

Diplomatic as ever, Masha starts her reply by describing how
wonderful everything is in Yalta now. Never has she known more
perfect weather, all the flowers are out in the garden, and their
new trees are already providing shade; the cracks in the plaster
caused by the settling of the house have been repaired, and the
walls whitewashed; and if Anton approves, she will have new
wall-paper hung in his study. As for Gurzuf and Kuchukoi, she
fears that she will only be able to sell them at a loss, and she
offers Anton a small piece of advice: not to be in a hurry to buy
a new property, since it will be hard to find anything to compare
with 'our wonderful house here in Yalta'. Her own mood, however, has been depressed. 'The depression increases in the
evenings, I can't get to sleep before about two. I keep thinking
and can't escape from my thoughts.'⁹

To this Anton replied: 'I don't understand why you write that
you're feeling depressed and have gloomy thoughts. Your health
is good, there's no one in the world who could have the least thing
against you, you have a job and a future like all respectable
people—so what's troubling you? You ought to go bathing and
go to bed later, cut out wine altogether or drink it only once a
week, and not eat meat at supper. It's a pity the Yalta milk's so
awful and we can't put you on a milk diet.'¹⁰

There is pathos in the fact that when Masha published her
letters to Anton in 1954, she had to *explain* the reason for her

depression: that she was worried by the thought of another major upheaval in their way of life. She had not complained at having to exchange Melikhovo for Yalta; now, five years later, they could begin to sit back and enjoy the fruits of their labours. Yet here was Anton, in poor health, apparently proposing to buy another estate which was bound to involve more work and fresh anxieties for both of them.

Did Anton really not see this for himself?

He may have felt that life was complicated enough already without Masha's depression, and that he would deliberately fail to see the implication of her remarks. But to accept this explanation is to accept an unattractive degree of cynicism in Anton's attitude towards his sister, for it would surely not have been necessary to deceive poor Masha with the elaborate rigmarole about reducing her wine consumption and cutting out meat. Or was he so determined to regard himself as a tolerably healthy, independent person, quite capable of organising his own life without Masha's assistance, that he genuinely failed to see what was troubling her? One must give Anton the benefit of the doubt and accept the second explanation.

Discouraged by Ostroumov's verdict, Anton and Olga called off the trip to Switzerland and accepted an invitation from a Mme Yakunchikova to make use of a large datcha on her estate. Its rural attractions were similar to those of Lyubimovka. In the grounds stood an old chapel which was to find its way into the stage directions for Act II of *The Cherry Orchard*. Anton's first enthusiasm, however, soon wore off. The river might be deep but he had no one to fish with. Nor did he find the company so congenial as at Lyubimovka. Only two people there—and one of them a servant—were worthy of respect, he told Olga some months later, adding that it would be difficult to find anywhere 'such a hideously empty, stupid and tasteless life' as in that white house of Yakunchikova's. 'The people there live exclusively for pleasure—to entertain General Gadon or to go out walking with the deputy minister.' Yet Vishnevsky looked up to such people as if they were gods![11] The rebuke was almost certainly intended for Olga also, since her attitude to the *beau monde* was much more ambivalent than Anton's. Though she felt that the theatre had enabled her to escape from her class background, she was still easily flattered by the attentions of the rich and well-connected.

Several excursions were made to look at properties, but Anton found travel exhausting in the hot weather. Masha, meanwhile, had been sending glowing reports of the beautiful summer in Yalta. Anton, one notices, is still writing of his plans in the first person, as if Olga either does not exist or will be making her own arrangements, but early in July they cut short their visit and set off together for the south.

The thought of having to spend the rest of the summer *à trois* in Yalta cannot have appealed to Olga. 'You're always nice to me, only not in Yalta,' she had written earlier to Anton, harping on an old theme. 'That's to say, you're nice, but you're not mine.' Carefully stepping round the point, Anton replied that she was prejudiced against Yalta because she had been ill there.[12] Nor was Masha at all pleased by their unexpectedly early arrival, which, it seems, had interfered with plans of her own. 'My trip's completely fallen through,' she wrote to Ivan Bunin. 'Antosha's arrived with his wife.' (She uses the distant *zhena*, 'wife', rather than her usual jocular *supruga*, 'spouse'.) 'Antosha's glad to be home, his wife's feeling bored, my spirits are drooping.'[13] Not a very promising start to the summer together.

A young artist who sketched Chekhov that August formed the impression that although everyone in the house talked loudly and cheerfully, they were secretly all preoccupied with Anton's failing health.[14] Whatever the underlying tensions in the household, to Stanislavsky Olga painted a rosy picture of her life in Yalta; she was up at six and swimming by six-thirty, and had become plump and sunburnt. Although rehearsals at the Art Theatre had begun in August, she received permission to stay in Yalta until the last possible moment. She was able to deploy a powerful argument: that in Yalta she could act as 'a kind of Cerberus', making sure that Anton was not interrupted in his work on *The Cherry Orchard*.[15]

Two full seasons had now gone by without a new play by Chekhov. Meanwhile his earlier plays continued to be the Theatre's 'battleships'; on the spring tour of St Petersburg it had not been *The Lower Depths* but *Uncle Vanya* that had captured the acclaim and the audiences. Their choice of new production for the first half of the 1903–4 season, *Julius Caesar*, was neither adventurous nor modern. '*Without Chekhov we cannot exist,*' Vishnevsky wrote to Olga, imagining what the reaction of his 'childhood friend' would be to those portentous italics; and to bring home to Chekhov the full seriousness of the situation, Olga was to tell him that his fellow pupil from Taganrog High School *had grown very thin* (Vishnevsky's italics).[16]

According to Olga, Chekhov had 'thought the play out fully in his mind' at Lyubimovka in the summer of 1902. As the winter went by and he showed no signs of putting pen to paper, she became increasingly tactless and impatient: 'What do you do with yourself all day long? In your position I'd spend the whole day writing.' Sensitive to such comments, Anton replied sharply: 'I've been telling all and sundry since the year dot that I'd be starting the play at the end of February or the beginning of March. My laziness has nothing to do with it. I'm not my worst enemy, you know, and if I were strong enough, I'd write not one play but twenty-five.'[17] Only in the summer, however, does the writing appear to be well under way. Olga had hoped to be able to take the completed manuscript with her to Moscow, but Anton fell ill and on September 17th she left for Moscow empty-handed.

Anton's reports on the final stages of work make painful reading. On the 30th he wrote of having been obliged to summon Altshuller by telephone. 'I'm telling you the gospel truth, darling, if my play's a failure, you can put the whole blame on my bowels.' Too many visitors had stopped him working on October 5th, and another visitor on the 6th had left him in such a bad mood that he was forced to give up writing for the day. Then came news that he was making a second fair copy. Olga's brother, Kostya, the railway engineer, had been to a restaurant for him and noted down billiard expressions to be given to the character of Gayev. 'Darling, how difficult it was for me to write the play!' he exclaims on the 12th; but two days later a telegram went off to Olga, who had threatened to divorce him if he did not send the play to her first, saying that the script was on its way.

Olga was in bed when the parcel arrived. Crossing herself three times for luck, she stayed there until she had read the play right through. Then she rushed round to the Theatre. Seven of them quickly gathered, the door was locked in case of interruptions, and Nemirovich began reading. Scarcely had they finished when Stanislavsky appeared. Without a word of greeting, he held out his hand to Olga for the manuscript. Olga sent off a congratulatory telegram, Nemirovich a telegram of a hundred and eighty words, while Stanislavsky in his telegram outdid them both in the lavishness of his praise.

Great was the excitement in Moscow and lengthy the discussions about the allocation of parts, but in Yalta there was only loneliness, ill health and ill humour. Anton was not pleased when Olga referred to him as a 'superman' and with grim Chekhonte humour signed himself: 'Your superman, who makes frequent visits to the super water-closet.' He deeply mistrusted the extravagance of Stanislavsky's praise ('I love every word, every stage direction, every comma,' the latter had written),[18] and was afraid that Nemirovich intended to allocate parts for diplomatic reasons. Any satisfaction that he might have derived from the Art Theatre's enthusiastic reaction was completely spoiled when the newspapers started printing an advance notice about the contents of the play, obtained from the Theatre, against Chekhov's express wishes, by the critic Efros. The notice contained many annoying inaccuracies, but Chekhov's reaction again seems quite out of proportion to the offence: he would never have given the play to the Art Theatre, he told Olga, had he known that this would happen. When Olga sensibly urged him to dismiss the whole affair from his mind, he replied that he felt like the father of a baby daughter, whom Efros had taken away and violated.

1 Olga Knipper, 1899. The photograph that prompted Chekhov to comment: 'There's a little demon lurking behind your modest expression of quiet sadness.'

2 Olga Knipper

3 Mariya Chekhova (Masha)

4 Anton Chekhov

5 Olga and Anton on honeymoon at Aksyonovo, 1901. 'In this
photograph you look like a little German, the kind, tender wife of a
doctor with no patients.' Anton to Olga, 11 November 1901

6 Family group, 1902.
Chekhov, his mother,
Olga (right) and
Masha

7 Olga and Anton, 1902

8 Chekhov reading *The Seagull* to the actors and directors of the Moscow Art Theatre, 1898.
L–R, standing: Nemirovich-Danchenko, Luzhsky, Ardreyev, Nikolayeva; seated: Rayevskaya, Vishnevsky, Artyom, Knipper, Stanislavsky, Chekhov, Lilina, Tikhomirov, Roksanova, Meierhold

9 Knipper as Irina in
   Tsar Fyodor, 1898

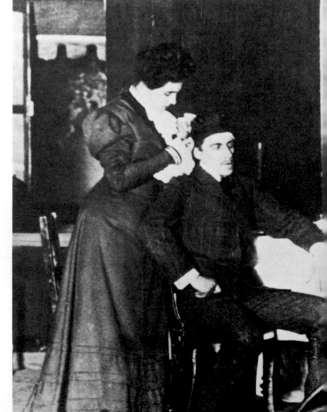

10 *The Seagull*, Act III,
    the 'bandage' scene:
    Knipper as Arkadina
    and Meierhold as
    her son

11 *Three Sisters*, Act I: Knipper as Masha

12 *Uncle Vanya*, Act I.
L–R: Rayevskaya as
Vanya's mother,
Stanislavsky as
Astrov, Knipper as
Yelyena and Vishnevsky
as Uncle Vanya

13 Cover of the first
edition of *Three Sisters*,
1901. L–R: Savitskaya as
Olga, Knipper as Masha,
Andreyeva as Irina.
Guarding the pram:
Luzhsky as Andrei

14 Knipper as Ranyevskaya
in *The Cherry Orchard*

15 *The Cherry Orchard*,
Act III: Kachalov as
Trofimov, Knipper
as Ranyevskaya, Lilina
as Anya

16 Knipper as Anna
Andreyevna, the Mayor's
wife, and Koreneva as her
daughter in Gogol's
The Inspector General.
Card sent by Knipper to
Gordon Craig (December
1908/January 1909) and
inscribed: 'With a nice
little kiss from a
big ugly woman Olga
Knipper Temple.'

17 'Early morning after a
night drive', 4 May 1909,
according to Gordon Craig's
diary. Photograph by him
of a group of Art Theatre
friends: Kachalov and Lilina
sitting down, Koreneva
(back left), Koonen (back
right) and Knipper for some
reason covering her face
with her muff

18 Knipper in America, 1923

19 Knipper as Ranyevskaya in
The Cherry Orchard at the
age of eighty, 1948

20 Masha and Olga
in the garden at
Yalta

21 The Chekhov
Museum at
Yalta, 1948. The
cypress on the
left was planted
by Masha in
1904, the year
of Chekhov's
death

Anton's Last Appearance

It had been arranged that Anton should be summoned to Moscow by Olga as soon as the hard winter had set in, but as ill luck would have it, winter arrived late that year. On November 16th the temperature was still 7° F. Anton could not contain his impatience. 'To Moscow, to Moscow! This is not Three Sisters speaking, but One Husband.' He sat in the study with his eyes glued to the telephone, waiting for the telegram that refused to come. Was Olga planning to send him a letter instead of a telegram? 'You've become such a miser you'll soon be sticking used stamps on your letters!' Did he still have a wife? Where was she? Fortunately, on the same day that he was asking these questions, November 29th, Olga sent off the telegram.

Anton plunged into the life of the Theatre with newly found energy. Not content with spending all afternoon at rehearsals of *The Cherry Orchard*, he proposed to return to the Theatre for evening performances. He had not yet seen *The Lower Depths*, *Julius Caesar*, or Ibsen's *Pillars of the Community*, in which Olga was taking the part of Lona Hessel. As usual, he claimed that his health was 'incomparably better' than it had been in Yalta, and he was still doing good turns: taking the Yalta headmistress's watch to the best watchmaker in Moscow, and choosing a new watch on her behalf after reporting that the old one was beyond repair.

Chekhov's letters give only slight hints of how rehearsals of *The Cherry Orchard* were progressing. He writes of 'having to get very worked up over trifles', and tells the headmistress that he is not expecting the play to be a great success.[19] Olga, however, states in her memoir that work on *The Cherry Orchard* was difficult and even agonising; directors and author simply could not understand one another and come to any agreement.[20] No sooner had the author turned up in Moscow, Stanislavsky recalled, than the blossoms on *The Cherry Orchard* began to wither, while Nemirovich writes that Chekhov became so irritated by rehearsals that after a while he stopped coming.[21] To some extent, this irritability was an expression of his morbid fear that nothing would go right for him with this play, but there was

137

also a broad difference of interpretation between him and Stanislavsky: he had called the play a comedy, but Stanislavsky insisted on treating it as a tragedy. Olga, in the central role of Ranyevskaya, found herself caught in the middle of this crossfire.

The first night had to be postponed until January 17th. Even so, neither of the directors felt that the production was ready. The date also happened to be Chekhov's forty-fourth birthday. Without his knowledge, elaborate plans were set in motion to honour him by celebrating, somewhat prematurely, the twenty-fifth anniversary of his literary début. This gala occasion might divert attention from any shortcomings in the performance of the play itself.

There was one snag. Chekhov had not attended any of his first nights since the *Seagull* disaster of 1896 and was not proposing to attend this one. He had to be lured to the Theatre by a note from Nemirovich: 'The play's going wonderfully. There were calls for you just now after Act II. We had to announce that you weren't in the theatre. The cast are asking if you could come in time for the interval after Act III, though probably there won't be any calls then for the author. But they'd like to see you.'[22] Needless to say, the calls for the author after Act III were numerous, and Chekhov was persuaded to come out and stand alone on the right-hand side of the stage. The applause was deafening, but when it died down and members of the audience had time to take stock of his appearance, they were shocked by what they saw. Very pale, thin, stooping and ill at ease, he stood there with difficulty and was unable to control a fit of coughing. 'A chair for Anton Pavlovich!' someone shouted in a loud voice from the auditorium; but Chekhov merely frowned and went on standing all through the lengthy ritual of congratulations, telegrams, speeches and presentations. Stanislavsky, who had delivered Gayev's speech beginning 'Dear and much respected bookcase', fancied that he caught Chekhov's eye when one of the speakers began his address with the words: 'Dear and much respected Anton Pavlovich!'[23] Nemirovich spoke movingly of the debt that the Art Theatre owed to Chekhov, who might justly claim: 'This is my theatre.'[24]

Olga's eyes were on Anton. He appeared to be listening seriously and attentively, but every so often he would toss his head back in a characteristic gesture, as if none of these proceedings had anything to do with him, and a smile would pucker up the corners of his mouth; and then she knew that he had noted something funny to chuckle over later.[25]

The directors had been right in their calculation. The evening would be remembered less for *The Cherry Orchard* than for Chekhov's appearance, though not in the way that they had intended. More like a funeral than a celebration, was Stanislavsky's final verdict on the occasion.

As for Chekhov, he made sure that he was not caught a second time. Writing a fortnight later to Olga's brother, Kostya, he explained his failure to visit St Petersburg by saying that 'they were threatening to honour me with some kind of jubilee celebration'.[26]

🙢

CHAPTER FOURTEEN

Badenweiler

For Chekhov the grass was always greener on the other side of the fence. Ironically, after his bitter complaints of loneliness in Yalta, he found Moscow life too much for him and began dreaming, 'not without pleasure', of returning to his Yalta Penates. He left Moscow with his mother in mid-February, but instead of an early spring, they found Yalta so bitterly cold that it made Moscow seem like the Riviera. Anton had brought with him Olga's dachshund, Schnapps. Schnapps had been auditioned for the part of the governess's dog in *The Cherry Orchard*, but Anton had vetoed him on the grounds of unsuitable appearance. This was probably as well, for he found Schnapps singularly unintelligent, though his deep bark was useful as a warning of impending visitors.

Anton's letters in February and March show him in unexpectedly good humour. He has to admit to feeling well, even though he is in Yalta; writes a couple of cheerful letters to his elder brother, Alexander ('It's not age that counts, it's brains. Keep well and tighten your braces . . .'); copes uncomplainingly with the task of combing through masses of stories by unknown writers in the hope of finding one or two suitable for publication in the journal, *Russian Thought*, of which he is now literary editor; is not writing much himself, but has been through his old notebooks and found enough material to last him for the next five years. With Olga too his tone is pleasantly relaxed. True, he complains bitterly about her glue-like ink, which forces him to prise the pages of her letters apart; upbraids her, in an ironic reversal of roles, for not sending a telegram about her health after writing that she has bronchitis ('it was only a chill,' she explained later); and is still thoroughly dissatisfied with the Art Theatre's interpretation of *The Cherry Orchard*. What good news that one of the actresses whom he particularly disliked had become pregnant and been replaced, and how sad it was that the same thing could not happen to some of the male performers. 'Stanislavsky has ruined my play,' he wrote,[1] and refused to be mollified when Olga told him that *The Cherry Orchard* was having a far greater success in St Petersburg than it had done in Moscow. In general, however, his letters show little of the ill humour and despairing loneliness that had so often come to the fore during the previous winter. 'I do love you, I love your letters, I love the way you act and the way you walk. The only thing I don't love is the way you spend ages at the wash-basin.'[2]

In February 1904 war broke out between Japan and Russia. Both Olga's uncles, Karl the doctor and Sasha the company commander, left early for the front. In March Anton announced that if his health had improved by the summer, he too proposed going out to the Far East as a doctor. Olga mocked him gently and advised her 'warrior' to spend the summer with her, fishing.

A more immediate preoccupation was 'the datcha question'. They had their eyes on a house at Tsaritsyno, within easy reach of Moscow and conveniently close to the railway station. Final negotiations would have to await Anton's arrival. In the mean time, Olga and Masha had moved to yet another flat, in the same block as the celebrated bass, Shalyapin. It was high up but had a lift: splendid, commented Anton, but lifts always seemed to be under repair whenever he wanted to use one. Now he was anxious to escape from Yalta as soon as Olga returned from the St Petersburg tour. 'I'll be in Moscow on April 31st,' she wrote. Anton reminded her that there were only thirty days in April and recommended May 1st. He would leave Yalta on the same day. Already he was dreaming of the summer's fishing, though probably his catch would consist of nothing more than 'one solitary gudgeon with suicidal tendencies'.

During April Anton's reports on his health had been less encouraging. 'Dr Chekhov is in love with his wife,' he wrote, 'and suffering from upset bowels.' He was also short of breath and coughing badly. Yet there was little to indicate that he would feel so ill throughout the journey that he had to be put to bed as soon as he reached Moscow. Olga called in her own German doctor, Taube, who diagnosed the familiar 'catarrh of the intestines' and pleurisy. On May 14th Masha left for Yalta. She was very reluctant to do so, in view of her brother's poor condition, but Anton insisted that she keep to her original plan of joining their mother, who disliked being left in Yalta with only the servants. It was a sad blow to Masha to realise that in this crisis she was not needed and that, as Anton wrote to a friend, a better nurse than Olga could not be imagined.[3] As Olga later admitted, there was bad feeling at this time between her and Masha. On reaching Yalta, Masha did not write to Anton straight away, as she usually did, to inform him of her safe arrival and their mother's health, but waited until the 20th. Then, pocketing her pride, she wrote that she was 'feeling fine and very glad to be home'.[4] Olga, meanwhile, was begging her to write to Anton: 'He's a sick man and mustn't be worried.'[5] So alarmed was Ivan Chekhov by his brother's sickly appearance that he could not sleep and kept deferring his own visit to Yalta. 'I just can't make out when he's leaving,' an unsuspecting Anton wrote to Masha.[6] After a slight improvement, Anton had another attack of pleurisy on the 20th, and later began suffering from agonising pains in the arms and legs, which made him very irritable and prevented him from sleeping. Olga was at her wits' end. But Anton rallied, on May 31st he went out of doors for the first time, and three days later, following Taube's advice to seek treatment at the small Black Forest health resort of Badenweiler, he left with Olga for Germany.

In Berlin they consulted a famous specialist in intestinal diseases, Professor Ewald. Olga recalled that after examining Anton, the Professor 'could think of nothing better to do than stand up, shrug his shoulders, say goodbye and leave', while

Anton gazed after him with a gentle, confused smile.[7] Schwörer, the young German doctor with a Russian wife to whom they had been recommended in Badenweiler, also expressed the opinion later that he could not understand how anyone as ill as Chekhov could have been advised to undertake such a long and exhausting journey.[8] Was it perhaps Chekhov himself who insisted? 'I'm going away to die,' one memoirist reports him as saying,[9] and Bunin also suspected that Chekhov had chosen to die abroad rather than inflict unnecessary suffering on members of his family.[10] The suggestion is plausible, yet if it were true, one must also add that in his letters from Badenweiler, Chekhov kept up a remarkable pretence of believing otherwise. His instruction to Masha in his letter of June 22nd—'don't throw away the stamp but keep it for me'—is not that of a man expecting to die, nor is his plan for returning to Yalta by sea via Trieste. Or was the pretence for his own benefit rather than for others?

The Chekhovs stayed at three different places in Badenweiler: the Hotel Römerbad, the Villa Friederike and the Hotel Sommer. At the Hotel Sommer they met two young Russian brothers, the Rabenecks: they were students at Moscow University, friends of the Alekseyevs (Stanislavsky's family) and through them of Olga Knipper, and had been among the group of young people who surrounded Chekhov at Lyubimovka in the summer of 1902. Olga explains that she and Anton left the Hotel Römerbad after a day or two because it was so fashionable and crowded, but Leo Rabeneck offers a different explanation. Chekhov always carried round in his jacket pocket a small blue spittoon, which could be sealed tightly and of which he made frequent use. The hotel management, reckoning that this indication of disease might put off other visitors, asked the Chekhovs to leave.[11] At the Villa Friederike, a private guest-house with a fine garden, they took a room on the ground floor. Anton would go out on his own in the mornings and lie in the sun—'which does not burn but caresses,' he told Masha—waiting impatiently for the postman to deliver his letters and the newspapers containing the latest reports on the Russo-Japanese war. It is from the Villa Friederike that he tells his mother that within a week he will be perfectly well again, and writes repeatedly of his health returning 'not by the dram but the hundredweight'. Within ten days, however, they had moved to the Hotel Sommer. The atmosphere at the Villa was very bourgeois, Anton explained to Masha, but Olga recalled that there was no sun inside their room, and that at night they could hear a very sick person coughing in the room next door.

At the Hotel Sommer Anton began to feel warmer and more cheerful. Every day they had lunch and dinner downstairs at their own individual table in the public dining-room. 'He spent a long time,' Olga recalls, 'lying in the hotel gardens or sitting on our balcony, where he followed what was going on in little Badenweiler with close attention. The unceasing activity at the post-office especially preoccupied him; he always had a soft spot for post-offices and postmen.'[12]

Anton now decided that for his return to Yalta by steamer he must have a new light-weight flannel suit—according to Rabeneck two suits, one white with a blue stripe, the other blue with a white stripe. He asked Olga to take an old suit of his with her to Freiburg and order the suits to be made up to his measurements. Olga invited young Leo Rabeneck to accompany her. As the day was fine, they decided to go sightseeing in Freiburg, and it was early evening before they returned to Badenweiler. Olga remembered Anton 'just coming out of the dining-room, obviously feeling proud of his independence'. Rabeneck recalled that Anton Pavlovich was 'walking quietly in the hotel garden with my brother. Seeing us come back with cheerful and happy expressions, he greeted us and looking at me through his pince-nez, said: "I suppose you've been paying court to my wife all day," which threw me into great confusion. I felt that this phrase of his, uttered apparently half-jokingly and seeming at first sight to be completely innocent, did in fact conceal Chekhov's grief and disappointment that it was not he but someone else who had accompanied his wife on an excursion which had given her such pleasure.'[13]

A heatwave began. On the morning of the 29th, while walking

along the corridor, Anton suddenly had an acute attack of breathlessness. 'The doctor says that because of the shocking state of his lungs,' Olga wrote to Masha, 'his heart is having to work twice as hard, and his heart is not very strong in any case.'[14] Oxygen, camphor, digitalis and ice on the heart were all prescribed. Anton insisted that they should move to a cooler, north-facing room on the top floor, which had a magnificent view of mountains and forests, and asked Olga to write to the bank in Berlin and instruct them to send on their remaining money. As Olga was sitting down to write, he said suddenly: 'Tell them to send the money in your name.' Olga protested that she never liked dealing with financial matters, but Anton insisted. That night his breathing became very bad again. He kept wanting to change position, sitting up and then lying down, and his mind began to wander. Olga gave him two injections of morphine, and towards morning he went off to sleep.

Next day he remained propped up in bed on five pillows, and only in the evening did he transfer to an armchair. He was not coughing at all. They had stopped taking his temperature, as he became nervous whenever it was slightly above normal.

The night of June 30th, Olga recalled later, was terrible:

It was very hot, storm after storm kept breaking, and there was no air. During the night Anton Pavlovich implored me to open the balcony door and the window, but the effect was uncanny: a thick, whitish mist came up to our floor and crept in to the room, filling it with ghostly, ductile shapes of the weirdest outlines. This went on all night. The electric light was off as it hurt Anton Pavlovich's eyes, there was only a candle end burning, and I was terrified that it would go out before daybreak; meanwhile the misty shapes kept stealing round the room, and it was particularly eerie when the candle died down and then flared up again. So that Anton Pavlovich should not be aware when he came to that I was not trying to sleep but keeping an eye on him, I picked up a book which I pretended to read. 'What's that you're reading?' he asked me, on coming round. It was a small volume of Chekhov open at the story, *A Strange Tale*. I told him. He smiled and said weakly: 'Silly thing, don't you know wives never take their husbands' books with them on holiday?' and again lapsed into un-consciousness. When I put ice on his heart, he pushed it away feebly and murmured indistinctly: 'Not ice on an empty heart . . .'

The combination of the night, so terrifying in its stillness, yet with a kind of life in every corner because of the swirling mist, and the silhouette of Anton Pavlovich, sitting almost upright and breathing with difficulty: there was such a tranquil solemnity about all this that it filled me with dread, and I waited impatiently for morning and the arrival of Dr Schwörer, so as to seek his advice and to summon Anton Pavlovich's sister or brother from Russia. I felt I might lose my presence of mind if I had to live through another night like that. Strangely enough, the thought of death, that this might be the end, never entered my head . . . The doctor reassured me, and talked in a kind and gentle way to Anton Pavlovich. Things became easier in the morning. Anton Pavlovich even managed to eat some thin gruel and asked to be installed in an armchair close to the window. Here he slowly played game after game of patience, with intervals between games.

At dusk I went off to the dispensary for oxygen, and he himself gave me orders to go for a swim in the pool, to take a walk round the park and have some fresh air, as I had not been out of the room once in three days. When I returned and saw the gentle smile on his face, I somehow became calmer and felt that with the passing of that dreadful night the most terrifying part of the ordeal was over. While we were talking, I missed the gong for dinner, and a servant brought me up something to eat. It was then that Anton Pavlovich began to invent a story of how the guests at a well-to-do health resort gather one evening, tired out after a day spent on various kinds of sporting activities, rich, well-fed Englishmen and Americans, all greedily looking forward to a satisfying dinner, when—

horror of horrors—it turns out that the chef has disappeared . . .
And what an effect this blow to the stomach would have on all
those well-fed, spoilt people.[15]

It was Chekhonte's last story. For a moment it seemed to Olga
just like old times. She sat back, roared with laughter as only she
could roar, and felt that a great weight had been lifted from her
shoulders. While he was taking his medicine, Anton instructed
her to remove the extra pillows and lay down as usual, saying
with a smile: 'I'm getting better already, I'm not so short of
breath today.' He soon dropped off quietly to sleep.

In another part of the hotel the Rabeneck brothers were sleeping soundly, having come back late from a day's excursion in the
mountains. Some time after midnight Leo Rabeneck suddenly
became aware of a loud knocking at the door. Olga was standing
there in her dressing-gown, looking very anxious. Would he dress
as quickly as possible and go to fetch Dr Schwörer?

At the doctor's house all the windows were wide open. 'Who is
it?' Dr Schwörer shouted down when the bell rang. Rabeneck
explained that he had come from Frau Chekhov and that her
husband was very ill. The doctor prepared at once to go to the
hotel and told Rabeneck to fetch a cylinder of oxygen from the
chemist's.

Olga had woken the hotel porter and told him to bring up some
ice. The expression on Anton's face was concentrated and
expectant, as if he were listening for something. The doctor
arrived and cradling Chekhov gently in his arms, began to say
something to him. Chekhov sat up very straight and in a loud,
clear voice said: 'I am dying. *Ich sterbe.*' The doctor soothed him,
took a syringe and gave him an injection of camphor. Rabeneck
came in with the oxygen. Chekhov was sitting up, supported by
Olga, and breathing with difficulty. After giving Chekhov the
oxygen, the doctor whispered to Rabeneck to run downstairs for
a bottle of champagne and a glass. Filling the glass almost to the
brim, Schwörer handed it to Chekhov, who turned towards Olga,
smiled, said 'It's a long time since I last drank champagne' and

drained the glass in one go. Schwörer took the empty glass and handed it to Rabeneck.

As Rabeneck was putting the glass down on the table, with his back to Chekhov, he heard a strange gurgling noise, rather like that which a tap makes when the air has got into it. Turning round, he saw that Chekhov, still supported by Olga, was lying on one side with his head resting on the pillows. For some time no one spoke. The doctor continued to hold Chekhov's hand. To Rabeneck it seemed that the worst was now over.

Dr Schwörer gently released his pressure on Chekhov's wrist, went up to Rabeneck, who was standing at the foot of the bed, and led him into the middle of the room.

'It's all over,' he said to him softly. 'Herr Chekhov is dead. Please be kind enough to tell Frau Chekhov.'

Olga had paid no attention to their whispered conversation. She was still leaning across from her own bed and supporting Anton. Rabeneck went over to her quietly, touched her on the shoulder, and signalled to her to get up. She carefully removed her arms from behind Anton's back.

'Olga Leonardovna, the doctor says that Anton Pavlovich is dead.'

After a moment of complete bewilderment, Olga threw herself upon the doctor, seized him by the lapels, and began shaking him with all her strength.

'*Doktor es ist nicht wahr, sagen Sie doch Doktor, dass ist nicht wahr!*' she kept repeating. 'Doctor, it's not true, say it's not true, Doctor.'

As Rabeneck and Schwörer were trying to calm her down, a huge black moth came flying through the open window and began crashing painfully against the walls, the ceiling and the lamp-shades, in a kind of death agony.

Before leaving, the doctor instructed Rabeneck to remove all the sharp objects from the table and to stay with Olga until early morning, when he and his wife would come to take Olga to their own home.

Suddenly, in the silent, airless room, there was a startling noise: the cork in the champagne bottle had gone off with a terrific explosion.[16]

Rabeneck took two chairs and persuaded Olga to sit outside on the balcony. 'You know, Leo dear, those weren't suits we ordered for Anton, but funeral shrouds.'

Dawn began to break and the electric lights were switched off outside the hotel. 'The birds woke up and started chirruping,' Olga recalled,

timidly at first, but soon their song became louder and more joyful. From the church, the notes of the organ, solitary and profound, began to pour forth on the fresh morning air. They seemed unreal: who could have been playing at such an early hour? All these sounds were like the first requiem. There was nothing mundane to disturb the feeling of majestic stillness, no unnecessary words or conversations, but only the peace and majesty of death. . . . The awareness of grief, of the loss of such a person as Anton Pavlovich, came to me only with the first sounds of human life awakening and when people began to arrive; that which I had lived through and experienced, standing by myself on the balcony and looking first at the rising sun and the vibrant awakening of nature, then at the beautiful face of Anton Pavlovich, whose expression was calm now and seemed to be smiling, as if he had just understood something— that, I repeat, still remains an unfathomable mystery to me . . . There had never been such moments in my life before, nor will there be again . . .[17]

CHAPTER FIFTEEN

※

Olga's Last Letters

Ivan Bunin was spending the summer of 1904 on an estate in the Russian steppe. He had ridden in to the village one morning to collect his mail and newspapers. It was a very warm day, with an overcast sky and a hot southern wind. He decided to have his horse re-shod at the blacksmith's. As he sat waiting outside the forge, he idly unwrapped the newspaper and began to scan its contents—'and suddenly I felt as if an ice-cold razor had been drawn across my heart'.[1]

Masha and her brother, Ivan, heard the news at Borzhom, an attractive spa in the Little Caucasus.

Reassured by Anton's encouraging letters and feeling the need of a change after those anxious weeks, they had left Yalta on June 29th for a short holiday, instructing their cousin, Georgii, who worked in Yalta for the steamship company, to let them know of any fresh developments. From Yalta they travelled by steamer across the Black Sea to Batum and then by train to Borzhom, keeping Georgii informed of their movements. Still very anxious, Masha insisted that they should call in at the post-office before setting off on their morning's sightseeing, and it was here that they received Georgii's telegram with the news of Anton's death.

The steamer that had brought them from Yalta had not yet left Batum on its return journey. They wired the captain from Borzhom, urging him to delay his departure. Masha remembered how she leapt down from the carriage taking them from Batum station to the harbour and ran at full tilt along the pier towards the steamer.

'Keep calm,' shouted the captain, 'we're waiting for you.'

At Yalta they faced the task of breaking the news to old Mrs Chekhov.

All the telegrams from Badenweiler had been sent off by the Rabeneck brothers. The Russian Resident Minister at the Court of Baden had arrived to take charge of official formalities, and Olga with some reluctance agreed to move in with Dr Schwörer and his wife. Late in the afternoon Rabeneck fetched her from the doctor's and they returned to the Hotel Sommer. All the blinds had been drawn and the light in the bedroom seemed dark after the brilliant sunshine outside. Chekhov's body was still lying on the bed, surrounded by flowers. Rabeneck left Olga alone in the room. It was late evening when she reappeared, but she looked calmer and more refreshed.[2]

That night, when the guests were all sound asleep, Chekhov's body was discreetly taken out of the hotel and transferred to a nearby chapel. The Rabenecks were deeply shocked to see that a long linen basket was to be used for the purpose. To the bearers' surprise the basket proved, however, to be not long enough: the body had to be propped up in a half-sitting position, and for a moment it seemed to Leo Rabeneck as if a smile of amusement flickered across the dead man's face.[3] Next morning, helped by Dr Schwörer's wife, Olga converted the small Catholic chapel into an Orthodox one with icons, and an Orthodox priest arrived from Karlsruhe to conduct the first requiem service.

From Freiburg Olga received notification that her husband's suits were now ready to be collected. More helpfully, the money arrived from Berlin. Arrangements for transporting Chekhov's body to Russia were complicated, because Olga insisted on travelling by the same train, but permission was finally granted for the carriage containing the body to be coupled to a passenger express.

On July 5th the Rabenecks accompanied Chekhov's coffin from Badenweiler to the local railway station. Here, in a siding, a second requiem service was conducted by Father Mal'tsev, whom Olga remembered as 'a man of wonderful spiritual qualities, highly intelligent and with a sense of humour'. Russian workmen had decorated the carriage with garlands of oak leaves, flowers and foliage. Because of a request by the authorities that no sound should be audible from outside, the whole service, including the singing, had to be conducted in hushed voices, but this, as Olga recalled, only made it the more moving and mysterious.[4]

Olga was accompanied on the arduous journey by her sister-in-law. At Berlin there was a long delay. 'No one could say when and by what train we were to continue our journey. Enquiries were coming in every day from Moscow and St Petersburg. Our embassy behaved rather oddly, as if setting out on purpose to keep us in ignorance, probably to make sure that there were no crowds or commotion when we arrived in Russia.'[5] When the train did reach St Petersburg, very few people were there to meet it. Those who were, and they included Gorky, might have noticed that Chekhonte had played another trump. At the frontier the coffin had been transferred to a drab, olive-coloured Russian goods wagon. On its doors someone had scrawled in large letters the words: 'For Oysters'.

At Moscow the station was swarming with summer holiday-makers. Chekhonte could not resist the temptation to play one more trick. Part of the crowd that had come to meet Chekhov began to follow the coffin of General Keller, a victim of the Russo-Japanese war, and could not understand why the writer was to be buried with full military honours and a military band.[6]

Gorky and Shalyapin were among the crowd of several thousand who followed the coffin on foot to the Moscow Art Theatre. Gorky had already been outraged by the 'Oysters'. 'It's all the same to him,' he wrote to his wife, not guessing at the truth of his words, 'if his body is carried in a dirty linen basket, but it's us, Russian society, that I can't forgive.'[7] Nemirovich, on the other hand, was only amused when, after Olga had stepped down from the train in full mourning, he walked silently alongside her towards the goods wagon and spotted the infamous inscription.[8] Now Gorky was further offended by the remarks of the crowds who kept gawping at him and Shalyapin. 'Doesn't Gorky look thin?' 'He's not like his pictures.' 'And look at his funny coat.' 'Shalyapin's not so handsome now he's had his hair cut short.' Not a word was said about the dead man. Chekhov would have smiled, but Gorky found it all 'a triumph of vulgarity'. Only when the procession stopped outside the Art Theatre for a short religious service did someone recall Chekhonte's short story, *The Orator*, about a man who delivers a funeral oration and then discovers that the 'deceased' is alive and well and standing beside him.[9]

The Chekhov family party, including old Mrs Chekhov, Masha, and her brothers, Ivan and Michael, had arrived from Yalta on the morning of July 9th, the day of the funeral. As the procession was already nearing the centre of Moscow, they took a cab to the offices of *Russian Thought*, where there was to be another halt. Too impatient to wait, they set off to meet the procession on foot. Masha was taken aback by the huge crowds: all traffic had been banned along the route and side streets cordoned off. To ensure order, the students and young men of Moscow had linked arms to form a chain preventing the curious from pressing too close to the coffin, and when Masha began to squeeze through the crowd, she found her way barred. No one paid any attention when she tried to explain who they were.

'Let me through,' the timid Masha cried out in despair and hurled herself forward. 'Let me through, I must go to my brother.'

At last they were recognised and allowed to break the human barrier. The procession halted briefly before going on to the offices of *Russian Thought*, where more prayers were offered. The final halt was outside the clinic in which Chekhov had been treated in 1897.

Order broke down when the procession reached the cemetery of the Novodevichy Convent, where Chekhov was to be buried in a simple grave next to that of his father. Crosses and tombstones were damaged, and branches of trees broken off, as the spectators scrambled to find vantage-points from which to view the burial. Gorky was still being appalled by the remarks around him:

'Which one's the wife? And the sister? Look, they're crying!'

'He hasn't left a thing, you know, it all goes to Marx the publisher.'

'Poor Knipper!'

'Oh, don't worry about her, she gets ten thousand a year from the theatre.'[10]

Some days later, in Yalta, Olga produced the will, in the form of a letter to Masha, that Anton had made in August 1901 and handed to Olga for safe keeping:

To Mariya Pavlovna Chekhova.

My dear Masha, I bequeath to you for your lifetime my house at Yalta, and the monies and income from my dramatic productions, and to my wife, Olga Leonardovna, my house at Gurzuf and five thousand roubles. You may sell my real estate if you wish. Give my brother Alexander three thousand, Ivan five thousand and Michael three thousand, to Alexei Dolzhenko one thousand and to Yelyena Chekhova (Lyolya), if she is unmarried, one thousand. After your death and our mother's death, everything that remains, apart from the income from the plays, is to be placed at the disposal of Taganrog Town Council for use in public education; the income from the plays to go to my brother Ivan, and after his death to be placed at the disposal of Taganrog Town Council for use in public education. I promised the peasants of the village of Melikhovo a hundred roubles to pay for a road; I also promised Gavriil Alexeyevich Kharchenko (Kharchenko House, Moskalevka, Kharkov) that I would pay for his elder daughter to go to High School until such time as her tuition fees are waived. Help the poor. Take care of Mother. Live at peace with one another.

Anton Chekhov[11]

The authorities refused to recognise the legal validity of this letter and in February 1905 a Moscow probate court divided Chekhov's estate between his three brothers and his widow. A month later, however, the four legatees made a legal gift of everything to Masha and empowered her to carry out Anton's instructions.[12]

So much of Olga's brief married life with Chekhov had taken the form of letters written by her from Moscow to Yalta that it does not seem surprising that when she returned to Moscow in August, she should have wished to continue communicating with him in that way.

'*August 19th, 1904.* At long last I can write to you—my dear, sweet Anton, so far away and yet so near to me. Where you are now, I do not know. I've waited such a long time for the day when I should be able to write to you. Today I arrived in Moscow and visited your grave . . . How pleasant it is there, if only you knew! The south has dried up completely but here everything seems so lush and fragrant, you can smell the earth and the greenery, and the trees rustle so softly. How impossible it is to realise that you are no longer among the living! There's so much, so much that I need to write to you about, to tell you everything that I experienced during the last part of your illness and after the moment when your heart stopped beating, your aching, exhausted heart.

'It seems odd to me now that I should be writing to you, but I want to, I want to desperately. When I am writing to you, I have the feeling that you are alive and waiting for my letter somewhere. My sweet, tender darling, let me speak tender affectionate words to you, let me stroke your soft, silky hair, let me look into your kind, radiant, affectionate eyes.

'If only I knew whether you realised that you were leaving this life! I think you did realise, vaguely perhaps, but realised it none the less. On June 29th, when you were taken ill, you told me to write off for the last of our money from Berlin through Iollos, and to ask him to send the money in my name. I didn't like the idea and didn't want to do it, but you insisted. Then you told me to write to Masha, and I did so immediately. We had parted bad friends when she left in May, but I had promised to write to her daily and did so, and then I stopped. You were writing to her frequently yourself from Badenweiler. Did you sense what was going on between us? It was really all a case of jealousy, nothing more. We were really very fond of one another. But she kept feeling that I had taken everything away from her—her home and you—and made herself into some kind of martyr. At first I kept having it out with her, talking a lot, trying so hard to persuade her, pleading with her; if only you knew how many tears we shed! But nothing would come of it, and eventually I stopped trying. If only she had known of our long talks in Aksyonovo, remember, about making sure that she did not feel left out of things. And after all I never showed the slightest proprietorial rights or inclinations, I always considered Yalta *her* home, and it was so painful for me to hear her say that now she had no home, no corner of her own, no garden. Heavens, why did it all work out like that? If only she had known of the cheerful expectations I had on the journey with you from Ufa to Yalta! It didn't go right from the very first day . . . Had everything turned out as I dreamed, I should probably have grown cold towards the theatre . . . But I sensed straight away that a completely satisfying life, complete harmony, would be impossible there. Oh, how I suffered during that month and a half in Yalta! And all those complications because of a church ceremony!

'*August 20th*. Greetings, darling! I've just come back from your brother Ivan's. They were deeply moved by my stories of you and your last days, but I felt they were glad to have heard them, even though it was painful. As for me, I could go on talking for ever and ever about it all, about you, about Badenweiler, about that great, majestic and inexorable event which took place in that lush little emerald-green spot in the Black Forest.

'Remember how we both loved to go on our little carriage expeditions, our *Rundreise*, as we used to call it? How tender you were, how well I understood you at those times. I had such a feeling of blissful innocence. Remember how you took my hand very quietly and squeezed it, and when I asked if you were happy, you just nodded to me in silence and smiled.

'With what veneration I kissed your hand on one of those occasions! You held my hand for a long time, while we drove through a fragrant pine wood. But your favourite spot was that little clearing of lush emerald green flooded with sunlight. The water gurgled so cheerfully along the little irrigation ditch, and everything was so rich and well-watered there. You always told the driver to slow down, so as to enjoy the view of the fruit trees, which occupied a huge open area and were quite unenclosed—yet no one broke them down or stole the pears and cherries. You were thinking of our poor Russia . . . And remember that enchanting little mill—how it stood down below somewhere, completely hidden in the dense greenery, and all you could see was the water flashing on the wheel? How you liked the clean, well-arranged little villages, the gardens with their inevitable beds of white lilies, their rosebushes and little vegetable plots! What pain there was in your voice when you said: 'Darling, whenever will our peasants be able to live in houses like that?'

'Darling, darling, where are you now!

'At first in Yalta I could feel you everywhere and in everything —in the air, in the foliage, in the rustling of the wind. When we were out on excursions, I felt I could see your light, transparent figure with a stick, now close to me, then far away, walking without touching the ground, against the bluish haze of the hills. And at this moment I can positively feel your head next to my cheek.

'*August 24th.* How long it is since I last wrote, darling! By evening I was so exhausted that I couldn't pick up a pen.

'Kundasova[13] has been sleeping here these past nights, Kostya arrived from St Petersburg and has been staying with me, so that also prevented me from writing to you. On Saturday Kundasova and I sat up until four chatting about you. On Sunday morning I drove out to the Novodevichy Convent. How joyfully my heart starts beating whenever the convent towers begin to appear! As if I were on my way to see you, and you were waiting for me there. How I cried on your grave! I could stay kneeling for hours, with my head pressed against the ground, against the little grassy hillock under which you are lying . . . Oh Anton, where are you?!

'This afternoon I finally plucked up courage and drove to the theatre. I entered the office and burst into tears. The theatre seemed so strange and meaningless to me without you. It was painful meeting all the others again. I sat for a while listening to a rehearsal. . . I wasn't listening so much as looking at everyone. Sitting with me were Butova, Rayevskaya, Luzhsky and Kachalov. Luzhsky kept telling me anecdotes to try and cheer me up. It seemed odd that they were all talking and walking about as before, nothing changed . . .

'I had your brother, Ivan, and his wife to dinner. They were talking with such absurd enthusiasm about the war, but I can't bear to hear about it. It caused you such pain, darling. How many German newspapers we read together, and how difficult it was for me having to translate all those scathing remarks about our poor Russia, when I felt how much they grieved you. If only this horror would end soon! And who knows how it will end.

'This evening we had a conference about *Ivanov*. Nemirovich gave the introductory talk, then we discussed parts. I found it distressing having to sit there and listen.

'Yesterday I went to the Convent again with Kostya. I'd like to go there every day. I also bought a stool yesterday and had it sent to the grave for me to sit on.

'Yesterday at Mama's I met the student, Rabeneck, who was with me all the time at Badenweiler. He's a fine boy.

'*August 27th*. I haven't written to you for two days, sweetheart, but it seems like ages. I'm attending rehearsals of *Ivanov*. The mood in the theatre is very flat, everyone seems to have lost interest, no one can work up any enthusiasm. It's a depressing time for us, what with your death and the war—oh, that terrible war. Is Uncle Sasha still alive?!

'I'm horribly lonely, darling.

'It's as if I'm still expecting you to come and see me again, and look at me with that wonderful radiant expression of yours, and stroke me, and call me your little doggie . . . Dearest, where are you?!

'I've turned your study into my sitting-room, it's terribly cosy.

Masha will be in our big bedroom, and my bedroom in what used to be Masha's little study. That naughty Masha seldom writes to me, though she promised to write every day. I'm keeping my word and writing to her frequently.

'I was at the grave today at dusk, round about seven. It was quiet and pleasant, just the noise of the birds flitting from tree to tree, and I could hear the hurrying footsteps of the nuns and make out their dark silhouettes. The icon-lamps that are always burning looked like glow-worms all round. There's one on your grave too, and somehow it makes you feel warm and at peace. I cried a little and kissed the green blades of grass on your grave. The stool is there now, so I can sit down. My thoughts went back to Badenweiler again and I tried to understand what happened there. Darling, I must tell you everything, only I cannot do so yet . . .

'When I saw the student again, every minute of that dreadful night came back to me with painful intensity. I could even hear the crunch of his footsteps on the gravel when he was going to fetch the doctor, amid the amazing silence of that grand and terrifying night.

'There *can't* be such a thing as death . . .

'More of that another time . . .

'We went over the *mise en scène* for Act I of *Ivanov*. . . .

'*August 30th*. The days and nights go by, all the same somehow. I've been sent another bouquet of wonderful roses and gladioli from the same mysterious donor. They touch me, these flowers.

'My darling, my treasure, my own one. When I write to you, I feel that we're only parted for a time. Masha is arriving on the 2nd.

'How depressing, how indescribably painful, my stay in Yalta was. And yet good too. I did nothing but moon about your rooms, touching and looking at your things, or dusting them. Everything is in its place, right down to the last detail. Your Mother has lit an icon-lamp in your bedroom. I wanted it so much. In the evenings I used to walk through your dark study, and I'd catch a glimpse beyond the carved door of the light flickering in the

icon-lamp. I kept waiting for you, every evening I expected to
see you in your usual place. I even talked out loud to you, and my
voice sounded so strange and lonely as it died away in the study.
In the mornings Masha and I went bathing as before. But I
didn't hurry home as I used to . . . No one was waiting there for
me before starting his morning toilet, no one was waiting in bed
for my arrival with a cunning expression on his face and making
rude gestures. Every morning used to be like that. And I would
feel cheerful, I would kiss and caress you, I wanted you so much
to share with me the feeling of the fresh sea and the delight of an
early morning bathe. How wonderful you looked lying there! I
couldn't take my eyes off you. And you kept talking nonsense and
making me laugh. . . .

'At last there was a telegram today from Uncle Sasha. . . .

'*September 11th.* Darling, my dear, tender one, it's so long since
I last talked to you! I've been nervy and restless, just the way
you didn't like me to be. How I wish I could kneel in front of
you now as I used to, rest my head on your chest and listen to
your heart beating, while you stroked me tenderly—remember?
Antonchik, where are you? Are you and I really never going to see
one another again?! That cannot be. Our life was only just
beginning, and suddenly everything's broken off, it's all over.
How wonderfully you and I lived together! You kept saying you
had never thought that life could be so good as a 'married man'.
I had such a blind faith that you and I still had a long, long time
ahead of us . . . Only a few days before your death we were talking
and dreaming of the little baby girl that we were going to have. It
fills me with such anguish to think that there is no child. You
and I talked so much about it. In November my little one would
have been two years old, but for the catastrophe. Why did that
have to happen! My child would have managed to pull through,
I feel sure. How you would have loved him! If only one could
still dream about it!

'The theatre, the theatre . . . I don't know whether I should
love it or curse it . . . Everything is so enticingly mixed up in
this life! Now there is nothing in my life apart from the theatre.

All those three years were a continual struggle for me. I lived with a constant self-reproach. That's why I was so restless and erratic, couldn't settle down anywhere and make a home. As if I were acting against my conscience all the time. And yet, who knows—had I given up the stage . . .'

CHAPTER SIXTEEN

Verdicts

So Olga's last letter to Anton breaks off, with an ambiguity worthy of one of Chekhov's own short stories. Had Olga given up the stage, would that have been the answer? There seems to be a strong suspicion in her mind that it would not.

In the role of Chekhov's wife, Olga Knipper has had a mixed press. Most of the adverse comments on her in the West have been based on uninformed prejudice, which previous chapters may have helped to dispel, but there are two Russian critics of the marriage, both of them with privileged viewpoints close to the individuals concerned, who have probably set the tone for much subsequent comment on Olga Knipper and whose criticisms need to be taken seriously: Chekhov's Yalta doctor, Altshuller, and the good friend of all three members of the emotional triangle, Ivan Bunin.

From a medical point of view, claims Altshuller, Chekhov's marriage was a disaster. Altshuller had hoped that Masha Chekhova would give up her job in Moscow to settle permanently in Yalta, and that with his guidance and support, she would establish the calm, regular routine essential for prolonging the life of a T.B. sufferer. Chekhov's marriage scotched this plan. Nothing could have been more calculated to provoke emotional and physical upheaval than the constant partings from, and reunions with, Olga, or those long journeys to Moscow, where he inevitably overexerted himself, returning to Yalta, however much he might deny it, in a far worse state of health than when he left. On receiving the telegram from Badenweiler, Altshuller felt painfully conscious that 'this untimely death might have been avoided'.[1]

But could the prescription of a calm, regular routine ever have worked for anyone like Chekhov? What appeal does a settled life have to someone for whom the grass always looks greener on the other side of the fence? Prolonged residence in Yalta, as we have seen, only made him feel incurably depressed. Ronald Hingley neatly sums it up when he writes that given the choice, Chekhov is likely to have preferred 'three hectic years as Olga's husband and Art Theatre dramatist to a longer period of inglorious coddling by his devoted sister in the doldrums of Yalta'.[2]

Ivan Bunin criticised the marriage for different reasons. He claims to have anticipated problems. 'I was already on friendly terms with Olga Leonardovna and realised that she came from a completely different background to the Chekhovs.' This was true but unimportant; from the outset Olga established friendly relations with several members of the Chekhov family that persisted long after Anton's death. Bunin also claims to have foreseen, rightly, that there would be trouble between Olga and Masha, but his claim that Chekhov would 'suffer acutely, now for one, now for the other, and then for both of them together', sounds exaggerated, as does his melodramatic description of Chekhov's decision to marry as an act of suicide.[3]

Bunin's most damaging observations, however, are to be found in two passages describing Olga and Anton as he saw them in Moscow in December 1903, prior to the *Cherry Orchard* première.

I used to call in every evening to see Chekhov, and sometimes stayed with him until 3 or 4 in the morning, i.e. until Olga Leonardovna returned home.

On most evenings she left for the theatre, but sometimes she went out to attend some charity concert. Nemirovich would call for her, wearing tails and smelling of cigars and expensive eau-de-Cologne. She would be in evening dress, young, scented and beautiful, and would go up to her husband with the words:

'Don't be bored without me, lovie—after all, you always like being with Bouquichon [a nickname Chekhov had given Bunin]. 'Goodbye, dear,' she said, turning to me. I kissed her hand and they left. Chekhov would not let me go until she came back. And these night vigils were especially precious to me. . . .

At about 4, and sometimes almost at daybreak, Olga Leonardovna would return, smelling of wine and scent . . .

'Whyever aren't you asleep, love? . . . It's no good to you. Oh, you're still here, Bouquichon—well, of course, he hasn't been bored then!'

I'd get up quickly and say goodbye.[4]

From this picture it is but a short step, which many have taken, to that of Olga as the selfish, career-minded young wife, bent on her own pleasures, offhandedly saying goodbye and tactlessly flaunting her youth and beauty in front of the sick husband whom she was so shamefully neglecting, etcetera, etcetera.

After Chekhov's death, Bunin remained on friendly terms with Olga and especially with Masha. His first reminiscences of Chekhov were published in 1904. To illustrate the intensity with which Olga lived through any experience, one of her memoirists recalls a story that Masha used to tell of how Bunin visited Olga's flat to read his reminiscences of Chekhov to her. 'She was sitting on her sofa, he on a chair in front of her. At first Olga Leonardovna made verbal comments on what he was reading, but then her responses became quieter and less and less frequent, and finally stopped altogether. Perplexed, Bunin leaned forward and stared closely at her—she had fainted.'[5]

She had fainted, not because she found anything offensive in the reminiscences, but because Bunin, a gifted mimic, had evoked the memory of Chekhov too vividly.

The damaging passages above were not in fact published until 1955, after Bunin's death. Only in 1953 did Bunin begin to assemble material for the longer memoir of Chekhov that he had always planned but did not live to complete. From 1920 onwards, he had been living in Paris, an outspoken critic of the Soviet regime, especially its cultural representatives. Nor did he spare old friends. Olga Knipper had also been in the West in the early 1920s, but had chosen to return to Russia and thrown in her lot with the new regime. Before starting work on his Chekhov memoir, Bunin had read Lydia Avilova's *A. P. Chekhov in My Life*, and had accepted without reservation her claim to have been Chekhov's one and only love.

Thus Bunin's whole attitude to Olga is immediately suspect. As a master of literary style, he knew how easily a person's character can be damned by the kind of suggestive psychological colouring that Chekhov himself used so skilfully to depict an unsympathetic character. Unfortunately, Bunin had learned the lesson too well, and Olga Knipper—like Gorky, to whom he hands out similar treatment—stands condemned.

Let us suppose, though, that Bunin was not motivated by a combination of revengeful malice and the desire to bring out his own special relationship with Chekhov, and that there was at least one occasion (bearing in mind how hard the Theatre worked her) on which Olga was escorted by Nemirovich to a charity concert from which she returned in the early hours of the morning. That she led a busy social life is beyond question. Anton knew this and approved of it. In Yalta he derived a vicarious pleasure from her accounts of her social activities, and wished that he could emulate them. Knowing his extreme reluctance to think of himself as an invalid, would he have had her curtail those activities to stay at home to look after a sick husband? It seems most unlikely that he would have agreed to accept that kind of sacrifice.

At the opposite extreme to Bunin and Altshuller, Professor Karlinsky has written:

Chekhov got exactly the kind of wife and marriage he wanted, the kind he described in advance to Suvorin about the wife who appears and disappears like the moon. . . . The marriage of Anton Chekhov and Olga Knipper was a partnership of equals and they arranged it to provide themselves with the independence they both wanted to be a part of that marriage. In the short time they had together, with all the occasional misunderstandings, with his deteriorating physical condition and her severe illnesses, with all the separations, they managed to give each other more real happiness than many other couples achieve in a long lifetime together.[6]

This is a welcome counterblast to denigrators of the marriage, but does it go too far in the other direction? Occasional misunderstandings? The Lyubimovka crisis seems to have been more serious than that. Looking at the marriage from Anton's point of view, however, Karlinsky is essentially right. In Olga he did get the kind of wife he wanted: not a pallid moon, though, but a shining comet, anxiously sought for in the heavens, trailing clouds of glory from Moscow and coming to light up his dull Yalta sky.

But what of the marriage from Olga's point of view?

She might be a shining comet whose appearance was eagerly awaited, but did it sometimes seem to her that she was more important to Anton in the awaiting than in reality? Was she his sustaining dream, like the dream of Moscow that sustains the three sisters in their wilderness? 'You won't notice Moscow once you're there,' Vershinin tells the sisters. Anton could not help noticing Olga, but it does seem that in his scheme of things there was a certain fixed role for her to play. Olga commented astutely on their relationship when she wrote that she had a very clear idea of everything that Anton liked. 'And I know how you like me to be. Only I can't always be like that. Does that disappoint you?'[7] And in her letters to him after his death, she wrote: 'I've been nervy and restless, just the way you didn't like me to be.'

The role in which Anton saw her was that of the glamorous, uncomplicated, good-humoured, morale-boosting companion. But that was not the role in which Olga wanted to see herself. She wanted to be something more, to be his intimate spiritual partner, responsive to his every thought and feeling. Had she been able to see herself in that light, she would willingly have sacrificed her independence and given up the theatre. 'Heavens, if only I knew that you needed me, that I could help you to live, that you'd feel happy if I were with you all the time! If only you could give me that assurance.'

Anton did not need a companion of that kind. The events of the marriage seem to show that he *had* passed a point of psychological no return, and that he was so used to living on his inner resources and leading a life of his own that he could not change. We have seen him at the start of the marriage referring to their joint arrangements in the first person and continuing to do so later, and it is ironical that in his very last letter from Baden-weiler, he has still not changed this habit of mind. 'I wanted to go to Italy, to Lake Como . . .' he writes to Masha, 'I thought of taking a steamer from Trieste to Odessa . . .'

And Olga?

The barrier between Chekhov and other people was not lowered, even in the case of his wife. At the time of the Lyubimovka crisis, Olga had tried unsuccessfully to break it down. 'I'd so like you to talk intimately with me,' she wrote a few months later, 'more intimately than you've ever talked with anyone else. Then I'd feel really close to you.'[8] But had he ever been intimate with, or felt really close to, anyone?

So Olga Knipper remains Chekhov's Leading Lady. Central to his vision of her was the romantic image of the highly talented actress and leading lady of the Art Theatre. That he loved her beyond all others, that she was his leading lady in that sense, seems likewise certain, but he loved her, as the Russians say, *po-svoyemu*, 'in his own way'. Would she in time have crossed the threshold between leading lady and intimate spiritual partner? That question seems to hover behind the agonised reflection in the last letter that she wrote to him after his death: 'I had such a blind faith that you and I still had a long, long time ahead of us . . .'

PART THREE

CHAPTER SEVENTEEN

First Revolution and First Tour

Writing to Nemirovich in the summer of 1904 about the
difficulties facing them in the coming season, Stanislavsky
pointed out that Olga Leonardovna, whom he regarded as
'absolutely indispensable', would need a long time to recover
from Chekhov's death. This was a misjudgement of her character.
She had often told Anton that there were only two things in her
life: him and the theatre. 'Now there is nothing in my life apart
from the theatre,' she wrote at the end of her last letter to him
after his death. Nemirovich, the shrewder psychologist, predicted that she would 'give herself up to the theatre entirely and
within a very short time'.[1] Less than two months after Anton's
death, she was already rehearsing the part of Sarah in Chekhov's
play, *Ivanov*.

Meanwhile, Russia's disastrous performance in the war
against Japan had led to a state of prolonged revolutionary
ferment at home. To political developments in the early part of
1905, Olga's reaction was one of eager excitement. If she lacked
the intransigence that made Anton condemn the 'hideously
empty, stupid and tasteless life' on the estate where they stayed
in the summer of 1903, she none the less had no difficulty in
coming to share to the full his liberalism and contempt for the
Tsarist autocracy. 'Do you realise,' she wrote in February to her
brother Volodya in Germany, 'that this is a real, thoroughgoing
ré . . . tion?' And in April she told him how greedily they seized
on the newspapers each morning for news of the latest strikes:
'It's like living on top of dynamite.'[2]

Olga spent the summer in Norway and on her return had thoughts only for the theatre. On September 9th, at a reading of the first two acts of *The Seagull*, she found it difficult to control her emotions: it was exactly seven years since her first meeting with Anton at the *Seagull* rehearsal. But the political situation could not be ignored. The revival of *The Seagull* with which they opened on October 1st failed to evoke any interest. Did it mean, Olga wondered, that only topical plays were needed? Or that the theatre as a whole had become superfluous?

Within a fortnight meetings of the company were being held at which it was decided to close the Theatre temporarily in sympathy with the wave of strikes breaking out all over the country. In a letter to Masha, Olga described the tense situation in Moscow, where water and electricity had been cut off, and life was at a standstill. Then, on October 17th, the Tsar issued a manifesto proclaiming a new constitution. Overnight Moscow came to life again. 'There were meetings everywhere, orators in the squares, red flags. Great excitement in the theatre, congratulations, shouts of "hurrah!" A group of us decided to go out into the streets, including me, of course. We joined the crowd moving along the Tverskaya towards the Governor-General's, carrying red flags, sang the *Marseillaise*, planted red flags everywhere, faces beaming, and just at the right moment the sun peeped through and lit up the jubilant crowd of a thousand.' When the Governor-General came out and made a short speech appealing to their patriotism, he was greeted by catcalls. Suddenly, as the procession moved on, they heard a shout that shots were being fired. 'The crowd scattered to either side, then came the sound of horses' hooves—there was a minute of silence and absolute panic. I decided that my time had come and ran towards the pavement, but I didn't follow the crowd, as I was afraid of being crushed in any case.' Fortunately the Cossacks' whips did not touch her, and she was sufficiently sanguine about the future to invite Masha and old Mrs Chekhov to visit her in Moscow.[3]

A month later, writing to Volodya, her mood was still exultant. The Theatre had reopened and she was too busy to attend all the political meetings that she would have liked. There had been times when the situation looked so grim that 'one wanted to throw everything up, join the revolutionary party and destroy everything. But those ardent moments passed. It's not revolution that one wants, but freedom, room to move, beauty, romanticism.' Though the future was uncertain, it seemed to hold the promise of something quite unexpected, of a new kind of life and a new brand of people. 'The age of whiners and depression is over,' she writes, 'an avalanche is bearing down on us' (an allusion to Tuzenbach's remark in *Three Sisters*). 'Heavens, there are prophetic hints of that life in all Anton's plays! I'm acting *The Cherry Orchard* with quite a new feeling.'[4]

But by December her mood was very different. Masha and Mamasha (old Mrs Chekhov) were now staying with her. 'Three times the government has come unstuck,' she wrote to Volodya, 'and now the revolutionary movement has failed as well. Poor Russia!' There had been fighting in the streets, with 'blood, horrors, barricades. Peaceful citizens like us were equally scared of the soldiers and the revolutionaries.' A period of reaction and government reprisals had set in: 'constant arrests, searches, policemen everywhere with bayonets, patrols going round'. On the previous day she and Masha had been unable to reach home; a nearby school was being searched, and the area was swarming with troops. They set off to spend the night at the Stanislavskys, since no one was allowed out after nine. Around nine they received word that the route was now clear and with some trepidation made their way back to the flat, where poor Mamasha was waiting in a torment of anxiety. 'So much for freedom,' Olga concludes.[5]

It was at this point that the Theatre decided to cut its losses on the Russian season and to stake everything on a foreign tour. Olga had only dared to speak so freely of the government, because her letter to Volodya in Dresden was being taken out of the country by Vishnevsky, on his way to Germany to make advance arrangements. 'Had there been a serious, single-minded revolution, one would feel ashamed of leaving, but now, on the contrary, one wants to get out and doesn't feel ashamed in the least.' Her position is understandable, if not very consistent. One feels that she would have had a stronger moral entitlement to blame the revolutionary movement for its shortcomings, had she herself been a more active participant. Attracted to the poetry and romance of revolution, to the red flags, the radiant faces, and the Chekhovian promise of a new life, she had recoiled from its prose—from the blood, the horrors and the barricades.

In Britain, readers of the theatrical journal *Era* were kept well informed of the Russian company's progress by the journal's Berlin correspondent.

'*February 22nd.* There is no doubt about it, Russia—poor, oppressed Russia—is the mode. In the street-cars and shops Russian is heard all around us—it is computed that there are upwards of 150,000 refugees in Berlin—and now we are being invaded by Russian plays and Russian companies.

'*March 3rd.* The Moscow Artistic Theatre Company, under the management of M. Stanislavsky, commenced its season at the Berliner on Friday. These artists have the reputation of being the best that Russia can produce; consequently, the house was filled almost to the last place. Neither were we in any way disappointed. *Tsar Fyodor* was splendidly acted and staged. The performance was an even one such as is seldom seen, each supernumerary playing his part to perfection.

'*March 17th.* The Moscow Artistic Theatre Company are doing excellent business at the Berliner. The performances are well-rounded, and, no matter how little the hearer understands of the language, he cannot fail to grasp the meaning and be moved by it. There is something very fascinating in the acting of these Russians, and it is no wonder the theatre is filled nightly, while our own actors may learn much from them. Chekhov's drama *Uncle Vanya* was given with much success last week. It has been done here in German, and was at the time detailed in your columns. New to Berlin was the four-act play *Three Sisters*—by the same author—which was given on Saturday, and received with cordiality. The chief attraction, however, remains Gorky's

Nachtasyl [i.e. *The Lower Depths*], which is so well known to Berlin audiences through its long run at the Kleines, that all the points can be followed and appreciated without difficulty. The interpretation, too, is a very fine one.

'*March 24th*. The Russian company at the Berliner announced Ibsen's *Enemy of the People* for Monday and the demand for seats was unusually great. Owing, however, to the Kaiser having expressed a wish to witness a performance of *Tsar Fyodor* on that evening the latter piece was—at some inconvenience—put in the bill. Both their Majesties put in an appearance, accompanied by Prince August Willhelm, and attended by a large suite. The Kaiser was delighted with the acting and the play, and told the directors, whom he received in the Royal box, that the latter reminded him of Shakespeare and from the former he hoped many German artists would learn.' (Though inconvenient at the time, this Royal visit not only transformed the attitude of the Russian Embassy in Berlin to the Theatre, but also ensured the success of the rest of the German tour.)

'*March 31st*. The Russian company left us on Monday for Dresden and left us sorrowing. It was among the most successful events in our theatrical annals, and the three weeks' season was all too short. The performance of Ibsen's *Enemy of the People* last week was one of the best-attended and perhaps the most appreciated of all. It was magnificently acted, the Dr Stockmann of M. Stanislavsky being a faultless rendering. The audience received the piece with acclamation, cries of "Stanislavsky!" reverberating through the house. The farewell performance took place on Saturday, Tolstoy's *Tsar Fyodor* having been chosen to conclude as well as commence the season. There was not a vacant seat in the theatre, the enthusiasm increased from act to act and as the curtain rose after the play was over for the artists to come forward, it rained flowers from all parts of the house.

'Altogether the Moscow guests have gained a series of triumphs all along the line, and richly-merited triumphs too. A crowd of Russian students as well as some of the members of the Embassy, assembled at the railway station on Monday to speed the parting guests, who had to submit—Russian fashion—to much indis-criminate kissing.'

Apart from a number of other German cities, the Theatre also played in Prague, Vienna and Warsaw. They were supposed to visit Paris, but Nemirovich became so irritated by the excessive demands made for advance advertising that he tore up the contract.[6] At one time there had even been talk of a visit to London,[7] but more than fifty years elapsed before such a visit materialised. The whole tour lasted four months and made the name of the Art Theatre well known outside Russia at a time when not only Russian theatre, but Russian ballet, art and litera-ture were being eagerly discovered in Europe and America. They returned home with an international reputation.

CHAPTER EIGHTEEN

Knipper the Actress

During the years before the war, the Art Theatre continued its policy of preparing very thoroughly no more than two or three new productions for each season, while established productions, such as *Tsar Fyodor* and the three major Chekhov plays—*Uncle Vanya*, *Three Sisters* and *The Cherry Orchard*—remained permanently in its repertoire. Of Gorky's plays only *The Lower Depths* retained its place. Both playwrights were far outstripped by Ibsen, nine of whose plays, beginning with *Hedda Gabler* in 1899 and ending with *Peer Gynt* in 1912, were produced by the Art Theatre. Ibsen's fellow Norwegian, Knut Hamsun, was represented by two important productions: *The Drama of Life* (1907) and *In the Claws of Life* (1910). The biggest commercial success was Maurice Maeterlinck's 'Fairy Play in Six Acts', *The Blue Bird* (1908), which gave the Theatre ample scope for ingenious stage effects, as in a different way did the four symbolist dramas of Leonid Andreyev. Apart from Andreyev, however, the Theatre paid little attention to contemporary Russian playwrights, turning instead to the classic Russian writers of the nineteenth century: Griboyedov, Gogol (*The Inspector General*, 1908), Ostrovsky, Turgenev (a memorable revival of *A Month in the Country*, 1909) and the novels of Dostoyevsky—dramatised versions of *The Brothers Karamazov* (1910) and of *The Possessed*, under the title of *Nikolai Stavrogin* (1913).

As this repertoire shows, the Theatre that had appeared daringly liberal at its inception could no longer be accused of 'corrupting Moscow's youth'.[1] They had never been allowed to carry out their original intention of putting on special Saturday morning performances for working people. Instead their patrons were drawn primarily from the well-to-do classes. The spirit of the times is well caught by a photograph taken in 1910 at the first of the Theatre's 'Cabbage Parties', held just before all the theatres closed for Lent. Patrons who had paid handsomely for tickets were first of all entertained to supper and then to a variety of comic turns and 'end of term' high jinks that lasted until nine the next morning. A very large sum was raised to help needy actors. Through the eye of the photographer one looks out from the stage towards the balconies, festooned with coloured lights and decorations. The foreground is crowded with elegant figures, among them Nemirovich and Stanislavsky, seated at their champagne-laden supper tables. It was clearly a very fashionable social occasion.[2]

Although she continued to be best known as an interpreter of Chekhov and for her Nastya in *The Lower Depths*, the name of Olga Knipper (or Knipper-Chekhova, as she now came to be known in the Theatre) figured prominently in many of the new pre-war productions. She was never content to rest upon her laurels. Sometimes, in accordance with Art Theatre practice, the parts that she was given were very small ones. Among her more important roles were four of Ibsen's heroines—Maya in *When We Dead Awaken* (1900), Lona Hessel in *The Pillars of the Community* (1903), Regina in *Ghosts* (1905) and Rebecca West in *Rosmersholm* (1908); the leading parts in both Hamsun plays; Anna Andreyevna, the Mayor's wife, in Gogol's *The Inspector General*, and Natalya Petrovna in Turgenev's *A Month in the Country*. Only with Leonid Andreyev and Dostoyevsky was her name not closely linked.

What kind of an actress was Knipper?

To a schoolboy who wanted to go on the stage Stanislavsky once wrote: 'Before anything else an actor must be a cultured person.'[3] With her varied cultural accomplishments, her participation in amateur theatricals and thorough training at the Philharmonic, Knipper's background was typical of the new

breed of intelligent actors and actresses recruited by the Art
Theatre. She was not an overnight star, relying on charm or
looks or stage presence to conceal a lack of training or education.
She did not cultivate a public, 'actress' personality; unlike many
of her colleagues, she did not even bother with a stage name. For
the liberal intelligentsia Knipper was very much 'one of us': a
frequent and enthusiastic attender not only at other theatres, but
at concerts, operas and art exhibitions.

Knipper did not bring to the stage any very striking physical
attributes, apart from her beautiful speaking voice and impeccable
Russian accent. This absence of striking features had its advan-
tages, however. Stanislavsky remained throughout his life a man
of dominating physical presence, but it cannot have been easy to
forget that the character on stage was anyone but Stanislavsky.
Knipper, by contrast, could transform herself: in her down-at-
heel Nastya from *The Lower Depths* the uninitiated spectator
would never have recognised the smartly turned out Arkadina of
The Seagull.

The most interesting of her memoirists is Kachalov's son,
V. V. Shverubovich (Kachalov was a stage name). Olga had
known him as a baby, and the names of Knipper and Chekhov
were among the first he ever heard. 'I don't know whether one
can say of her that she was a good actress,' he writes provocatively,
but goes on to explain: 'She was something else that is not
covered, not defined, by this professional title. A good actress
should be capable of working in other theatres, of being at home
in any theatrical company. But is it possible to imagine Olga
Leonardovna outside the Moscow Art Theatre?'[4]

Not a 'good actress' in the conventional sense, not a versatile
professional, but an actress of the Art Theatre, which she loved
with a fierce loyalty and served conscientiously for more than
half a century. Disciplined at rehearsals, never complaining of
overwork, always finding reserves of energy for a performance,
there was no one except Stanislavsky, writes another memoirist,
capable of creating round herself such an atmosphere of devotion
to the theatre.[5] If an experienced actress began suffering from

stage nerves, as happened to Stanislavsky's wife, Lilina, it was Knipper who took her under her wing, just as a reassuring word or nod of encouragement from Knipper might make all the difference to the inexperienced beginner. Once, in April 1903, she missed her entrance in the middle of Act I. 'The audience didn't notice anything, of course,' she wrote to Anton, 'but for me it was a catastrophe—the first time in five years. I cried all the way through the second Act. I just can't forgive myself.'[6]

But Knipper was an actress of the Art Theatre in a deeper sense than that. Those basic principles which had first inspired the founders of the Art Theatre—the rejection of theatricality, the emphasis on inner feelings as opposed to external effects, the importance of playing to the stage and not the audience, and the subordination of the individual to the ensemble—soon became second nature to Knipper. The comments that she made in a letter to Anton about a performance by conventional actors of a play by a successful conventional dramatist show how thoroughly she had learned those lessons. 'Just think of it: four acts, and during the whole of that time all the characters had dramatic, i.e. artificial, expressions on their faces and struck dramatic poses. No one said a single living human word, no one smiled. The impression was tedious and completely implausible; incomprehensible sufferings and incomprehensible individuals. We saw the famous Paskhalova, who spent all four acts making large eyes, wringing her hands and suffering frantically.'[7]

Chekhov's own attitude to drama and acting strongly reinforced in her the principles already implanted by Nemirovich and Stanislavsky. In a letter to Meierhold Chekhov wrote: 'The subtle emotions that are characteristic of cultured people must also be given subtle outward expression.'[8] Knipper's acting always remained firmly grounded within this tradition of psychological realism. In her book on Knipper's career as an actress, Turovskaya writes that she was capable of creating the most complex female characters and conveying the subtlest nuances in Chekhov's heroines, but was quite incapable of personifying abstract ideas and concepts. 'The main feature of her personality and of her talent was always a love of life, with all its earthly joys, sorrows, interests and passions.'⁹ This enabled her to act in Chekhov and Gorky, but prevented her from acting in Dostoyevsky and the symbolist theatre. The 'unreal' remained a closed world to her.

Once, in old age, she was asked what had been most precious to her in her life on the stage. 'Feelings,' she replied. 'The feelings that I experienced.'¹⁰ It was one of the Art Theatre's major innovations that they raised to a new pitch the 'lived' quality of their feelings on stage. During a performance of *The Seagull*, Lilina, as Masha, was living her part so intently that she failed to respond to Arkadina's cue. 'I waited quietly,' Olga wrote to Anton, 'then I let out a frantic yell—at last our Masha came to her senses. Her thoughts were so far away that if I hadn't shouted louder, she'd never have come to. How we all laughed.'¹¹ At a dress rehearsal of *Three Sisters*, Savitskaya, as Olga, was so overwrought by the final curtain that she had a hysterical outburst and kept shouting that such intense feelings were too much for her, and that scenes and words like that ought not to be written. Knipper, playing Masha, was also on the verge of hysteria, but they led her off quietly to a separate dressing-room.¹²

What of her technique as an actress?

One memoirist writes that having spent the whole of her life in the theatre alongside Stanislavsky, Knipper had mastered all the secrets of his 'system'.¹³ Knipper, herself, on the other hand, consistently claimed that she had no technique. Kachalov's son describes an incident that took place one summer in a fashionable *pension* at Kislovodsk, a health resort in the south of Russia, where Stanislavsky was the focal point of a lively company of artists and intellectuals. The high-flown discussions about art and literature struck the young Kachalov as artificial: to impress Stanislavsky seemed to be the chief aim of the participants. Knipper joined the company after a walking holiday in the mountains. At lunch on the first day, someone put a deep question to her about 'the psychology of artistic creation'. Instead of the sophisticated pronouncement to be expected from Chekhov's widow, Knipper replied: 'That's all a load of rubbish! I don't understand anything about it, and I don't need to. I act as I feel.' To Kachalov's son these unaffected words, so consistent with her unaffected character, seemed like a ray of light shining through obscurity. Stanislavsky burst out laughing and cried: 'Bravo, Olga Leonardovna, bravo!'[14]

From this it would be wrong to conclude that Knipper was a law unto herself as an actress. It is important to remember, however, that the critical influence on her approach to acting was not that of Stanislavsky, who only began to formulate his system of acting after 1906, but that of Nemirovich at the Philharmonic in 1895–98. After his death Knipper wrote of Nemirovich that she knew of no one 'who was a more subtle psychologist, who was more able to penetrate to the very heart of a human being'.[15] This would have been a far less appropriate comment to make about Stanislavsky, to whom she paid a different kind of compliment when she described him, in a memorable phrase, as 'the conscience' of the Art Theatre.[16] It is a paradox of Stanislavsky that for all his much publicised psychological approach to acting, he himself does not appear to have been a very reliable psychologist, whether in the theatre or in life itself. Students of Chekhov's life will be aware of the distorted impression of Chekhov given by Stanislavsky in *My Life in Art*, just as students of Chekhov's plays will know that Stanislavsky's productions ride roughshod over many of the psychological subtleties. Nemirovich, on the other hand, always seems to be more on Chekhov's wavelength. He was the more sensitive in interpreting an author's intentions, in analysing his characters, and in communicating the results of that analysis to the actors. Drawing up a chair on stage opposite the actor, he would expound the psychology of the character to be portrayed: quietly, without using any special vocabulary, and sometimes for as long as five hours at a stretch. He had worked like this with Moskvin at Pushkino in the summer of 1898, and between them they had created the memorable character of Tsar Fyodor.

Though he never appeared on stage himself, he was able to act for actors, to demonstrate, to indicate some small trait of character that made everything else clear and accessible. Give me the *mature* actor, he is reported as saying (contrasting himself in this respect with Stanislavsky, who preferred working with beginners), who is 'capable of introducing changes into his part after one brief remark, after a single conversation, not after lengthy rehearsals. My actor is the one who is capable of independent creative work. Then I can think when I see him acting: *we* did that together. Not *I* did it, not *he* did it, but *we* did it.'[17]

Knipper was this kind of actress. Once she had grasped the human content of a part, once she had understood the kind of person that she was portraying and the kind of feelings which that person was experiencing, all the detail would follow easily and naturally. Her acting always had to come from within; she found it impossible to learn by copying. When she had to spill a cup of hot tea over herself, she could not find the right reaction, in spite of Stanislavsky's repeated demonstrations; eventually, so the story goes, Stanislavsky had no choice but to fill the cup with boiling tea. The story sounds apocryphal but appropriate to Knipper. Nor did she find it easy to talk about her acting or to demonstrate to others. Once, in the 1930s, she was sitting in the wings waiting for her entrance and watching the young heroine rehearse a love scene. Without thinking, she began silently playing the heroine's part, registering every psychological nuance. The directors looked on spellbound, but when they asked her to repeat some of the passages, she was unable to do so.[18]

Though she needed parts that had emotional depth to them, Knipper was not a demonstrative actress. 'Dostoyevskian' parts were never to her liking. At first her acting might seem too low-key. Tone of voice, eyes, smile, gesture: these were the subtle and restrained Chekhovian means by which her feelings were expressed. With her hands she was particularly expressive—too much so when she felt nervous. Nemirovich sent a message round to her once in the middle of a rehearsal: 'One pair of hands is enough. Leave the other dozen pairs behind in the dressing-room.'[19] Her eyes and smile were both repeatedly described as 'clever' (*umnyi*) and as 'sly', 'crafty' or 'roguish' (*lukavyi*). The play of expression round her eyes and mouth seemed always to be hinting at something beyond: whether at a deep-seated unhappiness, or at high spirits on the verge of breaking out.

For Knipper preparing a part was like putting on 'a new skin'; the new part must fit 'like a glove'. Finding the right clothes was a matter of psychological importance. The initial process of comprehending the character seems, however, to have been a nerve-wracking, hit-or-miss affair. When things were going badly, she was liable to find Nemirovich telling her that her expression at rehearsals 'looked as if she'd just been sentenced to solitary confinement', or Stanislavsky dinning in to her that she was lazy and did not know how to work properly. The latter also criticised her for never being ready by the first night, only the fifteenth, but this did not worry Nemirovich so much, since in his view an actor should never feel that his job was complete and should always be looking for ways of re-interpreting his part. When things were going well, however, when the character suddenly came to life and she found herself thinking about her during every waking moment—at times such as those she experienced a wonderful feeling of creative exhilaration.

At the age of forty, Knipper went through a period of acute self-doubt as an actress. Writing to her brother Volodya in October 1908, just before the celebration of the Art Theatre's tenth anniversary, she described how she had been to visit Chekhov's grave and had gone over in her mind the previous ten years, so closely connected with him. 'For ten years I've been an actress, and in my opinion I've absolutely no idea of how to work or create, somehow I've never gone into things deeply, never adopted a thoughtful attitude to myself and my work. I want something different. I feel an emptiness, a dissatisfaction and a strong sense of having been spoiled; and when you realise that your youth has passed, you feel ashamed.'[20]

She had experienced this kind of dissatisfaction with herself as an actress before, but on this occasion, perhaps because it was associated with the onset of middle age, it seems to have been more deep-seated. In the following year there was a crisis while she was working on Turgenev's *A Month in the Country*. Despairing of her ability to grasp the character of Natalya Petrovna, Knipper uncharacteristically broke down in tears during a rehearsal with Stanislavsky, announced that she was unable to continue and went home. Next day she received a letter from Stanislavsky:

I am not coming to see you, so as not to cause you unpleasantness. You must be so sick of me that I'd better keep out of sight for a while. Instead of myself I am sending these flowers. Let them express the tender feelings that I nurture for your great talent. This love compels me to be harsh towards anything that threatens to interfere with the beautiful gift that is yours by nature.

You are now going through a painful period of artistic uncertainty. Deep feelings of suffering on stage are born through such anguish. Do not imagine that I am indifferent to your torments. I am continually anxious from afar, while knowing at the same time that these torments will bear splendid fruit.

Let someone other than me, Moskvin perhaps, explain to you what is yours by nature. I am ready to stand patiently aside and to admire the way in which your talent, rejecting what is superfluous, shall become free and manifest itself with all the power that is temporarily being held in check by the wretched craft of the actor. . . .

Should my help be necessary to you, I shall break your role down into sections and promise not to scare you with technical terms. That was probably my mistake.

I beg you to be firm and courageous in the artistic struggle that you must win, not only for the sake of your talent, which I love with all my heart, but also for the sake of the whole of our theatre, which is the meaning of my whole life. . . .

In each part of the role seek certain desires in relation to yourself and only yourself, and banish all other vulgar desires in relation to the audience. . . .

You are fortunate, you possess that scenic attraction which makes people listen to you, and so it is easy for you to do whatever you wish on stage.

For the rest of us it is more difficult, as in each role we have to think up, invent, create that attraction, without which an actor is just like a rose without scent.

Take heart and occupy once and for all your regal position in our theatre. I shall admire from afar or, if necessary, work for you like a common labourer.

Forgive me for the torments I have caused you, but believe me, they are inevitable.

Soon you will attain the real joys of art.

With heartfelt love from a worshipper of your great talent,

K. Alekseyev[21]

How clearly Stanislavsky emerges from this letter. The accompanying bouquet, no doubt, was wildly extravagant, just as the letter's sentiments are moving and generous. When he writes, 'Deep feelings of suffering on stage are born through such anguish', one realises that life on stage meant more to Stanislavsky, was in a sense more real to him, than the real world outside. Yet the very intensity of his dedication made him imperious and demanding towards those who worked alongside him. At this time he was striving to formulate in theoretical terms those fundamental principles of acting which he believed that he had discovered: those methods by which the actor calls up within himself the feelings that set in motion his brain and his body. *A Month in the Country* was in fact the first play that he produced in accordance with his system. The evolution of Stanislavsky's views on acting, with its cycles of hope and disillusion, is reminiscent of the spiritual development of a Tolstoy; and like Tolstoy, Stanislavsky was quite ready to overthrow everything in which he had believed previously and to be fanatical in the promulgation of the new truth. Olga Knipper was not the only one to be scared by Stanislavsky's technical terms. He himself describes how the older members of the company protested that they were being treated as guinea pigs and that rehearsals were being turned into an experimental laboratory. 'My obstinacy made me more and more unpopular. The actors worked with me against their wills. A wall rose between me and the company. For years our relations were cold.'[22]

There is nothing cold, however, about Olga's reply to Stanislavsky:

I cannot express how deeply moved I was by your letter and your sweet flowers, and since my tears were not yet completely dry from the previous night, they began flowing again, and had you been there then, I should have gone down on my knees and begged you with all my heart to forgive me for all the unpleasant, painful moments which I cause you through my total inability to work, my chaotic inner state and everything that makes it so difficult for me to live properly. And in return for one rehearsal that is just about tolerable you so easily forgive me for all your tedious work and bother with me—only you, with your pure, limitless and sincere devotion to art, are capable of that.

I am indeed going through a painful period now, but do not think that this has happened suddenly, because Natalya Petrovna is not working out. For some time I have been listening to myself on stage and it is better to do that too early than too late. Do not think that it is another case of faintheartedness. Probably this listening to myself is interfering with my self-confidence and my wholehearted devotion to my work. Why do you write about my talent? I have no talent, I probably have some abilities and, as you say, a certain scenic attraction, and thanks to the fact that you and Vladimir Ivanovich (Nemirovich-Danchenko) have worked with me all these years, I may have turned out a respectable actress. Believe me, I am speaking with complete sincerity. To act and to feel the whole time that

187

I am giving a fraction of what I should like to give, or even more horrifying, that I am not giving at all what I should like to give—that can be a terrible feeling. All this, of course, is accentuated by the fact of playing one role every two or three years, so that one's whole life seems to depend on that role, the more so for me since I have no life outside the theatre, and if my life in the theatre begins to fade—then one starts drawing certain conclusions. Of course, I shall now make every effort to master my role as well as possible, so as not to disgrace the Art Theatre too much by my acting. I do not know how it will turn out; I feel rather like Nina in *The Seagull*: 'I don't know what to do with my hands, I don't know how to stand on the stage, I can't control my voice. You can't understand what it's like to be aware that you're acting terribly.'

I do not know how to thank you for your deeply moving letter. I should like to act Natalya Petrovna so as not to disgrace myself in your eyes. In painful moments I shall re-read your letter. Forgive me for everything, and thank you for everything.

O. Knipper

Less florid in style than Stanislavsky's but equally emotional, Olga's letter is also very typical, with her self-castigation and unswerving loyalty to Stanislavsky and the Art Theatre.

Although, as Olga says, the crisis had begun before *A Month in the Country*, there can be little doubt that the confrontation with Stanislavsky's new methods brought home to her the limitations of her intuitive approach to acting. Where intuition failed her, she had no technique, no method, to fall back on. As she had written to Volodya, she had never *thought* about acting, had never 'gone into things deeply', had been spoiled by success. Yet at the same time her intuitive approach made her extremely resistant to Stanislavsky's theorising. Over the years, one imagines that the attitude she adopted towards the System was not unlike that of Stanislavsky's wife, Lilina. Lilina could not stand theorising either but she seized upon the *practical* application of the System and became one of its most successful exponents.

As for Stanislavsky, he achieved his immediate objective, in that Knipper applied herself with fresh determination, the crisis in self-confidence seems to have passed, and Natalya Petrovna became one of her most successful roles. The experience may have had a salutary effect in making him realise that there were limits beyond which even the most disciplined and dedicated artists could not be pushed. We do not hear of any further friction between him and Knipper. He was quite ready to admit that great artists like her should be regarded as special cases; only the lesser talents had need of systems. Already in his letter one sees him using concepts like 'great talent' and 'scenic attraction' that seem to be part of traditional theatrical vocabulary. And there was certainly nothing of the fanatic about his 'Bravo, Olga Leonardovna!' when Knipper asserted her right to act the way she felt.

CHAPTER NINETEEN

Knipper in Chekhov

'I wonder what we shall find in Berlin? I feel scared for Chekhov. There are new things happening in art and drama, realism is yielding ground and something new is taking its place, but that deep quiet poetry of Russian life and the Russian soul—that is deeply implanted in the human heart and will remain there for ever.' (Olga to her brother Volodya, on the eve of the Art Theatre's first European tour in 1906)[1]

Just as Chekhov the dramatist will always be associated with the Moscow Art Theatre, so Knipper the actress will always be best remembered for her performances in Chekhov's plays.

'We acted very well,' she wrote to him after a performance of *Three Sisters* in 1903, 'and the audience was wonderfully attentive. You see, you're *our* author, you must appreciate that, you must realise that we feel at home in your plays and perform them with love.'[2]

Of Knipper it was often said that she did not act in Chekhov's plays, she lived in them. His characters were as real to her as those of real life; in a sense, more so, for they did not age. Once, convalescing after a serious illness, she was staying in the Crimea at the cottage in Gurzuf which Chekhov had left to her in his will.

'I just lie here all day thinking,' she explained to her visitor. (She was forbidden to read.)

'What do you think about, Olga Leonardovna?'

'About Masha.'

Masha? The visitor was perplexed. Did she mean Chekhov's sister Masha? No, it was the Masha of *Three Sisters*, a part that Knipper had given up playing long ago; and she went on to talk about Masha and the other characters of the play as if they were all the familiar, intimate members of her own family circle.[3]

Chekhov's plays followed her through life. Fifty years separated her first performance as Arkadina in *The Seagull* from her last appearance, when she was over eighty, as Ranyevskaya in *The Cherry Orchard*. Around each of the plays clustered a whole set of memories and associations.

It was through *The Seagull* that she had first met Chekhov, so that it always occupied a unique place in her affections, as it did for the Art Theatre, which used the seagull motif on its curtain, programmes, stationery and even its tickets. Yet the play itself was performed rarely, for fear perhaps of not doing it justice; after the unsuccessful revival in 1905, it was not put on again until 1960. Thus, Knipper's performance as Arkadina, like so much else surrounding the play, remains something of a legend.

Her letters show that it was a part that she always enjoyed playing, even though Arkadina is not a sympathetic character. Thirty-two when the play was first performed, Knipper had the tricky task of portraying an actress whose real age is forty-three, but who passes herself off as thirty-two whenever her grown-up son is not present; an actress, moreover, of the old school of acting so much detested by the new Art Theatre. Arkadina does not love art, she loves herself in art. She loves the excitement of being a star, the applause, the gifts, the bouquets showered on her after her 'moving' performance in *La Dame aux Camélias*; she cannot contemplate the thought of growing old or of life without the fashionable wardrobe appropriate to one in her position. It was a feat of characterisation by Knipper, who had never rubbed shoulders with this kind of actress, but who may have understood intuitively Arkadina's greed for life, her desire to drink life's experiences to the last drop.

Knipper had far more problems with the role of Yelyena, the

beautiful young wife of the retired Professor in *Uncle Vanya*, though not because she failed to convey the glamour and mysterious appeal of the part. This will always be a difficult role, for Yelyena is important in the play not so much as a character in her own right, but for the way in which other people see and react to her. Arkadina fills her life with activity; Yelyena's life is empty. Stanislavsky, simplifying the psychology of the characters in order to bring out a sense of dramatic conflict, wanted Yelyena to be portrayed as a highly-strung, impressionable character, anxious to escape from the boredom in which an unwise marriage has trapped her. Knipper resisted this interpretation. She asked Chekhov about the scene in which Dr Astrov, played by Stanislavsky, says farewell to Yelyena. Her own judgement was confirmed when Chekhov wrote that Astrov should not behave towards Yelyena, as Stanislavsky was proposing, like 'the most passionate lover, clutching at his feeling like a drowning man clutching at a straw', and that such an interpretation would upset the whole quiet mood of the final Act.[4] By the time of the first night in October 1899, when her bad performance, as described in the letter to Anton quoted earlier, caused her such anguish, she was acting against the grain, unconvinced that the highly-strung image of Yelyena imposed upon her by the directors was preferable to her own. Later, in St Petersburg, she was criticised for going to the other extreme and making Yelyena too phlegmatic. In spite of this chopping and changing, she continued to play the part for a number of years, though Turovskaya considers it the least successful of her Chekhov roles.

When Chekhov in 1900 was creating the role of Masha in *Three Sisters* for Olga Knipper—and putting in to it Olga's 'little demon' qualities of outspokenness, quickness of temper and boisterous high spirits, as well as her capacity for feeling deeply— he and Olga were not yet married. In her private life Olga had yet to discover what it meant to 'take one's happiness in snatches', as Masha and Vershinin do, nor had she experienced the kind of pain that Masha feels when she and Vershinin have to part. After her marriage, Olga's private life and her stage life in *Three*

Sisters began strangely to overlap. On October 26th, 1901, she and Anton said goodbye and Anton left Moscow for Yalta. Their first long winter of separation lay ahead. That same night the Art Theatre was playing *Three Sisters*. Near the end of the play Olga as Masha stood listening to the sound of the regimental band fading away in the distance, and knew that it was taking Vershinin out of her life for ever. 'I couldn't stop the tears flowing,' she wrote to Anton, 'I kept seeing *you* and I can't remember how I spoke the final words; and when the curtain was drawn, I burst out sobbing, they caught hold of me and dragged me off to the dressing-room, so that I didn't even appear for curtain-calls. I just couldn't help myself.'[5] And in December it was surely the closing speeches of *Three Sisters* that were echoing in her mind as she wrote to Anton of the new life that awaited them both in the spring—'when you and I will start living again, darling'.[6]

Olga brought more depth of feeling to Masha than to any of her other parts. 'Usually I didn't go up to my dressing-room in between scenes,' she recalled, 'but sat in the foyer. But when I was playing Masha, before the farewell with Vershinin, I used to go off to my room and lock the door, so as to gather myself together. When the bell went, I would fly out of the dressing-room and run down to the stage with my heart pounding. And I offered up a silent prayer that no one would come up to me, stop me, or engage me in conversation, so that I would not spill the feeling that was welling up inside me.'[7]

Rushing up to Vershinin, she would suddenly stop short and her arms would drop down loosely by her sides. The brief scene that followed—Masha gazing into Vershinin's face as if to imprint it on her mind for ever, her single word of farewell, their last embrace and Masha's scarcely human, gasping sobs—this brief scene, as played by Knipper and Stanislavsky, was never forgotten by those who saw it, just as Masha quickly became established as the most moving and unforgettable of all the characters created by Knipper.

After Chekhov's death the personal associations of the play were intensified. Of course, any performance in one of his plays was a way of feeling in touch with him again and of helping to keep alive his reputation. But in each performance of *Three Sisters* Olga was re-enacting her life with Chekhov. Their time together had been so short, their happiness so fleeting, and now their separation, like that of Masha and Vershinin, was not temporary but irreversible. In public her ready smile gave no hint of private sorrows; but as Kachalov's son points out, everything tragic in her life—the unborn child, the last night at Badenweiler—could find an outlet through Masha.[8]

Though Masha does not have many lines to speak, the part is one of Chekhov's most effective, in that what appears on the surface of behaviour so skilfully suggests the complex patterning beneath. Chekhov can even conjure up her inner life without giving her any words at all. In the opening scene, while her sisters are reminiscing about their father's death, Masha, in her inevitable black dress, sits quietly reading her book and then, scorning social convention, begins to whistle; but it is Masha, not her sisters, to whom the audience's eyes turn, *her* life that one begins to wonder about. Or the words that she is given, as often happens in Chekhov, are not there to convey meaning but solely as a vehicle through which emotion can be expressed. This is true of the couplet from Pushkin—'A green oak by a curving shore, And on that oak a golden chain'—which Masha is saying to herself with gloomy absentmindedness not long before she meets Vershinin, and which turns up again, hauntingly, in her overwrought mind four years later, just after Vershinin has left. It is true also of the famous 'Tram-tam-tam' and 'Tra-ra-ra' of Act III, the musical language of love that Masha and Vershinin devise for themselves. This was not, Olga recalled, a signal that the two of them intended to throw themselves into one another's arms as soon as they had left the room; when she and Stanislavsky were 'fantasising' together (a method used by the Art Theatre to help actors to enter into their parts more fully), 'it always seemed to us that they would go off and wander the streets until morning, and that Masha might tell him about herself, or her sisters, or the conversation she had just had with them'.[9]

To all these moments Knipper brought a fine subtlety of interpretation.

Yet there had been a time when she was very nearly dropped from the role of Masha. Coming in on rehearsals at a late stage, Nemirovich objected to the excessive dramatisation that Stanislavsky had introduced into the play, especially in Act III. Why did there have to be such a frightful din? The noise of the fire in the town, as Chekhov confirmed, was 'only in the distance, dull and confused'.[10] And why was Knipper playing the so-called confession scene, in which she tells her sisters that she is in love with Vershinin, like something out of old-fashioned melodrama, throwing herself on to her knees and letting her hair fall loose? Answering Olga's query, Chekhov again supported Nemirovich when he wrote: 'Darling, Masha's confession in Act III isn't a confession at all, it's just a frank conversation. You're on edge but you're not desperate, so don't shout, put in at least an occasional smile, and in general let the audience feel the exhaustion of the night.'[11] Olga had to be quickly put through a crash course of remedial psychology with Nemirovich.

Unlike Masha, the part of Ranyevskaya in *The Cherry Orchard* was not written with Olga Knipper in mind. Chekhov originally intended Ranyevskaya to be considerably older. 'I'm not very keen on writing for your theatre,' he told Olga in April 1903, 'mainly because you haven't got an old woman. They'll go and land you with the old woman's part, but I've another part for you, and anyway you've already played an old lady in *The Seagull*'[12] (so much for Arkadina and her claim that she could still play a girl of fifteen!). In the event, Chekhov made Ranyevskaya middle-aged and the part was taken by Knipper, but only because there was no one more suitable.

Chekhov always regretted that Olga could not play the other part, that of the governess, Charlotte Ivanovna. Nemirovich also thought of her as an 'ideal' Charlotte. Olga herself was tempted: 'It's the most striking role and the most difficult one.'[13]

Inspired by the English governess at Lyubimovka, but made German in the play—with Knipper in mind?—Charlotte is eccentric. She goes out shooting on her own with a rifle slung over her shoulder and wearing a man's peaked cap, takes a long cucumber out of her pocket and starts to munch it, and performs all manner of conjuring tricks and acts of ventriloquism, which includes the imitation of a squalling baby. This was also one of Olga's party turns, given one evening in January 1902 backstage at the Art Theatre, where everyone congratulated her, she wrote to Anton, on producing a tiny Chekhov. Charlotte is by no means a purely comic character, but the fact that both Chekhov and Nemirovich saw Knipper in the part makes one regret that the comic side of her personality was not exploited more in the theatre: with her gift for mimicry, her lively sense of fun and awareness of the absurd that she shared with Chekhov, she would have made a good comedienne.

Kachalov's son has written of Knipper that 'she was Masha, she became Ranyevskaya'.[14] She was able to *be* Masha, in the sense of identifying herself totally with Masha's situation, whereas she had to *become* Ranyevskaya, whose situation—in particular, as a member of the gentry who has lost her wealth and position, and whose estate is about to be sold—was outside her experience.

Yet curiously, even though Chekhov may have written certain features of Olga's personality into the part of Masha, the broader parallels of character, though not intended by Chekhov, seem more apparent in the case of Knipper/Ranyevskaya.

Turovskaya's summing-up on Knipper that 'the main feature of her personality and of her talent was always a love of life, with all its earthly joys, sorrows, interests and passions' is particularly appropriate to Ranyevskaya. A love of life with all its earthly joys might also be attributed to Arkadina, of course; but there, because it is so self-centred, it only repels. Ranyevskaya's love of life, like Olga's, attracts others to her: the desire to radiate pleasure—not just to seek it for oneself, but to share it with others—is common to both of them. This attraction, this charm, is essential to the role of Ranyevskaya; it explains why two such opposing characters as the merchant Lopakhin and the 'eternal student' Trofimov should have gone out of their way to be present on the estate when Ranyevskaya and her daughter return from Paris.

Both Ranyevskaya and Knipper lived their lives on the emotional level. How one is feeling oneself, how others are feeling and how one relates to them emotionally: this is what life is all about. Money is too mundane to be taken seriously, so long as it is there—and even if it is not there; one is reminded of Ranyevskaya when Olga writes to Masha Chekhova in 1905: 'I'd like at least to subscribe to some journals but I've absolutely no money. I don't know what happens to it. I'll have to try writing down where the money goes'[15]—a good intention certainly never carried out. Ranyevskaya's capacity for giving herself up wholeheartedly to the emotion of the moment, and for switching rapidly from one mood to another, has already been noted in Knipper. So too has Ranyevskaya's inability to bottle things up inside her: that aspect of her own nature that Olga had become so keenly aware of whenever she began to think about the contrast between herself and Anton. In the famous duologue with Trofimov in Act III Ranyevskaya defends the emotional approach to life, defends the right to love, even though it be to love unwisely. Of Knipper in this scene Turovskaya writes that she was no longer the weak and sinful Ranyevskaya, robbed by a worthless lover. 'This was life itself, with its earthly passions, throwing down its challenge to Trofimov's bloodless intellectualism. There was something splendid and triumphant in the figure of Ranyevskaya at those moments.'[16] Knipper and Ranyevskaya were speaking with one voice.

When Olga told him how difficult the part of Ranyevskaya was, Anton disagreed. 'You need only to strike the right note from the outset, to think up a smile and a way of laughing, and to know how to dress.'[17] Olga followed this advice, introducing into her clothes that touch of Parisian chic which seemed so out of place on the dilapidated Russian estate; but she found her own clue to Ranyevskaya's inner nature. 'When I was preparing Ranyevskaya,' she recalled, 'I kept wondering why she was always dropping everything. It was obviously more than just a realistic detail on Chekhov's part. She's in a state of inner confusion, she doesn't know what to do with herself, how to live.'[18]

Knipper's hands in *The Cherry Orchard*: how clearly they expressed this confusion and how well they were remembered. Like those of her feckless brother, Gayev, played by Stanislavsky, whose raised right hand dangled in front of him like a dog's broken paw, they were hands that had never known work. They were kindly, graceful hands that played delicately with a handkerchief, fluttered nervously and seemed incapable of grasping or holding on to anything. When she looked in her purse to see how much money she had left after the visit to the restaurant, there was a helpless irritation about her 'Now I've gone and dropped it all', as if she had known in advance that this would happen, and that money was always destined to slip out of her grasp. When the drunken passer-by asks her for money, she fishes round helplessly in her purse and brings out a gold coin, unable to find anything smaller (in contrast to Arkadina, with her precise instructions to the servants that her one-rouble tip is to be divided between the three of them). Still every inch a lady, she holds it out to him with the very tips of her fingers. Kachalov's son remembers especially how she handled the telegrams from her sick lover in Paris. In the first Act the decisive way in which she tore them up indicated more clearly than words that she was 'through with Paris'; but how tenderly she stroked those little squares of paper in Act III, how much love and pity was betrayed by the ceaseless fluttering of her fingers.[19] And Cheryl Crawford, one of the co-founders of the famous Group Theatre in New York, watching Knipper in 1935 when she was long past her prime, remembers the moving moment after Lopakhin has announced that he is the new owner of the estate—when Knipper slumped into a chair, her eyes went dead and her large hands spread out helplessly along the table.

Knipper's last role was as Sarah in *Ivanov*, produced by the Art Theatre a few months after Chekhov's death. Sarah is the most obviously tragic of these Chekhov heroines. A Jewess, she has renounced her faith in order to marry the idealistic Ivanov, but when the play opens, Ivanov has lost his idealism, she is seriously ill with tuberculosis, and Ivanov no longer loves her. It was characteristic of Knipper not to bring out Sarah's quiet fading away so much as her defiant wish to go on living. In later years she had a soft spot for this play, remembering with particular vividness the feelings of loneliness and desertion that she had experienced as Sarah.

Knipper played opposite Kachalov as Ivanov. Kachalov's son, however, did not like Knipper's Sarah:

> Now that was a part she *acted*, executed the director's design, was sincere, worked herself up, suffered. Everything was as you would expect from a fine actress. Had it not been for Masha and Ranyevskaya, I might have reacted to Sarah differently, but I had seen and loved those two so much that there was no comparison. In those two, especially in Masha, there was a sense of creation, inspiration; in Sarah—only the execution of a role. . . .

> I have seen many good actresses, both here in Russia and abroad, but there was never one like her, nor could there be. There never was and I doubt if there ever will be. It was a unique matching of sound and echo, of beam and light, of Chekhov and Knipper. Only in her could he find such a sympathetic echo. Only reflected by her did his light begin to sparkle.[20]

CHAPTER TWENTY

Dear Temple

Only thirty-five when Chekhov died, still very attractive, famous as an actress in her own right, and now with the added glamour of being Chekhov's widow, Olga Knipper could not help being surrounded by admirers. One is bound to ask: were there other men in her life after Chekhov? Clearly there were, perhaps many of them; but it seems equally clear that none of them ever came to occupy the same place in her affections as Chekhov had done, and she never married again.

One of the most colourful men who passed through her life was the Englishman, Gordon Craig. Craig first came to Russia in 1905 with Isadora Duncan. The two of them had met in Berlin in December 1904, when he was thirty-two and she twenty-six. He was the illegitimate son of Ellen Terry but liked to think of himself as Irish on the strength of one Irish grandfather; she was born in San Francisco of American parents but claimed an Irish grandmother. Tall, with long hair and beautiful eyes, Craig was extravagantly handsome, but Isadora's appeal was as much in her personality as her good looks. With men she was relatively inexperienced, whereas Craig's amours, Max Beerbohm noted, were 'almost mythological':[1] he had already fathered seven children by three different mothers. For some years Craig had acted with Henry Irving but was now ambitious to revolutionise the theatre through his original ideas on stage design and production; Isadora's originality lay in her very individual style of free expressive dancing, which was rapidly turning her into a cult figure throughout Europe.

Dear Temple

Craig saw her dance and was captivated. As he put it later: 'She was speaking in her own language, not echoing any ballet master, and so she came to move as no one had ever seen anyone move before.'[2] They fell instantly in love, spending four days and four nights together in Craig's studio. The idyll came to an end when Isadora had to leave Berlin to give two performances in St Petersburg, which created a sensation: according to Diaghilev, the classical ballet of Imperial Russia received a shock from which it could never recover.

When Isadora returned to Russia a few weeks later to give further concerts in St Petersburg and Moscow, Craig accompanied her. Of Duncan's reception in Moscow Olga Knipper wrote to her brother: 'All the artists are raving about her, the musicians run her down because she uses classical music, but in my opinion she's such a great artist that it would be unthinkable for her to dance to music that was trivial. Let the young composers sit down and write music to suit her. She watched us give a performance of *The Cherry Orchard* and was in raptures; came round to my dressing-room and I went round to hers the next day. You know, she has a wonderfully refreshing effect on one, there's something so clear and pure about her, so fragrant and unaffected.'[3]

It was typical of Knipper's aesthetic sense that she responded with immediate enthusiasm to the emotional expressiveness of Duncan's dancing, in which the hands and facial expression played their part as well as the movements, while at the same time coming to feel that the 'Grecian' elements—the chiton, or flimsy Greek tunic, and the classical poses—were contrived and distracted attention from the natural human simplicity of her performance.

Among those present at the first concert in Moscow was Stanislavsky. The audience, he recalled in *My Life in Art*, was rather small ('??? What can he mean,' Craig wrote indignantly in the margin of his copy, '—the theatre was packed tight'), and at first the surprise of seeing 'an almost naked body on the stage' ('Not exactly the way to put it', comments Craig) prevented him from appreciating the dancer's art. By the time of the interval, however, he had been won over and hurried down to the foot-lights to applaud demonstratively.[4]

Stanislavsky attended all Isadora's Moscow performances, but did not meet either her or Craig. The first hint that Craig and Stanislavsky might work together appears to come in a letter to Craig from Isadora in June 1907, when she writes of having heard that the Art Theatre people 'are very anxious to meet you'.[5]

By this time, however, several events had taken place. In December 1906, Ibsen's *Rosmersholm*, produced by Craig and with Eleonora Duse as Rebecca West, was put on in Florence. 'Let our common sense be left in the cloak room with our umbrellas and hats,' Craig wrote in his programme note.[6] His set was completely unrealistic: Ibsen's 'sitting-room, comfortably furnished in an old-fashioned style', had been replaced by soaring, mobile nets in merging shades of blue and green, with a huge window at the back that looked like the entrance to eternity, as Knipper said of Craig's sketches.[7] Prior to this, in September, Isadora had given birth to a daughter. Though Craig was present at the confinement, relations between him and Isadora were no longer what they had been. She had quickly begun to realise, as Francis Steegmuller writes, that 'he was at least as devoted to his art not only as she was to hers, but as he was to her';[8] nor did he feel any sense of obligation towards his children. 'Why the very *Goo* of a Baby,' she told him, 'makes you look for a Time-Table book.'[9] Craig soon abandoned the ailing Isadora and her daughter, while continuing to look to Isadora's future concert earnings to provide him with financial support, and set himself up in Florence, there to pursue the writing, and the experiments in his theatrical workshop and with model stages, that were part of his campaign to revolutionise the theatre. The term 'sacred monster', writes Steegmuller, might well have been invented to describe Craig.[10] Because he was genuinely dedicated and a genuine innovator—'half-a-century ahead of his time', according to Stanislavsky[11]—he had to be forgiven for his monstrous shortcomings: his egocentricity, exploitation of the generous-hearted Isadora, chronic inability to work harmoniously with other people (within a few weeks of the *Rosmersholm* triumph he had fallen out with Duse) and incapacity for sustained human relationships. 'He was a great artist,' writes his son and biographer, Edward Craig, 'with a superb imagination but he wasn't a father, a husband or a real lover. Romantic yes.'[12]

In December 1907 Isadora again went on tour to Russia, this time without Craig, and was enthusiastically taken up by the Art Theatre, especially Stanislavsky. Like Craig, who had written in 1905—'Inspiration is given out by the thousand volt per second from Miss D. And I am alive again (as artist) through her'[13]— Stanislavsky was soon writing ecstatically to Isadora that she had given him a new insight into art and filled him with inspiration just when he felt on the verge of giving up his artistic career. To Craig Isadora described Stanislavsky as 'a wonderful man— really Beautiful & Great—I talked with him many hours about you. . . . He says he would give you a perfectly free hand in the Theatre.' She was to tell Mr Craig 'we are very simple people, that we care nothing at all for ourselves but very much for Art & that if he will come we will all be glad to follow his ideas'.[14]

Craig did come, arriving first in the autumn of 1908 and making in all four visits to Russia until *Hamlet* was finally produced in January 1912.[15] Craig could not be blamed for the typhoid fever that struck Stanislavsky down in the summer of 1910, resulting in the postponement of the autumn production, but he often behaved impossibly. Nemirovich would have been happy to see him go, and it says much for Stanislavsky's gentlemanliness and continuing faith in Craig's genius that *Hamlet* was ever produced at all.

When Craig arrived in Moscow at the end of October 1908, he was completely unprepared for the Russian winter. The Theatre fitted him up with a huge, old-fashioned fur coat from its wardrobe and took him on a tour of the Moscow night spots; they visited the gypsy singers and dancers, and did not disperse until six. Craig went to see all the current Art Theatre productions, including *Uncle Vanya* and *The Cherry Orchard*, finding them 'lovely', 'masterly', and 'beautifully acted'.[16] He remained in Moscow only four weeks, but it was long enough for a minor emotional explosion to take place between him and Olga Knipper, of a kind that was common in Craig's life and not perhaps so uncommon in Olga's. As in the case of Isadora, it was the artist in Knipper that Craig, like Chekhov before him, responded to first. He had nicknamed Isadora 'Topsy'; Knipper became 'Temple' (Temple of Art). On returning to Florence, he wrote to her that he was still trying to recover from the Theatre's hospitality, felt that he must travel to foreign parts, announced that he was dying and implored his Temple to send him her love, which he valued so highly.[17] In answer to her anxious reply, he wrote as follows (his epistolary style, like his spelling, was very much his own):[18]

11 January 1909
Dear Temple. I like answering a letter like yours—it lends itself to me to excersise my cynicism and affection on it.

I too send you my love . . . but I will not keep my cynicism to myself either. You are so charming—and so much more—something so mysterious that I can say at once

I love you very much—

I fear you very much—[19]

You tell me 'not to think that you have forgotten me' . . . of course I don't . . . I never do. I am so concieted that I know men and women never forget me—

You know that I am concieted—don't you? You ask what is the matter with me—that I am dying—must go to China Egypt—Temple darling, don't you know man, even now? don't you know he dies a death once a week if he lives a life once a week . . . I die, live, travel to India and back again . . . to Moscow and back—

This, and more (just as you are charming, and much, much more) I do in the space of an hour lying under a tree or sitting in my chair . . .

And you wonder why I am dying. Darling Temple I am

dying because I devour more time and expend more force in an hour than most people do in a year. That is to say I am 9570 years old—for I was born in 1900 . . . having been asleep until that year . . .

All of which I am sure, does not interest you at all! I wonder what does interest you—?

What can I say which will interest you who have known such dear and great things that all other things can but be senselesss—

Ah my dear Temple I see such wonders in your face—I see there the reflection of all the wonders you have looked at.

You ask where Isadora is? I am not quite sure whether she is in the island of St Helena or in Paris, but I have reason to suppose she is in Paris.

But why do you speak about Isadora? Do you think that she has anything to do with my 'dying'. . . .

When I look at you, and see on your face 'the eyes! the eyes!' the gravity of great beauty, then with my eyes I try to tell you all about this Love of Love for which I know we all care so little. . . .

So you are playing Revisor[20]—

How nice—I like to think of it.

And you in your dressing-room—half Japaneese and awfull jolly—not at all horibble. . . .

Olga had asked him where he would be in the summer, obviously hoping that they might arrange a meeting. Craig warns her that by then he may no longer be part of this world; there had been an alarming earthquake in Florence and another one was promised in a fortnight's time. 'All being well with my cieling and the top of my head I shall be in this room working like a good little boy. I may have one of my children here—a splendid boy[21]—but I dare say I shall be all by MYSELF. Isadora will be sure to come here but Isadora will be full of little ambitious plans—and only HUGE impossible plans please me——And *you*!'

From these remarks Olga might have found it difficult to

decide whether her presence in Florence that summer would be welcome or not. The problem, however, did not arise. Still in one piece, Craig joined the Art Theatre in St Petersburg on its spring tour and started work on *Hamlet*. 'Rehearsals have begun,' he wrote to his friend, Martin Shaw, '—in a most orderly fashion. The entire company, taking their lead from the manager, do *everything* I say. It may be a dream, dear old chap, but my God, it's like Heaven after years of Hell.'[22] Although Craig continued to place his dear Temple on a romantic pedestal, it seems likely that on this visit the amorous element in their relationship receded into the background, at least so far as Craig was concerned. His attentions were now directed towards the young actress with whom he was rehearsing Ophelia. In any case, Isadora was also in Russia on tour. 'Duncan was in St Petersburg,' wrote Stanislavsky, excusing himself for not answering a letter. 'Need I say more?' A friend joked to Olga that Russia's Gregorian calendar would have to be renamed the 'Craigorian'. Stanislavsky described them to his son as an entertaining couple, 'but they spend all the time quarrelling, or rather, Craig does the quarrelling, while she shrugs her shoulders and assures everyone that he's mad.'[23]

There exist three wildly differing accounts of an extraordinary farewell dinner party given by Isadora just before she was due to leave on the night train for Kiev. According to Isadora in *My Life*, only four people were present: herself, her young female secretary, Craig and Stanislavsky. 'In the middle of the dinner,' she writes, 'Craig asked me if I meant to remain with him or not. As I could not answer, he flew into one of his old-time rages, lifted the secretary from the chair, carried her into the other room and locked the door. Stanislavsky was terribly shocked and did his best to persuade Craig to open the door, but when we found that persuasion had no effect, we could do nothing but go the station, where we found the train had left ten minutes before.'[24]

Craig in *Book Topsy*, written in 1944 but not published, has the same four people sitting down to dinner. 'I suppose,' he begins, 'she thought she could do no better than play the whore, or pretend to, & so fixed on Stanislavsky—who *resisted* her superbly with a caution quite remarkable to observe. As soon as the 1st bottle of Champagne had been finished she began to encircle Stanislavsky's neck with her arms—& began to kiss him— he objecting most politely all the time—& she refusing to accept his objections. When I could stand no more of this rotten performance I took the other girl S by the arm telling her I had something to say to her *privately*—& mysteriously I drew her into the small room with the bed in it—I locked the door so that no one could come in any way.' Then follows a detailed account of how they wait until all is quiet, go out for a drive, engage another double room in the hotel and spend the night together, she 'apparently in church while in bed'. Next day, finding Isadora about to depart, he 'could not help saying with polite smiles that I hoped she had passed a pleasant evening anyhow. To this she said neither a yea or a nay but, as was her custom, when utterly bouleversé, she uttered a brief sermon—said she, "Try to emulate the virtues of the good *good* man with whom we supped last night," & signing to the coachman to jolly well drive on she drove away.'[86]

Stanislavsky's account is contained in the course of a letter to his son, written on April 21st, soon after the events described. Apart from himself and Craig, the guests at the dinner included Sulerzhitsky (Stanislavsky's close friend who had been appointed to act as Craig's assistant on *Hamlet*), Olga Knipper, and Maklakov, one of Olga's admirers. Stanislavsky does not describe the dinner itself but only the comic way in which it ended. They were suddenly informed that Isadora's train was due to leave in fifteen minutes. 'Everyone jumped up and began sorting the parcels. Duncan asked me to see her off. I hired a cab. "Which station?" I asked the hall porter. "Warsaw Station," he said confidently. It's miles from anywhere. We raced along and got there with two minutes to spare, only to be told that we should have gone to Tsarskoye Selo Station. So the maid and the heavy luggage left for Kiev, Duncan missed the train and her friends all went off in different directions with the hand luggage. We

returned to the hotel. Duncan's room was already being turned
out. Clouds of dust everywhere. Where could we go? Back to our
place. After the performance the actors came in and all hell was
let loose. Finally the friends joined forces, the luggage was found
and Duncan was reinstalled.'²⁶

The only fact to emerge with certainty from these three
accounts is that Isadora missed her train.

Neither Isadora's account, nor Craig's, strikes one as at all
reliable; on the contrary, they illustrate the complete unreliability
of such accounts, written long after the events by interested
parties. Perhaps Craig was not remembering the events at all,
but only what Isadora had written about them in her auto-
biography; he certainly seems unaware that in trying to denigrate
Isadora, he makes his own behaviour appear far worse than hers.
Stanislavsky's version is reliable but was it incomplete? The high-
minded Stanislavsky would not have mentioned Duncan's
amorous advances or the incident with the secretary to his
young son. Yet it seems almost impossible to imagine that
Duncan or Craig would have behaved so badly in the presence of
other guests, particularly Olga Knipper. No account exists by the
one person who might have shed light on the mystery: Isadora's
poor, unsuspecting young secretary.

In the spring of 1910 Craig came to Moscow to conduct further
rehearsals in preparation for the planned autumn opening. He
was now anxious for Knipper to play Gertrude. Stanislavsky told
Craig in July that he could not see her in the part and did not
believe it appealed to her; in any case she was busy enjoying herself in Paris. To Knipper he wrote that Craig still wanted her as
Gertrude, but 'I didn't think the part interested you, and to tell
the truth, I don't see any tender maternal feelings in you.'²⁷

With Stanislavsky's illness, all work on *Hamlet* ceased.
Nemirovich mobilised the whole company to put on *The Brothers
Karamazov*. Returning to Moscow, Knipper hurried down to
help Lilina in Kislovodsk, staying there until Stanislavsky was
out of danger. When work on *Hamlet* started again early in 1911,
Knipper took over the part of Gertrude from Savitskaya (who

died that year in her early forties), but Craig only learned of this change in October, when Lilina sent him a postcard; Stanislavsky had not been communicating so freely with Craig ever since a dispute over payment in February. Craig wrote off at once to Mrs Temple-Queensky: 'I cannot say how happy I am that you are to act the Queen. *You know how much I wished for that* and now *I have my wish.* Say to Kachalov that I will not disturb him until the work is done. I am sure he will be *noble* and that he will be *the first* STRONG HAMLET the world has seen.'[28]

The opening night was now scheduled for January 1912. Craig arrived late in December and put up at the Metropole. In the course of the play's first run-through, writes Laurence Senelick, 'a great hubbub breaks out in the audience, where no one at the Moscow Art Theatre has ever raised his voice during a rehearsal before. The word "stupid" in English is heard. Craig has come directly to the theatre and loses his temper on seeing that they have begun without him; he is asked to leave and not to return until the final dress rehearsals.'[29] Alone at the Metropole, Craig busies himself making a medallion to hang round Hamlet's neck. When Knipper suggests that he might prefer company, he replies:

Please Miss Temple-Knipper-Queensky do not send anyone to see me.

I think they would scarcely find me either—for I have only just found myself.

And you will understand that sometimes one does not want to see strangers even on business.

I wish to be as much alone as possible like the White Owl who sits warming his five wits in the belfry tower.

But I hope I shall see *you.* That would be a pleasure, but I do not ask you. You will come or not as you wish.

I am pleased about all I hear of *Hamlet* and I shall applaud the work of the actors.[30]

This resigned mood soon vanished, however, when he was at last able to attend a general rehearsal. He had conceived of the play as a monodrama, in which everything was to be seen from Hamlet's point of view. In the first Court Scene, Claudius and Gertrude were seated upon their golden throne at the back of the stage, surrounded by golden walls. From the King's shoulders, as Edward Craig describes it, there came 'an enormous cloak of golden material, which spread out towards the front, covering most of the stage. Through cuts in this enormous cloak appeared the heads and shoulders of fawning courtiers; facing their King and with backs to the audience, they were like so many gravestones in a golden graveyard. Down in front, silhouetted against this undulating background, the solitary black figure of Hamlet sat alone, part of a great shadow.'[31] But as the rehearsal continued, Craig became more and more dismayed to observe how many radical changes had been made in his absence. Matters came to a head over the lighting for the 'Mousetrap' scene, and the rehearsal ground to a halt while vehement argument raged at the directors' table.

Craig's decor consisted of a large number of wooden screens that could be rearranged in different ways for different scenes; instead of using the curtain, these screens were to be moved in full view of the audience. Everything was in position for the opening scene on the first night when suddenly, Stanislavsky recalls, 'one of the screens began to lean sideways more and more, then fell on the screen next to it, and the entire scenery fell to the floor like a house of cards.'[32] Hastily the curtain had to be lowered and the screens rebuilt while the audience was already entering the theatre, and to lessen the risk of further disaster, they had no choice but to use the curtain during the performance itself.

Unaware of this hitch, the audience gave the play an enthusiastic reception. So popular was Kachalov as Hamlet that the Theatre had to break its rule of no curtain calls for actors. 'An overwhelming success,' Craig wrote in his day-book. Was it with conscious irony that Nemirovich chose as the theme of his brief curtain speech 'the brotherhood of artists'? Next day Craig wrote to his sister: 'It will do its best under the disadvantage of having cost the management over £14,000', and appended

21 Sept. 1935.

My dear Gordon Craig,
Your book about Ellen Terry
was till the last days in the
theatre. I am just coming from
the Crimea. It is such a pity,
that they did not thought
about sending it to me to the
South – it would be so nice
to read this interesting book
in my nice cottage near the
Black See.
I send you my best, my
sincerest thanks for
having thought of me.
With great interest and
emotion I will read this
book and think of you,
my dear beautiful old
friend
Yours
Olga Knipper-Tchekowa

Postcard from Knipper to Gordon Craig.
Craig's book on Ellen Terry was published in 1931.

a sketch of himself jumping through Stanislavsky's hoop.[33]

Like so much else surrounding the man and the production, the critical success of Craig's *Hamlet* was far more controversial, but it remained a popular item in the Theatre's repertoire for a number of years.

No one liked Knipper as Gertrude. Even Craig later admitted that she had been a 'disaster'. Playing the part again in 1921, Knipper felt better pleased. 'I'm no longer the dead Queen that I was then,' she told Stanislavsky.[34]

As for Craig and Knipper, they did not meet again until April 1935, when Craig was staying once more at the Metropole. Always sublimely indifferent to the world of politics, he could not understand why it was that Nemirovich now had to open his own front door. At sixty-three he was still the object of admiring attention and his rages still a sight to behold.[35] On arrival he sent a note to his 'Dear Temple' and they visited old haunts together. Returning home, he sent her a present which she acknowledged in her postcard of September 21st (her English by this time had become a little rusty).

More than twenty years later, on New Year's Day, 1956, a much mellowed Gordon Craig wrote to 'Dear madame Knipper, dear Temple' from Vence in the south of France. He had read in the English newspapers that she had been present at two acts of Peter Brook's *Hamlet* in Moscow. He had informed his very gifted young friend, Mr Brook, that he would be happy to go with him to Moscow to play the part of Ghost, at which he excelled, but for some unaccountable reason his offer had been turned down. Of course, he explains to Olga, he *is* eighty-four, gallantly adding—'much older than you'.[36]

Knipper was then eighty-seven.

In the long list of women in Gordon Craig's life, Olga Knipper occupies an unusual but relatively minor position. For her sake one would not have wished it otherwise.

CHAPTER TWENTY-ONE

Upheaval

There were only two things in Olga's life: Anton and the theatre. In Masha's life there was only Anton. After his death, she took up once more her old role as Anton's 'right-hand man', devoting the rest of her long life to two main tasks: collecting and editing his previously unpublished writings, in particular his correspondence, and preserving and running the White House at Yalta as a Chekhov museum; tasks to which she addressed herself with great singleness of purpose and at times remarkable courage.

Just a few weeks before his death, Masha had written to Anton from Yalta: 'Three students—two boys and a girl—came today and asked permission to look round your house and garden. I showed them the garden and gave them some roses, but didn't let them into the house. They walked round the paths with an air of reverence, and the girl kissed the roses.'[1] When Anton died, Masha found that she could not bring herself to remove any of the carefully arranged objects from his study and bedroom. Everything was left just as it was, including six newspapers received while he was in Badenweiler and left unopened in their wrappers on his desk, his sweet box with two peppermints inside (still there, apparently, when the first guide to the Museum was published in 1937!) and the large notice on the wall requesting visitors to refrain from smoking.[2] When Chekhov-lovers came to the house, Masha found it impossible to turn them away or to show them round without speaking of her brother, so that the White House became in effect a museum right from the time of Chekhov's death.

After 1904, Masha and Olga quickly forgot the jealous rivalry of the past three years and resumed their former friendship. They saw one another at regular intervals, either in the Crimea or in Moscow, which Masha, like the three sisters, was to hanker after all her life. Olga also remained friendly with other members of the Chekhov family, and it was through her that Michael Chekhov, Alexander's son, received an audition from the Art Theatre in 1912 and was thereby launched on a successful career as an actor and producer in Russia, Europe and America.[3]

In time of war the theatre thrives. During the First World War the Art Theatre played to packed houses. Anniversaries, always religiously observed, came and went: the two hundredth *Three Sisters* in November 1915, the two hundred and fiftieth *Cherry Orchard* a few months later. In the summer of 1916, after a tour in the south, several members of the company went on to the Caucasian spa of Essentuki, where they stayed at the sanatorium run by Dr Zernov. Sonya, one of the doctor's four teenage children, has vividly described her memories of that summer: her first sight of a lady with very dark, laughing eyes, who looked at her attentively and turned out to be Olga Knipper; the dinner party, where they followed every gesture, every word, from Stanislavsky, Lilina, Knipper and the others, with rapt and admiring attention; Stanislavsky deserting the adult table to find out the young people's views on art; excursions into the steppe, where Olga Leonardovna proved to be an excellent walker; being introduced by her to Kachalov, whose charm was so individual, his velvety voice so irresistible, that she felt an involuntary stiffening of resistance; a visit to the travelling circus, where Olga Leonardovna laughed so much that she could not stop crying; and the concert at the sanatorium, of which she writes: 'In their lives there had been so many concerts and evenings like that one. So many young people had surrounded them with worship and adoration, whereas for us meeting the Art Theatre was something special, unique and unforgettable.'[4]

By this time, the founder members of the company had dwindled in number. Already approaching fifty, Olga was used to thinking of herself as one of the 'old brigade'. Her reputation was secure. Once the war was over, she could look forward to many more Art Theatre anniversaries, many more serene years of worship and adoration; yet the most strenuous part of her career now lay ahead.

The Zernov children's next meeting with Stanislavsky was in Moscow, in February 1917. What had seemed so unattainable in 1905 was already a *fait accompli*. The old regime had fallen, the Tsar had abdicated, and power was in the hands of the Provisional Government. In Moscow the revolution was bloodless. Red flags again decorated the streets. Walking into the centre of the city, where huge crowds of soldiers and civilians were milling about aimlessly on the pavements, the Zernovs and their father encountered Stanislavsky. What struck them was not only his jaunty step, but the sight of his fur coat, thrown wide open with theatrical panache to reveal a large red bow on his chest.[5]

Because of the uncertain political situation there was no spring tour to Petrograd in 1917. Olga spent the summer in the Crimea. When the Theatre began its new season, the audience no longer consisted of the rich and well-educated, but was taken from all classes of society. Stanislavsky has described a performance of *The Cherry Orchard* given on the very eve of the Bolshevik take-over. They were afraid of trouble: how would this new audience react to Chekhov's gentle evocation of the life of the landowning class? But the play was listened to with close attention and received a tremendous ovation. After the October Revolution the composition of their audiences changed again. Many of the exclusively working-class spectators had never been inside a theatre before, let alone the Art Theatre, where audiences were traditionally expected to behave with the same sense of decorum and dedication to Art as the artists themselves. Stanislavsky found himself having to go in front of the curtain to remonstrate with them and on one occasion spoke 'more sharply' than he should have done. How did it happen, he wonders ingenuously, that within a very short time the attitude of audiences changed completely and boys scattered at his approach to warn the others that *he* was coming? To us the situation seems less puzzling. Stanislavsky in a towering rage must have been enough to inspire awe even in the boldest spirits.[6]

Late that autumn, Masha came to Moscow, where her nephew had recently died, but during her visit she contracted typhoid and was ill for two months on her return to Yalta. 'I'm almost well again,' she wrote to Nemirovich in February 1918, 'and my shaven head has already become covered with vegetation. I must still be needed in this world if I've managed to survive such a serious illness!!' She was hoping that Nemirovich might be able to send her some money from Chekhov's Art Theatre royalties. 'I've no cash at all, though there's money in my current account. But the bank's giving out such a tiny sum it's not even enough for food.' What made matters worse was that Mamasha (old Mrs Chekhov) simply could not grasp the implications of the social upheaval going on around her and did not understand the need for economies.[7] Masha was so heavily in debt that she was forced to do something that she had last done as a young girl, when the Chekhov family was living in the Moscow slums and desperately trying to keep its head above water: she had to earn money by taking in sewing.[8] 'I could just picture you,' Olga wrote, 'sitting with your needle in Anton's bedroom.'[9]

Meanwhile, in Moscow, the Art Theatre was continuing to function as best it could. Although it enjoyed special privileges, no one was spared the hardships of that first post-Revolutionary winter. Audiences in the unheated theatre might bundle themselves up in fur coats and hats; not so the actors. Olga was one of the lucky few who escaped serious illness, though she was exhausted by the daily walk to and from the Theatre, lost weight ('there are endless conversations everywhere about flour, butter, bread') and found her hair becoming greyer from day to day; had she not been playing Masha in *Three Sisters* without a wig, she would have been quite happy to go completely white. At night, she wrote to Masha, 'like you I've been playing desperate games of patience, glancing up every so often at the lights blazing in the row of requisitioned houses on the other side of the boulevard and at the reflection of the brightly lit windows in the liquid mud of the street—it's like being in Venice. From Gurzuf I received a letter with some violets inside—they made such a touching contrast to all the devastation and neglect, the filth and chaos, in which we're living. . . . I'm so tired mentally that on stage I lose all sense of shame and don't even try to *act* when I feel exhausted. Sometimes during a performance I think how easy it would be to go mad because you cease to understand what's going on around you and don't react to anything.'[10]

At the time of the 1905 Revolution, Olga had never doubted her ability to judge the situation: she had felt confident that Anton would have shared her initial hopes and later disappointments. Her reaction to the Bolshevik Revolution, like that of so many intellectuals, was one of bewilderment and disorientation. Everything was so new, so alien, that the mind could not keep up with the rapidly changing course of events. If only Anton were still alive, 'how skilfully he would be able to sort everything out, to grasp what is real and essential, and reject everything superfluous. . . . I look round at Anton's portraits and think: why isn't he alive at a time like this? It would make life so much easier!'[11]

But Anton was not alive and Olga did not know how to speak for him. Whatever her other feelings may have been—and one recalls her earlier comment: 'It's not revolution that one wants, but freedom, room to move, beauty, romanticism'—there can be no doubt that she was too far removed from feelings of class hatred not to have been completely horrified by the ruthless pursuit of 'class enemies' in Russia after the Revolution. In 1905 she had written: 'How many victims there were who belonged neither to one party or the other.'[12] How many more such innocent victims she must have known after 1917.

In her attitude to religion, as in her social attitudes, Olga was more ambivalent than Anton. Anton could write with remarkable sympathy about religious figures (in *The Bishop*, for example) and was characteristically helpful and generous to such people in real life; but he remained uncompromisingly a non-believer.

Olga told him once that she had given up praying after her father died,[13] but this emotional withdrawal from religion was less absolute than Anton's intellectual repudiation. It was not social convention alone that made her anxious to arrange the requiem services immediately after Anton's death. In 1918 one notices that she has begun to write 'Christ be with you' at the end of some of her letters.[14] The phrase is conventional, used in the way that 'God bless' might be in English, but acquires significance at that time and in that context. It may be interpreted as an unspoken reaction against the aggressive godlessness, callousness and philistinism of the age—not a narrowly religious reaction, but a reaction in the name of those humane values that she had absorbed from Anton.

CHAPTER TWENTY-TWO

The Years of Wandering

The cold hungry winter of 1918–19 was even more arduous than its predecessor. 'Everyone has work on the side,' Olga wrote to Masha in January, 'as it would be impossible to live on one's salary.' When she is given a hard-boiled egg as a present, she bears it off home 'like a precious object': it is the first egg that she has seen for three months. Horse-flesh is being eaten everywhere, dogs are being sold. How she longs for the south—for warmth, the sun and the sea![1] Before sending off this letter, Olga received a telephone message from Yalta to say that Mamasha had died.[2] She was in her early eighties and had outlived her famous son by more than fourteen years. Olga grieved to think that it had not been possible for her to be buried next to Anton, and recalled the images of Mamasha that remained most vividly in her memory: playing patience, whispering prayers in her little white room with its icon-lamp, swopping newspapers with Anton, and telling stories about her youth: 'How seriously and intently she always described everything!'[3]

Since food was still relatively plentiful in the south, it was proposed that the whole Art Theatre company should go on an extended southern tour. This plan had to be abandoned, however, because the chaotic state of the railways would have made it impossible to transport all their bulky paraphernalia. Instead, with the Theatre's official blessing, arrangements were made for a smaller group, led by Kachalov and Knipper, to present a three-week season in Kharkov. Administration was in the hands of Nemirovich's assistant, Sergei Bertensson, who later settled permanently in America and from whose account much of the following information is taken.

They left Moscow on May 1st, 1919. As cultural emissaries, they were given V.I.P. treatment: exclusive use of a third-class wagon (there was no other class), recently disinfected to protect them against typhoid, and with Red Army guards to protect them against the hordes of would-be passengers who besieged the train at every station. Their mood was carefree after the rigours of Moscow. They were travelling light, since the weather was already warm, and the further south they went, the more plentiful food became.

In Kharkov they lived in the Hotel Russia, which had long since ceased to function as a hotel and needed thorough cleaning, but still retained an air of pre-Revolutionary elegance. They opened to an enthusiastic reception with *The Cherry Orchard*. In Moscow they had paid little attention to the reports of civil war in the south, but now they found that Kharkov was on a military footing. Theatre performances had to begin at six; a curfew began at nine. Once they inadvertently broke the curfew and were all arrested. At night convoys of lorries began passing through the town in increasing numbers. All civilian rail travel was stopped. The newspapers exhorted the population to remain calm, and printed inflated accounts of Red Army successes.

The swift dénouement, however, took everyone by surprise. At six o'clock on May 24th, the curtain went up as usual on *The Cherry Orchard*. Scarcely had the second act begun when Bertensson was disturbed by strange noises from the street. Running out to investigate, he found that Kharkov had already been occupied by the White Volunteer Army under General Denikin. No hint of what was going on had reached the packed auditorium. The curtain was drawn, an explanation given, and the audience told that the theatre would remain locked until the streets were quiet. Loud applause then greeted the announcement that the performance would now continue from the point where it had been interrupted.

So, less than a month after leaving Moscow, the Kachalov

Group, as it came to be called, found itself cut off from Bolshevik Russia and the Art Theatre. One of the actors, Podgorny, anxious to rejoin his wife in Moscow, decided to take a chance on crossing the front line. Thanks to an officer friend in the Volunteer Army and his official Art Theatre papers, he reached Moscow without difficulty and was welcomed back with open arms. But if one had returned, why not the others? The Group was to hear later that they had been denounced in Moscow as traitors, who had cunningly planned their defection to the Whites before their departure. This was untrue, and as Bertensson points out, for one person to negotiate the front line was very different from a whole theatrical troupe carrying all its costumes in huge, unwieldy baskets. Nevertheless, had any of them felt strongly committed to the Bolshevik cause, they could have followed Podgorny's example. Instead, like many others, they preferred to await further developments from the relative comfort and security of the south.

In Kharkov there was general rejoicing and they were asked to extend their season until the end of June. Then they disbanded for two months' holiday in the Crimea, having agreed to reassemble in Sevastopol at the beginning of September (unless, of course, Moscow had fallen before then).

From Sevastopol they sailed to Yalta, where they gave two performances and were warmly welcomed by Masha Chekhova at the White House. Knipper's seaside cottage at Gurzuf, 'The Blue Gate', then became their artistic headquarters while they prepared the coming season's repertoire, for whatever happened, they were determined not to let down the good name of the Art Theatre. Their first engagement was in Odessa. Denikin's spectacular advances, however, had been followed by an equally spectacular retreat, and the anxious inhabitants of Odessa were in little mood for theatre-going. Their next engagement, in Rostov, meant crossing the Black Sea to Novorossisk. Because of the influx of refugees from the north, Novorossisk was in a state of chaos, and they had to spend the night sitting jammed together on the floor of the filthy railway station. Worse was to follow in

Rostov. The town was in the grip of a typhoid epidemic and their theatre had been turned into a hospital. Fortunately, they were able to hire another one and attracted large audiences despite the epidemic, but they could not wait for the day when they were free to travel south to Yekaterinodar.

Here life was still relatively normal and they were looking forward to a long season. It was not to be. Soon came news that Rostov had been evacuated. Electric lights were banned after seven except in government buildings, hospitals and theatres. Audiences went on trudging to the theatre through the unlit streets in undiminished numbers, but it was clearly only a matter of time before Yekaterinodar had to be evacuated.

Where could they go next? Apart from the Crimea, there was nowhere of importance still in the hands of the Volunteer Army. To the south lay Georgia, formerly part of the Russian Empire, but at that time an independent republic. The director of the State Theatre in Tiflis, the capital of Georgia, was a former pupil of the Art Theatre school. Would he be willing to receive them? He cabled back that he would be delighted.

To reach Tiflis, they had to return once more by train to Novorossisk. It was now February 1920. There were no passenger coaches, so they had to travel in goods wagons, where they either froze to death, or almost expired when the iron stoves heated up too rapidly. Since there was not the slightest chance of finding living accommodation in the town, these goods wagons, standing in sidings outside the station, became their permanent home for several days while they tried to find a boat to take them on to the Georgian port of Poti. Kachalov's son remembers Olga Knipper at this time. A fierce north-easterly gale was blowing from the sea, whipping up the dust and sending it whistling through the loose slats of the wagon. Inside, everyone lay huddled in corners, staring fixedly ahead or trying to sleep—everyone, that is, except Olga Leonardovna. There was never anything defensive about her attitude to life. Sitting bolt upright on a suitcase in the middle of the wagon, with another case propped up beside her on which she had placed a lighted candle, she was absorbed in reading. The book was in a gilt morocco cover and had an ivory paper-knife inside. Neither the dust and discomfort, nor the distant sound of gunfire, seemed to touch her in the least.[4]

After numerous refusals from foreign captains who became immediately suspicious on hearing that they were a company of actors from Moscow, they eventually found an Italian steamer willing to take them to Poti as deck passengers. They had to carry all their luggage and costume baskets by hand from the railway sidings to the harbour. As they approached Poti, the relief at leaving revolution and civil war behind them was tempered by uncertainty: how long would they have to remain in Poti before being summoned to Tiflis and what would they live on? Then came a stroke of luck. Among those waiting at the harbour was the head of the local militia. He had been a student in Moscow, and could scarcely believe his eyes when he recognised on board the faces of so many of the theatrical idols of his youth. He immediately offered his services. They were all taken to stay with private families, a telegram was sent off to Tiflis announcing their arrival, the immediate financial problem was solved by a swiftly arranged concert performance, while a generous advance from government funds was more than enough to tide them over until they began earning again. A comfortable passenger coach was put at their disposal for the journey to Tiflis. After the crowds and the squalor, after the filthy goods wagon in Novorossisk and their begging approaches to foreign captains, this sudden reversal in their fortunes seemed almost too good to be true.

The same spirit of generosity and admiration for the Art Theatre was to characterise the whole of their stay in Georgia. Arriving in Tiflis at the start of spring, with a bleak Russian winter just behind them, they were overwhelmed by the warmth and colour of the southern capital, with its exotic mixture of East and West, of Europe and Asia. For the rest of the season they shared the State Theatre with the national opera company. They polished up existing productions and introduced new ones. They were acclaimed not only by the Georgian public but by the many Russian refugees for whom Georgia was providing a half-way house while they waited to see if they would be able to return to Russia.

With funds restored, they left to spend July and August on holiday in Borzhom, where the Georgian government had offered them the use of the former hunting lodge of the late Grand Duke Nikolai Mikhailovich. They were due to return to Tiflis for the start of the autumn season. Borzhom was the attractive spa in the Little Caucasus, surrounded by richly wooded hills, where Masha and Ivan Chekhov had first heard the news of Anton's death. It was to imprint itself on Olga's memory also, for it was here that she had to take the most difficult decision of her life.

After those few months of respite, the political situation had begun to close in again. There was every reason to think that before long the Bolsheviks would take over Georgia, despite its independent status. The Group had to act quickly. Until this time all their plans and movements had seemed provisional, but the decision that faced them now was stark and perhaps irrevocable: whether or not to leave for the West.

On September 11th, Olga wrote from Tiflis to Masha:

So it seems as if we're almost certainly leaving, Masha. We'll travel via Sofia, the Slav countries, Prague—then maybe Berlin, Paris? I don't know. I've written to the Maklakovs in Paris. . .

For a whole month in Borzhom I went through agonies and couldn't make up my mind to go to the West; in the whole of my life I don't think I've shed so many tears. And I wouldn't give my consent. I kept expecting that at any moment we'd be summoned to Moscow. From Moscow we received heaps of letters, all very touching and full of lyricism, but no one would take the definite decision to recall us, i.e. officially. We had a crazy day—we were in conference from morning to night and couldn't decide what to do. They sent us the minutes of conferences at the Theatre. It gave me such a pang to be suddenly reminded of the atmosphere of our Theatre like that!

How I want to go to Moscow! How tired I am of wander-

The Years of Wandering

ing!... There's no hope of seeing Moscow, the graves. We're thinking of leaving at the end of September. You wouldn't come with me, would you, Masha?

We've been back in Tiflis for a week now.... We're giving nine performances here, finishing with *The Cherry Orchard*.

Masha, think of me when our little steamer takes us across the Black Sea. Heavens, how ashamed and disgusted I feel at going abroad! Life's just the same here, Masha, you can buy what you want, though prices have shot up—but oh what boredom, what boredom! There's food for the body only....

Well, Christ be with you! We'll both go on living and maybe we'll see one another again! I think of Gurzuf with such tender love and longing—everyone starts looking brighter when we recall it.[5]

Although they had avoided any political involvement, the Group had obviously been hoping that a White victory would enable them to return to a Moscow liberated from the Bolsheviks. They had gambled and lost. Olga Knipper was under no illusions about the seriousness of the decision now facing them. 'Maybe we'll see one another again,' she writes to Masha—clearly envisaging that they may *never* be able to do so. Younger members of the Group may have seen only the short-term excitement of new adventures in new countries; others may have felt that exile was preferable to enduring the material privations of life in Russia under a political regime which they detested. For senior members like Knipper and Kachalov, the dilemma was more acute. The Art Theatre, *their* Art Theatre, was still in Moscow; to be split in two could only multiply its already acute problems. For them Nemirovich and Stanislavsky were not just the Theatre's directors, but close associates in a successful communal enterprise of twenty years' standing. Should not allegiance to the Art Theatre override all other considerations? Knipper, it seems from her letter, would have gladly responded to an official recall from Moscow, but the Group was officially still in

225

disgrace; Nemirovich and Stanislavsky dared not make any move on their own.

Counterbalancing allegiance to the Theatre in Moscow was the knowledge that without her the Group was liable to collapse. By Art Theatre standards their repertoire was large, but their numbers were so small that such unlikely people as the wardrobe manager's son were having to walk on in *The Cherry Orchard*. They had only three major artists: Kachalov, Knipper and Maria Germanova. If any one of these were to defect, it would be fatal. Their decision, in other words, had to be unanimous: either they all went to the West, or they disbanded. How difficult for Knipper to let down the others after all they had been through as a group in the previous fifteen months.

There was one further consideration in her mind that did not apply to the others and which made her decision so agonising. This was Anton. Her farewell letter to Stanislavsky is full of Chekhovian motifs. 'Our life and work together have come to an end . . . "Life in this house has come to an end", as they say in *The Cherry Orchard*. . . . I'm echoing Irina's words: "We shall never, never go to Moscow". ' There is even an echo of Arkadina's speech to Trigorin when she refers to Stanislavsky as 'a huge chapter in my life'. [6] Knipper's tone in this letter, though regretful, is calm and in no sense apologetic. It is the letter to Masha that shows how deeply undecided she was, how torn between conflicting emotions. There is something shamefaced about the question—'You wouldn't come with me, would you, Masha?'— and Olga answers it herself when she asks Masha to think of her as their steamer crosses the Black Sea. Olga must have known that Masha would never leave Russia, would never leave the White House at Yalta that was shortly to become the official Chekhov Museum. There were only two things in Olga's life: Anton and the theatre. In Masha's life there was only Anton.

So the decision had been taken; but would it be so easy to carry out? The Georgian government was willing to issue them with Georgian passports, but at the last moment had to withdraw its offer of a loan. On the very day, however, that this disastrous news was broken to them, they were unexpectedly approached by a Russian émigré organisation, which was planning to open a cinema studio in Milan. The organisation offered the Kachalov Group a substantial advance in Western currency if the latter agreed to be in Milan by January 1st, 1921, for the filming of their production of Hamsun's *In the Claws of Life*. Should the film company default, the advance was not repayable. And that in fact was exactly what happened: before January the company went into liquidation and the Group kept the money.

In Sofia they introduced *Three Sisters* into their repertoire. They did not have the music for the famous Skobelev March that is being played in the background while Masha is saying farewell to Vershinin in the final act, but Bertensson recalls that he managed to obtain a march 'close in mood to the Skobelev' from one of the local military bands. Kachalov's son tells a different story, more colourful but in essence perhaps more credible. At rehearsals the March had been picked out on the piano by the producer. A military band was engaged only in time for the dress rehearsal—the bandmaster wearing lots of braid and sporting a huge military moustache. At the right signal the band struck up, but horror of horrors, instead of the evocative melody familiar to Olga Knipper for twenty years, they launched into a rousing Prussian march. Olga rushed towards the orchestra pit, looking like some wounded bird in Masha's long black dress. Hurling some incomprehensible words at the startled musicians, she rushed back again and fled towards her dressing-room. Here they found her sobbing uncontrollably, her head resting on the table, vowing that she would never play Masha without the Moscow music. The young Bulgarian composer employed as the theatre's musical director was hovering in confusion in the background. Even the bandmaster was there, plucking nervously at his moustache. They were all anxious to help. Kachalov whistled the Skobelev March to the composer, within a couple of days the latter had orchestrated it, and on the following day the band performed it without a hitch.[7]

Such an outburst would certainly have been consistent with

the homesickness that Olga experienced throughout the 1920–21 season, when the Group's main engagements were in Sofia, Belgrade, Zagreb, Vienna, Prague, Berlin and Copenhagen. As in Anton's time, her own life and her life on stage in *Three Sisters* began to coincide; like the sisters, she longed desperately for Moscow and feared that she might never be able to reach it. The mere mention of the word 'Moscow' was enough to make her burst into tears. In the spring of 1921 the Group was joined by a young actor-producer from the Art Theatre, Richard Boleslavsky, who had managed to slip out of Moscow with the aid of his Polish passport. The news that he brought confirmed their suspicions. The Theatre's repertoire had been reduced to three old war-horses: *Tsar Fyodor*, *The Lower Depths* and *The Blue Bird*; Nemirovich had started an Art Theatre Musical Studio. They were clearly needed back without delay, and Olga was hoping for the arrival from Moscow of a go-between—the actor Podgorny, who had left the Group in Kharkov—to discuss with them the terms of their return. Neither she nor Kachalov would let the others know before August 1st whether they intended staying or not.[8] But no go-between appeared, August 1st came and went, and theatres had to be hired for the coming season. 'You mustn't think that we don't want a reunion,' Olga wrote to Stanislavsky in September. 'When we're all together, it's my dream that Stanislavsky will spread his wings and create the kind of theatre that is needed now, and that it will be in Russia!'[9]

On September 18th, 1921, in Prague, they gave the première of their first independent production: a free adaptation by Boleslavsky of the Craig-Stanislavsky *Hamlet*, with Kachalov and Knipper in their former roles as Hamlet and Gertrude. Prague had already become a centre of Russian émigré life, and the Group was asked by a Russian publishing-house to contribute articles to a book on the Art Theatre. Olga Knipper was persuaded to write on the Art Theatre and Chekhov. She had always resisted attempts to persuade her to write her Chekhov memoirs, and if she changed her mind now, perhaps it was because in exile she felt so cut off from her Russian past.

Bertensson, Kachalov and his wife were invited to her hotel room in Prague to listen to the draft, which culminated in her description of the last days at Badenweiler. 'When the reading finished,' writes Bertensson, 'for several minutes none of us could bring ourselves to utter a word. Dusk was falling, it was getting dark in the room, but it didn't even occur to anyone to switch on the light or start talking. . . . Her narrative, so simple and yet so profound, revealed in her the presence of a genuine literary talent that no one had previously suspected. And she herself probably least of all.'[10]

Prague, Vienna, Bratislava, Vienna again, Berlin . . . Ahead of them lay Dresden and Leipzig, then Copenhagen and a tour of Sweden. The longer they stayed away, the less chance there seemed of being able to return. It was true that at long last they had begun to receive letters from relatives and friends in Russia, which spoke of certain changes and improvements there . . . but everyone was completely taken by surprise when in February 1922 they were contacted by Nemirovich with a formal request to return to Moscow. The Theatre had been invited to America for the whole of the following season. Without the Group this venture could not be undertaken, and Nemirovich listed those whose participation he regarded as particularly vital. In the mean time he was sending Podgorny to Berlin to discuss all the details with them.

Podgorny arrived promptly, proving that it was no longer impossible for Russians to travel abroad. With the introduction of NEP (the New Economic Policy), life in Russia, he explained, had returned more or less to normal; there were goods in the shops again and travel was no longer difficult. As for all the rumours that the Group had been proscribed for plotting to defect to the Whites, these were quite false (though in that case it is hard to see why no attempt had been made to recall them earlier). They were free to return with absolute confidence that no reprisals would be taken against them.

The Group deliberated for several days. From the outset there had probably been a wide spectrum of opinions among its members about the desirability of returning to Russia. Eventually a sizeable minority opted to stay in the West, and Maria Germanova became the leading figure in what was later known as the Prague Group of the Moscow Art Theatre. (In 1928 a group led by her presented a season at the Garrick Theatre in London, and annoyed the Soviet government by styling themselves the Moscow Art Theatre Company.)

There was never any doubt that Olga Knipper would be among those to return. She wrote off at once to Nemirovich, saying how much she was looking forward to helping 'to rebuild a single, and as you write, "magnificent" theatre'.[11] For Olga, as for Anton, the grass was always greener on the other side of the fence.

Having fulfilled all their engagements and said goodbye to the 'exiles' at a farewell supper party in the little Berlin restaurant where they gathered after performances, the Moscow party left for Russia towards the end of March, 1922.[12] They approached the Soviet border with mixed feelings. They were returning to their home country, but they were also entering the Soviet Union, as the archway at the entrance to the frontier station, adorned with the hammer and sickle, and the inscription 'Proletarians Of All Countries, Unite', so clearly reminded them. There was nothing, however, to remind them of the Russia they had known in 1918–19. The customs officials were brisk and polite, the porters looked like the porters of Tsarist times, and the stations were no longer swarming with crowds of dirty, dejected travellers surrounded by heaps of bundles and suitcases. It was a fine spring day as they approached Moscow, like the one on which they had left Moscow for Kharkov almost three years before. They reached Moscow early in the afternoon. A joyful throng of relatives, friends and colleagues had gathered to greet them. The years of wandering were over. They were home.

CHAPTER TWENTY-THREE

The White House

However great its psychological turmoil, Olga's life from the spring of 1920 onwards had at least been one of material comfort and security. Not so that of Masha. The pleasant summer of 1919 soon became a distant memory. During the Civil War period power changed hands several times in the Crimea. Masha once told her niece that the White House had been searched on no less than nine occasions for such things as weapons, gold, uniforms, and even barrels of fish stolen from the harbour, and that during the last of these searches she had seen an order for her own arrest.[1] In November 1920, when Soviet power finally became established in the Crimea, she was appointed official custodian and director of the Chekhov House and Museum.[2] She does not appear to have been tempted by Olga's invitation in the previous September to accompany her to the West or to have experienced any qualms about entering Soviet employment. Her first duty was towards Anton and his memory. To fulfil it, she had to remain in Russia, and she was quite prepared to efface herself and to make the necessary adjustments to whatever happened to be the prevailing political regime.

Anxious since the early days of the Revolution about the fate of the Chekhov archives which had been left in her flat in Moscow, Masha decided that she had no alternative but to go to Moscow herself in the summer of 1921, leaving the house in the care of her brother Ivan and his wife. It was not an easy decision to take. The conditions of rail travel were appalling, and she was now approaching sixty. The journey that in Anton's time had taken just over two days was to take Masha more than three weeks.

At Simferopol she boarded a coach full of soldiers and peasant women, and managed to secure a position on the top shelf, normally used only for passengers' luggage. The air was heavy with cigarette smoke. All the passengers were arguing and swearing. Catching sight of Masha, they began shouting and calling her a bourgeois, demanding that she should be put off the train at the nearest station and her place given to 'one of our own people'.

In the midst of this uproar Masha happened to notice that a boy travelling with his mother on the shelf below was reading Chekhov's famous short story, *Van'ka*, about the nine-year-old shoemaker's apprentice who writes a homesick letter to his grandfather in the country.

'Do you know who wrote that story?' she asked him.

The boy told her.

'Well, I'm his sister.'

The boy's mother asked Masha all about herself. When the peasant women heard who Masha was and that she was planning to undertake the whole of that arduous journey entirely unaided, they immediately became sympathetic and offered her food and drink.[3]

Having completed her mission, Masha returned to Yalta, more or less intact despite further unpleasant travelling adventures, only to find that in Yalta alarming news was waiting for her. Chekhov used to joke that his house would make a perfect target for the British fleet. Eyecatchingly white, perched on the hillside and framed by the mountains beyond, of irregular design, with a curious tower on top in which Masha had her bedroom, it was one of Yalta's most obvious landmarks. Not only, however, from the sea. It was also an irresistible temptation to the groups of anti-Bolsheviks and bandits still hiding out in the mountains behind Yalta. During Masha's absence the house had been attacked by one of these groups. All her clothes, she wrote to Nemirovich, had been stolen, leaving her with nothing but what she had arrived in.

The White House

My brother defended the house courageously! They fired on
mother's old room, where my brother and his wife were living.
The bullets pierced the window-panes and lodged in the walls.
Now I'm entirely alone in the house at night and can scarcely
sleep a wink, of course. I'm frightened and don't know how I
shall go on living. It's a gloomy prospect—famine, armed raids,
no money to live on! The town's completely dead, especially
the part where our house is. Please don't forget me, remember
how frightened I am and what I'm going through. If there's
any money to spare, please send me some—from royalties.
Please. How I'd like to live in Moscow! There's still a pleasant
atmosphere in your theatre—one's reminded of the old days
and it's comparatively clean![4]

Masha's fears were justified. 'There's been another raid,' she
wrote in February, 'on this occasion Shalyapin's trunks suffered.'
(Shalyapin had entrusted furniture and possessions to Masha's
care when he and his family left the Crimea for Moscow in
February 1918.) 'I'm living on a powder keg! They'll be sorely
tempted to come back for the rest of the trunks.'[5] Unable to face
any more nights alone, she had to engage a woman to live in, but
feeding her meant having to go short herself. She was invited to
Moscow to organise a Chekhov museum there, 'but if I leave this
house, not a thing will remain untouched, they'll strip the
window-frames, the doors and the floorboards, just as they did
with Dostoyevsky's house.'[6]

That same winter, the young Konstantin Paustovsky, who
later became one of the best known Soviet writers, was travelling
by boat from Sevastopol to Yalta. As the evening light faded, he
searched the coastline for some sign of life, but could not make
out even the glimmer of a candle. Apart from an occasional rifle
shot in the distance, Yalta was quiet and pitch dark. They were
advised not to go into town, as you risked being stopped by bandits
and stripped naked or even killed; and if not by bandits, then by
the Whites still hiding in the mountains. Though he knew that he
was foolishly tempting fate, Paustovsky felt an irresistible urge to

walk into the town. 'The night held its secret, and I could not live until I had found the clue.' He walked for a very long time, moving stealthily, hugging the walls, though occasionally when the wind rose and rustled in the cypresses, he walked more boldly. Then, after bumping into a stone wall, he came upon a gate with a name-plate beside it. Beyond the wall he sensed that there was a thickly grown garden, although not a rustle came from it.

I took out my matches and struck three at once, so that the flame should be as bright as possible: I had decided to read the name on the plate.

By the light of the yellow flame I had time to read the words: *The House of Anton Pavlovich.* . . .

Then the matches blew out in the wind and, immediately, a shot came from somewhere above the Autsky highway. The bullet zoomed low over the wall, and with a soft crackle snapped a twig.

The second bullet went higher and was lost in the gloom in which lay the benumbed sea.

I squeezed myself into the recess of the wicket-gate. At once, everything was forgotten—my strange state, so like a sickness of the spirit, and the whole of my strenuous journey, as on a tight-rope, across the sinister town to this place, to Chekhov's house.

I had been to this house as a boy in 1906, two years after Chekhov's death, and had now come back after sixteen years.

Why I had come all the way to this remote suburb and to this particular house, I could not understand . . . but of course it already seemed to me that I had come deliberately, that I had known my destination, that I had something urgent on my mind which had brought me here.

What could this be?

Suddenly and deeply, I felt the bitterness and pain of all I had lost in life. . . . I pressed my face against the stone wall and, trying hard not to, wept all the same.

I wished the gate would creak open, and Chekhov come out and ask me what was wrong.

I raised my head. Pale in the darkness, the mountains shone with a magical and steady light. I guessed that snow had fallen on them—crisp dry mountain snow that crunches underfoot like gravel.

And suddenly I felt the nearness and certainty of happiness. Why, I don't know. Perhaps because of that pure snow-whiteness which looked like the distant radiance of a beautiful country, or because of my sense of sonship—long unexpressed and driven to the back of my mind—towards Russia, towards Chekhov.[7]

Happiness would come again, he believed, to the starved and frozen Crimea. And indeed, with the passing of winter, life began to look a little brighter for Masha. The bandits did not come back after all for the rest of Shalyapin's trunks. Olga had returned to Moscow and in June sent Masha the royalties that she had collected from the productions of Chekhov's plays by the Kachalov Group. She had written several letters to Masha while abroad, but none of them had got through. 'I'd come down to the Crimea myself if I were free. Drop me a line or two about the Gurzuf cottage . . . Heavens, what a lot of gravestones have sprung up!'[8]

Olga also wrote of the Art Theatre's proposed visit to America. Masha had accompanied the Theatre on its first foreign tour in 1906, and the thought of exchanging troubled Russia for America must have filled her with longing. But Masha knew that her future lay in Yalta, showing visitors round the Museum and gradually reconciling herself to 'the smell of sweat and cheap perfume' in Anton's study.[9] Although she might complain, with justification, that she felt tired to death, she was still driven on by the determination to preserve her brother's White House intact for future generations.

CHAPTER TWENTY-FOUR

❦

Knipper in America

How green was the grass on the other side when Olga returned
to Russia in the spring of 1922?

To Masha in June her tone was cautious. 'Here I am in
Moscow,' she wrote, 'and so far I'm glad to be in Russia; but I
don't know what things'll be like in future.'

Writing in August to one of the Kachalov Group who had
remained in the West, she made no complaint about the home
that she now shared with other members of her family. It was on
the outskirts of Moscow, in the workers' barracks of a brick
factory that had been closed since 1915. She delighted in being
able to gaze at the simple Russian countryside again, and in
making a fuss of her great-niece—'catching up, I suppose, on
what's been missing in my own life'.[1]

And the Theatre?

Here the grass did not look green at all. 'How tired I am of
listening to conversations about the Theatre, I want to talk and
think about Art.' She was glad that the edition of Anton's letters to
her that she was preparing for publication offered a pretext for
not becoming too involved in theatrical affairs. For some reason
she had not spoken once to Nemirovich, 'and I think it's better
that way'. Apart from the estrangement caused by their exile,
Olga found it hard to reconcile herself to the idea that Nemirovich
was now producing operetta within the walls of the Art Theatre—
those walls which seemed to cry out for something more original
and inspiring.

All this was very far from the magnificent new theatre, united

236

and harmonious, that Olga had dreamed of in exile. The Art Theatre had lost its way. What kind of role was there for it under Bolshevism? In February 1923 Stanislavsky wrote to Nemirovich: 'One must get used to the idea that the Art Theatre no longer exists. You seem to have understood that sooner than I did.'[2]

The irony was that Stanislavsky wrote those words just when the Art Theatre was in the middle of its most successful foreign tour.

In accepting the invitation from the impresario, Morris Gest, to visit America, the Theatre was in a sense putting off the evil hour—extricating itself from an awkward situation, just as it had done at the time of its first foreign tour in 1906.

So, after only six months in Russia, Olga Knipper found herself on the move again. 'I seem to be getting out of the habit of leading a settled life,' she complained to Masha.

At that time, the Art Theatre was still an independent body, financed by its shareholders. 'It is hard to believe now,' writes Bertensson, 'that we left Russia without any political commissars attached to our organisation to keep an eye on our behaviour, and to tell us what to do and what not to do.'[3] Their tour took them first to Berlin, and then to Prague, Zagreb and Paris. Olga was very nervous before the first Paris performance of *The Cherry Orchard* and could not sleep afterwards. What feelings this play was bound to evoke in the hearts of their émigré compatriots: all those former Grand Dukes, Grand Duchesses and Ambassadors, who, as the *New York Times* reported, had sacrificed their last penny to buy a seat.

On December 27th, 1922, they embarked at Cherbourg on the White Star liner *Majestic*, bound for New York. For months Stanislavsky had been nervously anticipating the voyage. Was the *Majestic* absolutely seaworthy? How many funnels did it have? On learning that it had three funnels, he felt a little safer. Olga Knipper, as one of the few English speakers in the company, had to work hard as an interpreter. On New Year's Day they gave a charity concert and Knipper sang some songs. 'I'm not an admirer of hers as a singer,' commented Stanislavsky, 'but on

237

this occasion it wasn't bad.' Then in mid-ocean they suddenly struck a force 10 gale. Stanislavsky was confined to bed for two days. His fears were not entirely misplaced, for the *Majestic* was only on its sixth voyage and had never had to face storm conditions before. Reports appeared in the American press that the ship was in danger, but Stanislavsky strongly suspected that these were inspired in New York by Morris Gest with the aim of creating the maximum publicity for their arrival.

Born in Odessa, the enterprising Gest was the son of Russian Jewish parents and had come to America as a young boy. Only with difficulty had he been persuaded that it would be inappropriate to invite a local Russian bishop, in return for a contribution of a thousand dollars to church funds, to greet the company on the quayside wearing full ceremonial robes and carrying a cross. Instead the Mayor of New York was supposed to present Stanislavsky with the keys of the city, but this also fell through because of the ship's late arrival. Even without the Mayor and the bishop, the reception on January 4th was lively enough. Reporters swarmed on board before the ship had docked to interview Stanislavsky, who was annoyed at having to miss the Statue of Liberty. Newsreel shots were taken of him apparently waving to a huge crowd of well-wishers. In fact, only a small group of friends was waiting on the quayside, and just as the *Era* correspondent in 1906 had referred to the Russian fashion of 'much indiscriminate kissing', so the *New York Times* described the Russian men 'rushing into one another's arms, with salutations upon both cheeks, while those of this country contented themselves with hearty handshakes.' Traditional gifts of welcome were supposed to be offered, but the bearers had become so tired by the long delay while the ship docked that all the gifts had been piled up in the car that was waiting for Stanislavsky. 'Later,' he wrote, 'these gifts were taken off to be photographed. Where they are now, I don't know. Maybe they were hired!!!' As Stanislavsky, Gest and Bertensson, followed by a convoy of cameramen, sped through the streets of New York on their way to the Hotel Thorndyke on 56th Street West, a policeman stood on the running-board of their car, whistling furiously to warn other policemen to clear the route.

The visit had already provoked a controversy in the press, which, as Christine Edwards writes in *The Stanislavsky Heritage*, 'was a stronger force in promoting the advance sale of tickets than all the expensive advertising indulged in by Gest'.[4] On December 25th, under the headline 'Calls Art Theatre Agent of Soviets', a report appeared of an allegation by the American Defense Society that one third of the receipts from the tour would be paid to the Soviet government, that members of the company had pledged themselves to return to Russia and not to conduct anti-Soviet propaganda, and that those who agreed to conduct propaganda on behalf of the Soviets would be shown special preference. Gest denied the charge, pointing out that a clause in his contract specifically prevented any of them from engaging in propaganda work. Stanislavsky had already been questioned in Paris by reporters who refused to believe in the Theatre's independent status. Cross-examined by the American press, he stated: 'We have no connection with the Soviet government. We are interested only in art. It is our art that we have come to bring you, not politics.'[5]

On January 8th they opened at Al Jolson's Theatre on 59th Street with *Tsar Fyodor*. There had been a veritable fever of expectation, wrote the *New York Times*, the theatre was packed with people who could not even get standing room, and the evening proved to be one of intense excitement. Not even a ghastly hitch before the second scene could mar the triumph. Misinterpreting the assistant stage manager's signal, the American stagehand raised the curtain while the actors were still hurrying to their positions. To the credit of the audience, no one so much as giggled, even at the sight of the Patriarch clutching his heavy robes round his middle and scurrying across the stage in a pair of ordinary shoes. When the curtain had been lowered again, Stanislavsky, pale as a sheet, rushed backstage and urged the cast to save the Theatre's reputation by redoubling their efforts. 'Never before have we scored such a success, either in

Moscow or elsewhere,' he reported to Nemirovich, who had decided to remain in Moscow, to look after his Musical Studio. 'They're saying that it wasn't a success, but a revelation.'[6]

Such a reception was extremely gratifying, although Stanislavsky could not forget that the production of *Fyodor* was now a quarter-of-a-century old. Equally venerable were the other main items in their repertoire: *The Lower Depths, Three Sisters* and *The Cherry Orchard*. This did not matter at all, however, to audiences who were seeing the Theatre for the first time. 'The most distinguished company that has visited our shores in modern memory,' John Corbin wrote on January 23rd; and on March 4th he affirmed his conviction, 'very strong from the outset, that we have here the most competent theatre of the modern world and the most stimulating'. Small wonder that 'the box-office at Jolson's these days frequently bends around the corner and a new record for receipts is being established'; and that the original eight-week season had to be extended to twelve.

'To tell you the truth,' Stanislavsky wrote to Nemirovich, 'I quite often wonder why the Americans praise us so highly. Our ensemble! Yes, that impresses them. But what impresses them infinitely more is that in a single company there should be three or four individual artistic personalities whom they discovered straight away and appreciated more highly than in Europe.' And there were others in the company for them still to discover. An American company might possess one outstanding talent— Stanislavsky was highly impressed by the Shylock of David Warfield and found John Barrymore as Hamlet 'far from ideal but very charming'—but not three or four talents all appearing in the same play. In the same letter in which he wrote that 'the Art Theatre no longer exists', Stanislavsky could also write that after seeing the best that Europe and America had to offer, he was in no doubt that 'ours is the best theatre in the world'.[7] This was less of a paradox than it might seem, for most of the individual figures who had so impressed American audiences by their acting were members of the 'old brigade': Kachalov, Knipper, Moskvin, and, of course, Stanislavsky himself.

Knipper in America

Their box-office success was due largely to New York's Russian population. Stanislavsky reckoned that the number of spectators who could afford their fantastic prices and understand at least some Russian was fifteen thousand, but these spectators visited the theatre and even the same play many times over. Cultured Americans accounted for about a quarter of their audiences. It seems unlikely that the average New Yorker was tempted to sample the exotic fare being offered at Al Jolson's. His reaction, had he done so, is imagined in a poem which appeared in the *New York Times* on February 11th, 1923, and which amusingly catches the spirit of the times. (The reference to a 'great big goof' is to Stanislavsky in the part of Gayev.)

A 100 Per Cent American Speaks

The wife says 'What you want to see them for?
It's only a bunch of dirty Bolshevicky
That's tryin' to turn the country upside down
The way they done their own. Why don't they stay
In Russia, where they belong?' And so I says,
'Well, I'll go there and give the stuff the razz.'

I stands in line for a couple of hours or so
And finely gets a seat in the gallery
In with the foreigners and all the garlic.
The name of the show was called 'The Cherry Orchard',
And the first two acts was sure the bunk to me—
A lot of people runnin' up and down
In a great big room, carryin' suitcases and trunks,
And whisperin' in the corners. After that
They sat around in a silly-lookin' field,
With hay, and done a whole lot more talkin',
And it sounded like they was talkin' English
But makin' up words just while they went along.
I couldn't make out nothing from the program,
And so I ast one of them Bolshevicky

Chekhov's Leading Lady

Behind me if he wouldn't put me wise
And so he says it was a real rich family
That didn't know how to manage property
Because they couldn't keep their minds on it
And when they tried to talk, got makin' jokes.
And one of the birds that useta be a slave,
Or I guess his old man was, well, anyway,
This bird was tryin' to tell 'em what to do.
He says that they should take the Cherry orchard
And cut it up in little lots—you know,
Like Pleasant Heighths—suburban subdivision—
That sort of thing, and sell 'em. And that way
They could save half the old farm. See? But they
Just wouldn't listen. They was nice enough,
But nit-wits, see? And in the third act, then,
They're havin' a dance, and waitin' for the news
From the auction sale. The brother went to the auction
With money that they borrowed from a aunt,
And just when they're havin' the swellest kind of a time
The brother comes back. And he says the money
Wasn't enough. And so they lost the place.
And what do you think? The guy that was a slave
He went and bought it! And he comes in soused,
And yells around about how proud he is.
So then the last act's where they got to move,
And packin' up the stuff, and sayin' good-bye,
And—listen, I can't make out yet how it happened
But when that great big goof looked at the orchard,
And I could hear the axes cuttin' the trees,
And all of a sudden this six-foot bird breaks down,
And stuffed his handkerchief right in his mouth,
And real tears in his eyes—can y' imagine?
I just set there and blubbered like a baby.
I sure do hope nobody didn't see me.
Just think of a bunch of low-down Bolshevicky
That can't talk even a word of English, makin'

242

Knipper in America

A hard-boiled egg like me cry like a kid!
And me not understandin' what they said!
I tell you what. It's just like I was watchin'
A movie where somebody told me what
Was goin' on, and not a wild movie, either,
Hardly anything happenin' at all,
But with the best actors that ever was.
Why did it get me? I ain't goin' again.
I don't like things that I can't understand,
And yet can get me like them foreigners did.

John V. A. Weaver

Not every reaction to the tour was favourable. The American patriots who regarded the company as a group of Soviet agents were matched by those Bolshevik sympathisers for whom the Theatre was too reactionary. One trouble-making correspondent to the *New York Times* claimed that it had always been out of touch with the people, putting the blame on the 'multi-millionaire' (!) Nemirovich-Danchenko for choosing plays of a conservative character, and claiming that the Theatre refused to put on their cherished Chekhov 'for the new audience of "dirty Red guards and common rabble that filled every seat", as Kachalov said in the course of an interview in Berlin two years ago.'[8] (One cannot imagine him saying anything so tactless.) More serious reservations were expressed by the critic, A. E. Thomas. His attack was not on the Russian actors—'thoroughly drilled by a fine director'—but on the 'neurasthenia' with which they had been greeted. Were all those superlatives that had been trumpeted up and down the land generated by sincere enthusiasm, or by the desire to run after what was novel? 'Slopping over is one of our failings as a people. It is still possible for some of us to hear the names of Kachalov and Stanislavsky without genuflecting.'[9] He may have been thinking of the enthusiast who declared that 'his experience at Al Jolson's made him fervently pray that he might never again enter an American theatre'. How

243

could such people be sincere when they did not understand a word of Russian? In 1906 the *Era* correspondent had written that 'no matter how little the hearer understands of the language, he cannot fail to grasp the meaning and be moved by it'; but he also noted that *Three Sisters* had been greeted with less enthusiasm than either *Tsar Fyodor*—a historical drama with relatively simple characterization—or *The Lower Depths* and *Uncle Vanya*, both familiar to Berlin audiences from recent productions in German. In New York Gest had English translations printed of all the plays, but Corbin wrote that 'where effects are to be achieved only by the subtlest intonation, the most delicate phrasing,' (as in Chekhov's plays) 'it fares ill with those whose entire vocabulary is da, da.'[10] This is well put, but Thomas overstates the case by his arbitrary assertion that 'Russian psychology and feeling and character are utterly foreign to Occidental comprehension'. Bertensson recalls the sight of one young American girl watching the last Act of *Three Sisters*, holding the English translation in one hand, while with the other she wiped away her tears with a handkerchief.

Because of the venerable repertoire, Olga Knipper had to take on a very heavy load of work. Of her Irina in *Tsar Fyodor* Corbin wrote: 'The manner in which the actress holds her due place in scene after scene with no uttered word, and with rarely a turn of the head or a glance of the eye, is truly amazing, or would be if it were not shared by all the principals.' His description of her Nastya in *The Lower Depths* as 'a very solid figure' is more double-edged: though still as upright as ever, Olga by this time had become round and matronly. Corbin also found it difficult to associate her 'Junoesque form and demeanor' with Ranyevskaya in *The Cherry Orchard*, the prey to disjointed emotions, just as the herculean presence of Stanislavsky and his vigorous, vibrant voice seemed ill suited to the feckless Gayev; but he admitted that ignorance of the language made it impossible for him to judge these characterizations. Candour compelled him, however, to make the 'ungracious' comment that the heroine in Turgenev's *A Lady from the Provinces* 'did not seem to be the requisite thirty-eight but rather to belong to the generation of the old dandy Count whom she was twirling around her little finger'.[11] But it was as Masha in *Three Sisters* that this discrepancy in age should have been most glaring. Here was Knipper, aged fifty-four, playing the part of a lively young woman who is twenty-four when the play begins and still only twenty-eight at the final curtain! Yet such was the conviction of her acting that this discrepancy appears to have been ignored. 'They've taken a liking here to my Masha,' she wrote modestly, 'and many people understand her very well indeed.'[12] American women sent her fan letters and 'wept buckets', according to Stanislavsky, as they watched the play.

It was a rule at New York's fashionable Colony Club for women that men were never invited. As a mark of special esteem, the Club decided to break its rule by giving a banquet for the Art Theatre. For two hours Stanislavsky listened to speeches of which he understood not a word, including one by John Barrymore, who said that he was proud to belong to the same profession as the Moscow actors. Afterwards the visitors sang Russian songs and Knipper read two of Chekhov's stories in English. 'With new-found boldness I stopped at the end of the first paragraph and asked: "Do you understand me?"—whereupon the whole hall burst into applause.'[13] Later she gave a matinée on her own, reading in English her reminiscences of Chekhov and some of his short stories.

Olga found America hard to fathom. It was like 'some kind of mechanism that's been wound up, everything's going round, each little wheel engaging with the next—and you keep crossing your fingers and hoping that nothing's about to fly off. The expressions on people's faces are quite impassive—so everything must be all right!'[14] She did not take to the noise and bustle, to the garish advertisements that lit up the streets at night-time, and the crowded cinemas and dance-halls—'oh, those dances of theirs!' Stanislavsky's particular aversion was to the revolving glass doors in restaurants and apartments. 'Many a time,' wrote an American journalist, 'he has been caught, to spin round and round until rescued.' But there were compensations: the Negro Theatre; grapefruits ('it's worth living in America for them alone,' wrote Stanislavsky); and the fulfilment of Olga's dream of a lifetime— to be able to have a hot shower in her room after returning from an evening performance.

As for the people, her immediate impression was that they did not have an ounce of artistic appreciation between them, so that she felt disgusted at first by the Theatre's huge success in New York. (She had been equally scathing about the French, who struck her as narrow-minded *bourgeois* for all the incredible beauty surrounding them in Paris.) She modified this opinion after *Three Sisters* and *The Cherry Orchard*, when members of the audience came round to her dressing-room, and she realised that those impassive expressions did not tell the whole story; but she seems never to have shared the wholehearted enthusiasm for the Americans that was constantly expressed by Stanislavsky. 'They are charming, simple and hospitable people,' he wrote home, 'without European snobbery, most like the Muscovites of Tsarist times.'[15] A Frenchman in the theatre, he told an interviewer, takes nothing for granted and leans back to scrutinise you, but the American is with you from the outset and follows the action with the credulity of a child. Among Germans, Russians feel obliged to speak quietly; in America you can talk and shout in Russian, and everyone is simply delighted. 'They are the most like Russians of any foreigners I have met.'[16]

By the end of February Olga felt completely exhausted. This, of course, was the commercial theatre; in Moscow she would never have been expected to give eight performances in six days for two weeks running. Between the matinée and evening performances on Fridays and Saturdays she tried to sleep on a camp-bed in her dressing-room. She was suffering from insomnia: not getting to bed until about two, sleeping for a couple of hours, lying awake until eight or nine, then dropping off for another hour or so and waking up feeling dreadful—'I'm just not used to sleeping late.' Many of the company were struck down by Spanish influenza and bronchitis. To the young friend in Moscow,

Liza Konshina, who was helping her with the edition of Anton's letters, Olga wrote that she had felt weak and ill during the première and first week of *The Cherry Orchard*. In fact, as Stanislavsky reported, the situation had been very much more serious. On the morning of the première Knipper's temperature was over 101°. 'She didn't dare take it in the evening. We had no one to replace her. I rushed round to Gest. "The performance must go ahead. I can't allow a change of play. Let anyone take the part. It's no business of mine if you've not brought enough actors. You'll have to stand all the losses." Knipper, ill, with a temperature ranging between 101° and 103°, played all sixteen performances and saved us.'[17]

When the New York season was over, the Theatre went on tour to Chicago (where they were able to celebrate the Russian Easter in traditional style), Philadelphia and Boston, returning for a short farewell season in New York.

On June 2nd, after a performance of *Three Sisters*, the curtain came down for the last time. What followed was one of the most remarkable demonstrations in the history of the American theatre. The curtain was raised and lowered dozens of times. Stanislavsky was prevailed upon to address the audience in French, but still the demonstration continued. Then he addressed the audience in Russian. Nearly half-an-hour passed before the applause finally subsided.

Stanislavsky had already signed a contract with Gest to bring the Theatre back to America for the following season. Rumours were rife that he intended to settle permanently in America, but although he gave careful thought to a proposal that he should spend six months in the year helping to establish an American national opera company, it seems that he never seriously entertained the idea of leaving Russia. Explaining why he had agreed to a second season, he claimed that so far the Theatre had been merely preparing the ground in America and would now be able to reap a rich harvest, and that this would give them the financial security needed to prepare a new repertoire, without which, it seemed to him, the doors of the Theatre in Moscow might as well remain closed. There was also a pressing personal reason. Stanislavsky was a great family man. His son, Igor, had been suffering for some time from T.B. and needed to spend the next four or five years in Switzerland. To pay for this costly treatment, Stanislavsky was banking on the royalties from two books for which he had signed contracts with an American publisher. In the summer of 1923 he was feverishly at work on what became the best-selling and widely translated *My Life in Art*. It was essential for the book's success that it should appear while Stanislavsky was still a public figure in America, where, thanks to the popular newsreels, he was recognised in the street far more often than in Moscow.

The summer of 1923 was a disaster for the Art Theatre. Proposed seasons in Germany and England had to be cancelled. They were forced to spend several weeks rehearsing in France, where the cost of living was far beyond their budget. The short Paris season failed to pay off their debts, and they were only able to sail to America by pawning valuables and putting in money of their own.[18]

Eleonora Duse, the last of the great tragediennes, now aged sixty-four, was already in New York, giving two matinée performances a week to capacity audiences. 'She can't act any more,' Stanislavsky wrote of her performance on November 11th in Ibsen's *The Lady from the Sea*, 'but there's still a kind of music in her.' Olga found the experience harrowing. 'You felt that you wanted to carry her off the stage and surround her with care and kindness, just so that she shouldn't act.' After the performance, Stanislavsky and Olga presented her with bouquets, and Stanislavsky made a long speech in French. 'She held my hand,' Olga wrote, 'and was trembling all over.'[19] On the 19th Duse attended the Art Theatre's opening night—a performance of *The Brothers Karamazov* given in her honour—but stayed only for one act, as she was performing herself on the next afternoon. Always a great admirer of the Theatre, she surprised them by returning on the following evening after her own performance and watching the play through from beginning to end.

For one matinée by Duse the box-office takings might be as much as $10,000. The Art Theatre's taking for eight performances in their first week were only $14,000, compared to $45,000 in the previous season. As Olga had anticipated, their novelty had worn off, in spite of a much wider repertoire. All Gest's flair for publicity was now being lavished on Duse and Max Reinhardt's company. Stanislavsky's forecast of a rich harvest proved absurdly wishful thinking; as the tour continued, the only question was whether they would earn enough to pay off all their debts. Eventually, the actors had to forego their salaries.[20] After New York, they spent three weeks in Chicago, one week respectively in Philadelphia, Boston, Washington, Pittsburgh, Detroit, Cleveland, Brooklyn and Newark, and three days each in New Haven and Hartford. Their success was phenomenal, but the profits from these short visits were offset by the huge cost of transporting all their personnel and paraphernalia from one place to the next. In Washington Olga Knipper was among the delegation of senior members of the company who shook hands with President Coolidge at the White House.

Yet their success with the critics remained undiminished. Of *Ivanov* Corbin wrote that the Theatre had not played more brilliantly in New York, and he singled out Knipper's Sarah as a superb performance. In a leading article he referred to their 'highly original and, as we hope, epoch-making art'. Stanislavsky told Nemirovich that if their success in the first season had been noisy and popular, on this second visit it had been 'more aristocratic'. He rightly judged that they had made a lasting impression on 'the genuine intelligentsia and the few Americans who are exceptionally cultured and crave for genuine art'—on those individuals, in other words, who were most likely to shape the American theatre of the future.[21]

As for Olga, in December she wrote cheerfully that she was 'acting a lot but finding life easier than last year'. She had recently given her lecture on Chekhov ('fifty minutes in a foreign language—can you imagine?'), followed by four of his short stories; and she was clearly one of those artists of whom

I

Stanislavsky writes that they 'are accepted in society here and regarded not only with respect but genuine affection'. In February Stanislavsky wrote that the long tour had demoralised everyone apart from Luzhsky and Knipper, 'who complains least of all and is always happy to fall in with everything'. By this time, however, even Olga was beginning to wilt. Her whole life seemed superficial and mechanical, she wrote from Chicago, and she felt tempted just to run off the stage. 'The day after tomorrow I'm reading Chekhov's stories in English for 100 dollars in a rich American private house on the shores of Lake Michigan—see what I've come down to!'[22] Yet their success in Chicago was fantastic. Crowds blocked the street outside the theatre, invaded their hotel and burst into the railway carriages to bid them farewell.

Whatever the state of their morale, whatever the rebellious noises being made behind the scenes about the non-payment of salaries, they finished in a blaze of glory. At New York's Imperial Theatre they gave a farewell week with a full programme of revivals. At the final performance on May 11th both Stanislavsky and Knipper made speeches. On the following Monday they gave a single farewell concert performance, for which hundreds were unable to obtain tickets. Various scenes from the plays were acted, Chekhov's rollicking one-act comedy, *The Marriage Proposal*, proved ideally suited to the occasion, and Olga gave a reading of his short story, *The Student*. What the *New York Times* referred to on May 13th as 'the disturbance occasioned in this country by the Moscow Art Theatre' did not die down until the early hours of the morning.

Beneath the columns describing the Moscow players' glorious farewell, a small news item appeared. Its headline ran: 'Duse Buried At Asolo'. She had died while on tour in Pittsburgh, and her body had been taken back to Italy to be buried in the little cemetery of her home town.

CHAPTER TWENTY-FIVE

The Difficult Years

Although the Art Theatre's visit, and Stanislavsky's System in particular, subsequently had a great influence on the theatre in America, in post-Revolutionary Russia the Art Theatre was no longer in the forefront of theatrical developments. Its position on the right of the Soviet theatrical scene was not unlike that of the Imperial Theatres in Tsarist times: it enjoyed considerable prestige, continued to emphasise the basic theatrical skills and to value excellence above experimentation, and in time developed into a huge state-run theatrical bureaucracy. Throughout the twenties, although it went some way towards conforming to the spirit of the times and put on a certain number of plays by Soviet writers, it found itself exposed to steady criticism and abuse from the theatrical left for the conservatism of its methods and repertoire. Contrary to Stanislavsky's fears, however, Soviet audiences did not tire of the Art Theatre; with so much that was novel going on in other theatres, it must have provided a reassuring link with the older cultural tradition.

If Russian theatre in the early years of the century had been dominated by Stanislavsky and Nemirovich, the man who imprinted himself on Soviet theatre in the twenties was Meierhold: Knipper's fellow student at the Philharmonic, one-time actor of the Art Theatre and creator of the roles of Kostya in *The Seagull* and of Tuzenbach in *Three Sisters*; the champion of the theatre of show, of spectacle (not for one moment was the spectator to be allowed to forget that he was in the theatre), at the opposite extreme to Stanislavsky's theatre of authentic emotion (where the spectator should be made to feel how easy it would be to join in the conversation taking place on the stage in front of him); Meierhold with his daring transformations of the Russian classics —grotesque distortions, his critics called them; Meierhold the anti-traditionalist and Bolshevik sympathiser, who later fell foul of the Soviet regime while the more conservative Art Theatre survived.

By the time of her return from America, Olga Knipper was in her mid-fifties. 'I was told that you sometimes feel depressed about your artistic career,' Nemirovich wrote to her. 'But I take the opposite view. The youthful roles are behind you and you'll be starting a splendid new life as an actress.' Olga replied that she was looking forward eagerly to working in a disciplined theatre again, to acting and not just parading herself before an audience.[1]

The future, as always, looked full of promise, but the reality, as in 1922, proved otherwise. She gained no satisfaction from repeating two of her old roles in the 1924–25 season. When the Theatre held its traditional party on New Year's Day, 1925, Knipper was conspicuously absent. 'I think she feels,' her friend Liza Konshina explained,

> that she's been cast to one side and isn't needed any more. But, of course, the theatre means everything to her and it's a tragedy for her now to feel unwanted. Sometimes she comes out with the remark: 'How I wish I could start speaking from the stage in my own voice!'[2]

Speaking in her own voice could mean only one thing for Knipper: acting in the plays of Chekhov. But until 1928 she had no opportunity to do so. The reason was simple. Chekhov was not performed by the Art Theatre during those years. Writing in October 1922 from Berlin, Stanislavsky himself had expressed the feeling that he no longer wanted to act in Chekhov. 'When I'm playing the farewell scene with Masha in *Three Sisters*, I begin to feel embarrassed. After everything that we've lived through, it's impossible to shed tears because an officer is going away and the officer's lady has to stay behind.'[3] During the

The Difficult Years

1920s Chekhov's plays, but not his stories, were widely regarded in Russia as bourgeois and counter-revolutionary. Had he staged them, Stanislavsky would have been handing ammunition to those critics who already accused the Art Theatre of living in the past.

Olga soon learned at first hand that although Chekhov's literary status might be assured, his ideological status was still a matter of dispute. In October 1924 she took part in a Chekhov Evening to commemorate the twentieth anniversary of his death. It had not been a pleasant experience, she reported to Masha. She had protested unsuccessfully against the use of a huge ceremonial hall for the occasion, since she needed a more intimate setting in which to read her reminiscences of Chekhov. The audience had been divided into 'two sharply opposed camps'—presumably those who insisted on seeing Chekhov in political terms and those who refused to; so that what appealed to some seemed completely irrelevant to others. Masha had anxiously wanted to know what attitude Lunacharsky, the Commissar for Education, would adopt to Anton's work 'in the light of the present situation'. His speech was very long, Olga wrote, 'but I wasn't listening. I told him I wasn't going to. I think it was about how the "Chekhov world-view" has been misunderstood, but no one could give me a clear idea.'[4]

In the autumn of 1926 she fell ill and went down to Yalta to convalesce at the White House with Masha. There had been a break in the friendship while Olga was in America, perhaps dating back to an earlier period (although Olga continued writing to Masha from exile and in the summer of 1922); but whatever the cause, the breach was healed by an exchange of letters in the autumn of 1924. Now, after Olga's return to Moscow, the sixty-three-year-old Masha writes in terms that recall the earliest days of their friendship. She had woken up next morning, looked sadly at the empty bed opposite and said mournfully to herself: my echo has disappeared! How pleasant their life had been together! Now the Museum work had piled up again, but she did not feel in the mood for sitting down at her desk and going through a heap of boring papers. 'Keep well, God bless, I send you more kisses than you can count.'[5]

Knipper's habitual good humour in the Theatre only ever deserted her when she did not have enough to do. There were painful and sometimes stormy scenes with the casting director. She eagerly seized the opportunity to play a very small part in Vsevolod Ivanov's *Armoured Train 14–69*, which had its première in November 1927 and was the first play to be performed by the Art Theatre with a contemporary Soviet theme. Then in May 1928 Stanislavsky revived *The Cherry Orchard*, using the pre-Revolutionary decor. (One Soviet critic, sympathetic to Chekhov, later protested that the play was kept in the repertoire merely as a 'museum piece'.)[6] Knipper retained the part of Ranyevskaya that she had created twenty-four years earlier. Was this an act of kindness by the Theatre? Not entirely. In September 1928 Olga was sixty, but still sufficiently youthful and attractive to carry off the part of the middle-aged Ranyevskaya; though audiences who watched her playing the part throughout the 1930s must have felt that they were looking at a page of theatrical history. But her first real 'break' in the 1920s did not come until she was chosen to play the lead in an adaptation of Dostoyevsky's short novel, *Uncle's Dream*, a production that took so long to reach the stage that it was nicknamed 'the slow goods train'.

The autumn of 1928 was more like old times. Olga found herself hectically busy with rehearsals, performances and concert appearances. At the end of October the 30th anniversary of the Art Theatre was celebrated with a lavishness that made up for their inability to celebrate the 20th anniversary in 1918. Lunacharsky delivered his usual long speech. Stanislavsky and Nemirovich exchanged their usual pleasantries but the undercurrents of tension between them did not escape the audience. For all their long collaboration, they were never close friends, and the association had recently been under great strain when the Art Theatre refused to make a rehearsal room available for Nemirovich's Musical Studio. Among the items included in the jubilee concert on the following evening was the first Act of *Three Sisters*, which received a tremendous ovation. Towards the end Stanislavsky, playing Vershinin, began to experience a feeling of tightness round his chest. As the pain became worse, only his sense of artistic discipline prevented him from running off the stage. When he finally staggered to his dressing-room and collapsed, the doctor diagnosed a violent heart attack. Stanislavsky, sixty-five, had acted for the last time, and his health remained precarious for the remaining ten years of his life.

During the 1929–30 season Knipper had two important first nights. In *Uncle's Dream* she took the leading part of Moskaleva, and in *Resurrection*, an adaptation of Tolstoy's novel, she played Countess Charskaya. According to Turovskaya, these two satirical roles marked a new stage in Knipper's development as an actress, but both roles were taken from the classics and from upper-class society. Her casting as a 'woman of the people', as Klara, the old working-class revolutionary in *Fear* by the young Soviet playwright, Afinogenov, was a completely new departure. For this reason Knipper must have expended even more than her usual amount of time and nervous energy on preparing the part. The play was to be the Theatre's only new production in the 1931–32 season. At the end of the dress rehearsal Stanislavsky found himself in an awkward predicament. For the sake of the production, however, he decided without a moment's hesitation to drop Knipper from the part of Klara and replace her by another actress. True to the discipline of the Art Theatre, Knipper accepted the decision without a murmur, and the incident would later be quoted as a model example of how uncompromising the Theatre could be in its artistic standards. Within a day or two Knipper reappeared in the Theatre, outwardly composed and in good humour. One is left to imagine how much effort that composure had cost her, and how bitter the pill had been to swallow. Much later she admitted that Stanislavsky had been perfectly right—Vilenkin states categorically that Knipper could never portray working-class women or peasants, and certainly not women revolutionaries—but then, as if thinking aloud about something very important and painful, she added: 'The theatre can be a cruel place. Cruel and even merciless.'[7]

* * *

In the summer of 1929, following his heart attack of the previous autumn, Stanislavsky went to convalesce in Badenweiler, where he was treated by the same Dr Schwörer who had attended Chekhov a quarter-of-a-century earlier. Sonya Zernova, the young girl on whom the Art Theatre had made such an impression in the summer of 1916, wrote to him there from Paris. In his reply Stanislavsky recalled his years of friendship with her family and thanked her for sending him such a charming and undeserved letter. 'In our coarse and cruel age, when, like everyone else, even the young folk are withdrawn or filled with hatred or malice, such letters as yours are a rarity, and I thank you for it twice over. I am delighted that since I am temporarily abroad, I am able to answer it, as I should not have succeeded in doing so from Russia.'[8]

'Our coarse and cruel age': they were words that Olga Knipper would certainly have echoed; and the age was to become very much crueller.

Having been made an Artist of Merit of the Republic in 1923 and a People's Artist of the Republic in 1928, Knipper enjoyed official favour in the Soviet Union, but she was in complete sympathy with the Theatre's policy of rejecting plays that were crudely political in character. 'It's good,' she wrote of a play they were considering in 1929, 'but again it's all about Mensheviks, Bolsheviks, Social Revolutionaries and so on.'[9] We do not know, but we can guess, what her reaction was in 1932 when the Soviet government replaced Chekhov's name in the Art Theatre's official title by that of Gorky. Was this because Gorky had become the Theatre's favourite playwright, just as Chekhov had once been? Not at all; they had not staged a single new production of a play by him since the Revolution. The decision had been handed down from above. Gorky was close to Stalin, had come to occupy the leading position in the official literary hierarchy, and in 1932 became the first head of the newly-founded Writers' Union. There followed a predictable spate of Gorky productions by the Art Theatre. To Lilina, then in France

The Difficult Years

with Stanislavsky, Knipper wrote in January 1934 that they were 'obliged' to put on Gorky's play, *Enemies*. Nemirovich had offered her a part. 'I said yes, of course, being so starved of work, but it's rather a dated play and in my opinion, not very interesting.'[10]

The founding of the Writers' Union, and the elevation of the tenets of 'socialist realism' into an official orthodoxy from which no deviations were to be allowed, brought to an end the comparative freedom that had existed in literature and the theatre in the 1920s. Realism alone was permissible; all other forms of theatrical experiment were liable to be branded as 'formalism'. The voices of the theatrical left, including those of the Art Theatre's noisy critics, began to fall silent. Not that the Art Theatre itself could afford to take liberties. Bulgakov's play, *Molière*, had to be withdrawn after only seven performances in 1936, because the theme of how Molière's life and artistic freedom were poisoned by a bunch of hypocritical officials struck too close to home.[11]

Visiting Paris in 1934, Stella Adler and Harold Clurman, of the Group Theatre in New York, met Stanislavsky. 'Regally handsome, with beautiful white hair,' Stanislavsky told them that he enjoyed a special relationship with Stalin, but they noticed that when any question relating directly to the regime came up, he 'glanced about to see if some stranger might be listening. Once he murmured "There are things going on . . ." but stopped himself from saying any more.'[12]

To Clurman, visiting Moscow in the following year, the theatrical scene seemed full of excitement. Theatres were packed and there was no shortage of interesting productions. With Cheryl Crawford he met Nemirovich, 'trim and elegant with a finely-cut aristocratic beard', at a preview of *Romeo and Juliet*, where the play's director leaned forward to hear Nemirovich's opinion 'with a reverence approximating anxiety'.[13] The American visitors were not aware of any undercurrents of change, though a Russian student told Clurman that Meierhold's 'experimental' productions were now being frowned upon as 'formalist'.[14]

Chekhov's Leading Lady

In August 1937 the Art Theatre went on a short tour to Paris. At first sight there is something incongruous about such a tour taking place at that particular time, when the Stalinist Terror was at its height and well known figures in the literary and theatrical worlds were being hounded, sent to labour camps or lined up in front of firing squads; but perhaps that was precisely the point—to say to the rest of the world: 'Look, here is our famous Art Theatre bringing the new Soviet culture to the West. Why should you imagine that anything untoward is happening in the Soviet Union?'

There are no published letters by Knipper from Paris, but on her return she wrote an article about the tour for the press. She seldom wrote articles of this kind, and from the anxiety with which she falls over herself to say all the right things, one may infer that its contents were officially inspired.

Before leaving Moscow, she writes, they had been given a very interesting briefing on the political situation in France. The success of their opening performance, of Gorky's *Enemies*, had exceeded all expectations. Visiting the World Exhibition, they had been immediately struck by the gleaming whiteness of the Soviet pavilion and its uplifting, all-embracing theme. She had been to see a French version of Gorky's *Mother*. So popular was its political message that the actors sometimes had difficulty in making themselves heard above the constant bursts of applause! When they returned to their native land, it was with the feeling that their trip had demonstrated over and over again the power and strength of their country.

This article does not add to Knipper's reputation as a writer. It might have been written by any hack journalist of the time (and perhaps was). Fortunately, however, there are two other, more convincing, pictures of Knipper in Paris to set alongside this official one.

The first is provided by Sonya Zernova. On August 19th she wrote to her sister:

Yesterday I was at the last performance given by the Art

The Difficult Years

Theatre—*Enemies*. It's the only play where the acting is good, especially Kachalov and Knipper. After the performance I went up to Knipper in the street. She didn't recognise me, of course. When I told her my name, she seized hold of her head in her hands. She asked after you and all our family. She was dressed in a bright red dress and a bright red cloak, with a wonderful fox fur, a real 'people's artist'. I asked her if it was all right for me to walk along with her, she answered that there was no label on my head saying who I was and no one would guess, but she said this in such a hesitant tone of voice that I realised it would be better for me not to. I also said to her how strange it was that there should suddenly be this rift between Russian people, and she said: 'Yes, we're living in terrible times, the only question now is how to stay alive and in one piece.' She looks very strong and healthy, she's become a stout, imposing old lady.[16]

The second picture is provided by Leo Rabeneck, the young student at the hotel in Badenweiler in 1904, with whom Olga had continued to be on friendly terms up till the Revolution. He writes:

The last time I saw Olga Leonardovna was in 1937, when the Art Theatre was on tour in Paris.

At the end of the performance I went along to a small *bistro* where the artists usually had supper after the theatre.

As I entered, I caught sight of Olga Leonardovna sitting at a table between two men I did not know. On catching sight of me, she quickly looked down at her plate and did not look up again until I had gone past. I concluded that she was unable to see me for a talk.

Early next morning I was walking along the *Champs Elysées* when suddenly, quite by chance, I came face to face with Kachalov. We stopped, embraced one another and kissed, and I said to him: 'I'm so glad to see you. I was at your theatre yesterday, I wanted to see Olga Leonardovna and went along to the *bistro* where you all have supper, but when she saw me come in, she stared down at her plate and I decided she didn't want to meet me.' To this Kachalov replied:

'But Lev L'vovich, didn't you realise she was sitting with two of our archangels, how could she possibly have spoken to you? We're kept under very tight control here and not allowed to mix with the émigrés.'

Kachalov began glancing round and I realised that he was afraid of being seen with me . . . We said goodbye and kissed one another, and I asked him to kiss Olga Leonardovna's hand 'on my behalf' and to tell her that in view of the conditions they were living under, I should not persist in trying to see her.[17]

Both these pictures are distressing, but there is something peculiarly abhorrent about the thought of Olga Knipper flanked by her two archangels and unable to speak to the person who was with her at the time of Chekhov's death.

In August 1938 Stanislavsky died at the age of seventy-five. Not long before, he had performed an act of courage and generosity. Meierhold's position had been steadily deteriorating throughout the 1930s; in January 1938 his theatre was liquidated, and he found himself out of work and ostracised. At this point Stanislavsky stepped forward and invited him to assist on the production of *Rigoletto* that he was preparing for his Opera House. But fate was not to be cheated much longer. Meierhold was arrested in June 1939 after making a speech at the All-Union Congress of Stage Directors: a speech in which he did not recant as expected, but outspokenly criticised the state of the Russian theatre (where you could only tell one inept production from another by the degree of its mediocrity), and defiantly asserted that if this was the best of which socialist realism was capable, he would rather be called a formalist. A fortnight after his arrest, his wife, the famous Jewish actress, Zinaida Raikh, was found murdered in their apartment, her body horribly mutilated; the 'intruders' were never caught. Meierhold's end is obscure. A story was put about that he had been transferred to the provinces at his own request, but it has since been stated that he died in Moscow in February 1940. It is unlikely that his death was natural either.[18]

In April 1940 Nemirovich presented a new production of *Three Sisters*, the first new Chekhov production since the Revolution. The part of Masha was to be played by Alla Tarasova, the Theatre's most distinguished actress in the years between the wars. 'I just can't imagine what my feelings will be like when I watch it,' Olga wrote to Masha in Yalta.

As the final Act was drawing to a close on the first night, one of Knipper's younger colleagues, Maria Knebel', arrived at the Theatre in time to take part in the backstage celebrations. On entering the building, she caught sight of Olga Leonardovna, standing alone in the dark empty foyer. Her forehead was pressed against the wall and she was crying. Knebel' was already too close to be able to pass by unnoticed. 'It's all gone,' Olga Leonardovna said to her, wiping away her tears and smiling. 'All gone.'[19]

Was it only, as Knebel' assumed, 'her' production of *Three Sisters* that Knipper was regretting? Or did her tears express an accumulation of grief: grief at the realisation of everything that had gone during those difficult years?

There was Stanislavsky, the most famous of her dramatic partners: Astrov to her Yelyena, Gayev to her Ranyevskaya, and —best remembered of all—Vershinin to her Masha in *Three Sisters*. With his death, even though the octogenarian Nemirovich was still alive and working, the Art Theatre as Knipper knew it may be said to have ceased to exist. Perhaps there were thoughts in her mind of Meierhold, the Tuzenbach of the original *Three Sisters* production. Her association with him went back even further than with Stanislavsky. He was the most brilliant of her contemporaries. In the debates of the twenties and thirties she had never adopted a partisan attitude, taking the view, as Trigorin does in *The Seagull*, that 'there's room for everyone'. Now his career was over and his fate unknown. Even his name dared not be mentioned. But above all there was Chekhov, Chekhov's world, the world of *Three Sisters*, with 'its deep quiet poetry of Russian life and the Russian soul that is deeply implanted in the human heart and will remain there for ever'.

In that coarse, cruel age, where had *that* gone?

What had happened to the hopes expressed in the finale of *Three Sisters*: 'Our sufferings will turn into joy for those who live after us, peace and happiness will reign on earth, and we who are alive now will be remembered with affection and gratitude'?

How unbearable to have to listen to *those* words again in the light of everything that had happened in the course of the difficult years.

When the performance was over, Olga went backstage to congratulate the new cast and firmly disagreed with those who tried to assure her that the old production had been far superior.

CHAPTER TWENTY-SIX

辈

Olga's Last Appearance

Knipper's old age was inevitably saddened by the deaths of those with whom she had been most closely associated in the original Art Theatre family. Nemirovich-Danchenko, Lilina and Vishnevsky all died in 1943. One link with the past remained, however, and the most important link of all. Masha was still alive and living in Yalta. Or was she?

On November 8th, 1941, Yalta was occupied by the Germans. Masha had written earlier that whatever happened, she had no intention of leaving the White House. For months Olga heard nothing. She herself had been evacuated from Moscow in August with other theatrical veterans. On her return in the autumn of 1942 she received a letter from the front, written by a former doctor in Yalta and describing his last visit to Mariya Pavlovna on November 3rd. As dusk began to fall, they had sat on the covered terrace overlooking Chekhov's garden and talked anxiously of the future. All day long there had been air-raids. With each explosion the ground vibrated underfoot, window-panes rattled, and even the mountains appeared to be shaking. Now the silence of the mild autumn evening seemed brooding and unnatural. Next day he had telephoned Mariya Pavlovna to say goodbye . . .[1]

When the Germans entered Yalta, Masha decided to leave the Museum exhibits exactly as they were, but instructed her four female assistants to take down all the portraits of Party leaders from the walls. Then she placed a postcard of the German dramatist, Hauptmann, in an eye-catching position in the front of a show-case filled with photographs of Chekhov's literary contemporaries. Masha was told that the Museum might remain open, but the house would be lived in by a Major and his staff. The Major would take over Anton's study and bedroom on the ground floor. At this, something in the diplomatic Masha's nature snapped. 'That's quite out of the question,' she said, firmly locking the study door, and the Major had to be content with Chekhov's dining-room.²

The occupation lasted two and a half years. During this time one of Masha's assistants died of starvation.³ They kept the life of the Museum going as best they could: showing round occasional German visitors, reading Chekhov's stories aloud, working on a new edition of his letters, and marking each Chekhov anniversary by some modest celebration. Masha, who was eighty in 1943, survived two very serious illnesses: pneumonia, and for the second time in her life, typhoid. The typhoid was concealed from the authorities, as it would have meant her being taken to hospital. Her assistants kept up a round-the-clock vigil at her bedside, and somehow managed to get her on her feet again.⁴

When the Germans evacuated Yalta on the night of April 15th, 1944, they carried out a last bombing raid. Four bombs fell in the garden of the White House, blowing out all the window-panes and shattering the glass in the show-cases. Two months later, the house remained wide open to the elements, and Masha could still hear broken glass crunching beneath the feet of the visitors. But the immediate shock of the bombing was absorbed by the joy of liberation and re-establishing contact with Moscow. Only later did a reaction set in. By June 10th Masha felt certain that her life was coming to an end. One hope alone sustained her: that of seeing once again her beloved Olya (who was herself then lying ill in Moscow) and being able to talk, talk, talk.⁵ Masha slowly rallied, and in August the convalescent sisters-in-law were reunited in Yalta.

With the death in 1946 of Moskvin, the original Tsar Fyodor, Knipper became the last surviving founder-member of the Art

Olga's Last Appearance

Theatre. Kachalov, who had joined the company soon after the start and whose stage career had run so parallel with hers, died on September 30th, 1948, at the age of seventy-three. 'In his final years,' Vilenkin writes in his book about him, 'as their colleagues slipped away one by one, he and Olga Leonardovna became inseparable companions, to the delight of the rest of us, for when they were together, they immediately evoked the distinctive poetic atmosphere of the old Art Theatre. Not because they wallowed in the past, far from it, but because of their generous simplicity of tone, their lively, subtle wit and their genuine interest in what was going on in the world, both in the arts and outside.'[6] Olga recalled him a few weeks before his death, at the sanatorium where they were both being treated, deciding to try out his famous voice and reading with great inspiration a long passage from Tolstoy's *Resurrection*.[7]

Kachalov's death occurred just after Olga's eightieth birthday. In spite of mixed health, she had continued to act right through her seventies, creating her last new role, as Lady Markby in Oscar Wilde's *The Ideal Husband*, in 1946. Her final appearances in Chekhov took place in the 1948-49 season, at the time of the Theatre's fiftieth jubilee celebrations. To her niece she described the special gala evening on October 24th:

I'd been thinking of playing the whole of *The Cherry Orchard* but took fright and limited myself to Act III. . .

When I made my entrance after the *grand rond*, the audience all stood up and went on clapping and clapping—I felt moved to tears. And at the end they stood for more than half an hour, shouting, calling me back time after time—I don't know how I managed to stay on my feet. My dressing-room was one mass of flowers. There's been so much genuine love shown towards me and the Theatre. I'd never really thought of myself as an individual but only as part of our unforgettable team, and now I'm the only one left to accept the spectators' joyful appreciation of what our Theatre has achieved.

When we were already in the car about to leave and they

265

opened the gates, a huge crowd of young people surged forward and for about half an hour wouldn't let the car through. The din was unbelievable. For some reason the lights had gone out inside, so they kept striking handfuls of matches and wouldn't go away. At home quite a crowd of friends had gathered for the evening—we'd taken the precaution of getting food in. I spent the next day in bed, of course.[8]

This spontaneous demonstration of enthusiasm for a non-political figure like Knipper is easy to understand against the background of those bleak post-war Stalin years.

Knipper in her eighties retained something of the vitality that had characterised her throughout life. She suffered from chronic breathing difficulties, her sight began to fail and her daily routine became more and more restricted, but well-intentioned visitors to the small flat that she shared for twenty years with her faithful companion-secretary, Sofiya Baklanova, were in for a surprise if they thought to console a poor half-blind old actress by politely recalling her past triumphs; for the conversation was likely to be subtly turned towards an examination of *their* aims and attitudes in life. Knipper did not indulge in any cult of the past. Material possessions had never meant much to her; most of the ramshackle furniture in the flat belonged to Sofiya. An old icon hung over the bed in Knipper's sparsely furnished little bedroom. The battered armchairs creaked in the dining-room, but there were flowers everywhere and the piano was good enough for Richter to play on. On the walls hung photographs of Chekhov, of the house at Yalta and the cottage at Gurzuf. But as Turovskaya discovered when she began collecting material for her book on Knipper's stage career (to be published in 1959, not long after Knipper's death in April), Olga Leonardovna took no pleasure in recalling the past for its own sake. As in her youth, she displayed an insatiable curiosity about life, wanted to hear all about the latest play or novel, and was always making plans. When her thoughts did go back to the past—and nothing in fact was easier than to set her talking about her favourite Chekhov roles—

she illustrated her remarks so vividly that Turovskaya would suddenly glimpse the charming, youthful smile with which Knipper had captivated audiences as Chekhov's Masha. When her sight failed and she could no longer read, she amused herself on sleepless nights by going over all her old parts—not re-living past glories, however, but discovering how far she had failed to understand the part properly. 'Ah, if only I could play that part *now*,' she would confide.

For many years the big event in the lives of both Olga and Masha was Olga's summer visit to the Crimea. Though five years older, the frail-looking Masha seems to have remained physically the more robust of the two, continuing to supervise all the affairs of the Museum and to preside over all the Chekhov celebrations. When the sisters-in-law were together in Yalta, Anton's name was frequently mentioned, not in tones of hushed reverence, but casually, almost as if he were still a living member of the household.[9] One is reminded of Tuzenbach's remarks to Irina in *Three Sisters*, when he is about to leave for the duel: 'Look at that tree over there. It's dead and withered, but it's still swaying in the breeze with the others. That's how I feel. Even if I die, I'll still have some part or other to play in life.'

In April 1951, following Olga's serious illness of the previous autumn, Masha wrote to her:

> You say I mustn't count on your visit. And whose visit do you expect me to count on? No one in the world is as dear to me as you are, and you know that perfectly well. No one else shall stay in your room while I am alive. You are as much the mistress of the Yalta house as I am, if not more so.[10]

Olga did visit Yalta that summer, only to learn to her dismay that the Gurzuf council was proposing to develop the small headland on which stood her cottage, 'The Blue Gate', with all its Chekhov and Art Theatre associations. She tried at once to rally support: could not the Theatre take over her cottage and its neighbour, put up a more solid dwelling nearby that could be used for actors' vacations all the year round, and so preserve this area of great natural beauty as a memorial to Chekhov and herself? Sadly, her efforts were unavailing. The bureaucratic wheels were slow to turn—or perhaps Olga fought a stubborn rearguard action—but in 1956, by which time she was no longer able to travel there herself, the cottage was boarded up for good while work proceeded on the construction of a military sanatorium. Three shrubs—two oleanders and an agave—were rescued from their tubs by the last tenant, the writer Boris Lavrenev. In 1958 the cottage was sold.[11]

Both sisters-in-law were ill during 1954. 'I feel I shall die soon,' Masha wrote,

> and I'm afraid of not seeing you again. How I'd love to have a talk!
>
> I'm writing in bed and get tired quickly, like you. My heart keeps thumping away and won't give me any peace. The nights are the worst time!
>
> I've been in bed for more than two weeks; even here, of course, I have to go on working.
>
> Olechka, I love you also, you're the person closest and dearest to me—closer than anyone . . . Now, when my life is coming to an end, I feel I want to say so many tender things to you, to say how deeply devoted I am to you . . .[12]

Masha's life was not yet over, but Olga's visit to Yalta that summer was to be her last. Their subsequent communication was by letter and telephone.

September 18th, 1956. Moscow. Dear Mashenka, I was so alarmed by the sound of your tears, I decided something must have happened, but when I realised that your tears were caused by the unexpected nearness of my voice, I became very agitated myself and took a long time to calm down at the end of our conversation.

How can we arrange to see one another? I'd been dreaming of visiting Yalta, if only for a few days, but our journey at the beginning of June showed me that I can't manage even fifty minutes in a car. . . .

Olga's Last Appearance

Writing is difficult for me, but oh, how I'd love to talk!

Masha dear, that's all I can manage. I kiss you and please, don't cry. I'll write again.

October 25th, 1956. Moscow. Dear Masha, the last time you spoke on the telephone, your voice sounded so clear and youthful, as if you were feeling especially pleased about something, am I right?

End of 1956/beginning of 1957. Yalta. Olechka, my dear, my own one, I'm pining for you desperately. I want to see you, I want to talk and talk and talk, complain against fate and so on and so forth. I'm ill all the time and waiting for the end, but still I don't want to die without seeing you again.[13]

On the back of this postcard Olga wrote: 'Masha's last card'. She died on January 15th, 1957, in her ninety-fourth year, having served her brother faithfully to the end as director of the Chekhov Museum.[14]

Masha had gone, the emotional triangle had been finally dissolved more than fifty years after Anton's death, but the Art Theatre remained. Alas, the Theatre was no longer what it was. 'I haven't appeared on stage for a number of years now,' Olga wrote in August 1957 to Massalitinov, one of the members of the Kachalov Group of the twenties, who had settled in Prague. 'Our Theatre gives me absolutely no pleasure, such a glorious beginning and such a miserable end. I'm one of its founders and was a member of our glorious team, so it's not easy for me to feel reconciled.'[15]

Yet she was to be seen once more on the stage of the Art Theatre. By then her appearances in public had become rare events. In the autumn of 1955 she had been to see two acts of Peter Brook's *Hamlet* with Paul Scofield: 'I liked the production very much indeed. They had a terrific success, although some people remained critical.'[16] Deeply rooted in the European cultural tradition, she must have rejoiced to think that with the coming of Khrushchev's Thaw, Russia had abandoned its policy of total cultural isolation, and when in 1958 the Art Theatre made its first ever visit to London, she went out of her way to send English audiences her heartfelt greetings.

The English *Hamlet* may well have been her last public appearance, however, before the evening of October 22nd, 1958, when the Art Theatre decided to celebrate Knipper's ninetieth birthday and the sixtieth anniversary of her stage debut.

Surrounded by celebrities from the theatre and the arts, she took up her seat at the centre of the stage, in the unaccustomed glare of the spotlights. The lengthy ritual of speeches and congratulations began. After a while, reports Turovskaya, 'Olga Leonardovna began to look a little tired by all this ceremonial.' Did her thoughts drift back to a similar occasion in that same theatre many years earlier? January 17th, 1904. The first night of *The Cherry Orchard*. Anton Pavlovich's forty-fourth birthday. She had promised not to breathe a word to him about the elaborate celebration that was planned. How he loathed any kind of fuss or formality. Perhaps he would refuse to come to the theatre after all? That would make a good anecdote. But no, they had fetched him in time for the final interval. And how the audience had cheered. He kept trying to smother his cough and tossing his head back, as if to say: 'There must be some mistake, you know—this really has nothing to do with *me*.' The last time that he had appeared in public. Then Badenweiler, the student's footsteps crunching across the gravel . . .

They had stopped applauding at last, and she was being helped to a seat in one of the boxes. From the stage they still went on offering her presents and congratulations. A group of young actors appeared, wearing old-fashioned officers' uniforms. Of course, *Three Sisters*! And that must be Fedotik coming over towards her, just as he did in the play with his present for Irina: 'By the way, I've something for you. It's a humming top. Makes a wonderful sound.'

Olga Knipper had never been one to miss a cue.

'A green oak by a curving shore,' came the sound of Masha's next lines being spoken from the box in a voice that was cracked but firm and confident.

And on that oak a golden chain,
And on that oak a golden chain.

'For a moment,' writes Turovskaya, 'the clock seemed to turn back. An almost uncanny silence fell on the audience. All that could be heard was the wonderful sound of Fedotik's humming top. Then with one accord everyone stood up—in the stalls, the boxes, the circle . . .

So for the last time on the stage of her beloved Theatre, Knipper spoke the words of her favourite author from her favourite role.'[17]

Notes and References

Chekhov's letters to Knipper are indicated below by dates rather than page references, so that they can be more easily referred to in his *Collected Works*, especially the 1974–82 edition, of which the relevant volumes of Letters have not appeared at the time of writing.

Omissions from quotations are indicated by the insertion into the text of four dots for major omissions and three for minor ones, but minor omissions have not been indicated where this served only to interrupt the flow of the text.

Where a chapter has drawn heavily on a particular source or sources, the latter have been listed at the start of the notes to the chapter.

The abbreviations 'D1', 'D2' and 'V1', 'V2' refer to the Derman and Vilenkin two-volume editions. 'Stanislavsky' refers to *My Life in Art*, except where a volume number is given, in which case it refers to his *Collected Works* (e.g. Stanislavsky 7,267). 'Nemirovich' refers to Nemirovich-Danchenko's *My Life in the Russian Theatre*. Full details of all titles are to be found in the Bibliography.

INTRODUCTION, *pp.* 1–4
1. Chekhova *Pis'ma* 186. 2. V2,146.

1. FINDING A VOCATION, *pp.* 7–17
   Turovskaya 13–23; V1,41–45.
   1. Not 1870, as given in a number of sources. Her year of birth was wrongly entered as 1870 on her passport. In 1940 the Art Theatre took advantage of this mistake to present her with a congratulatory address on the occasion of her 'seventieth' birthday. The victim willingly connived at this deception which persisted for a number of years (see V2,391). 2. Rabeneck 120. In Russian their surname was spelt *Zal'tsa*. 3. D1,22. 4. Nemirovich 203. 5. D2,482. 6. Rabeneck 119. 7. D1,161–62. 8. D2,259. 9. V1,217. 10. Nemirovich 49. 11. V1,91. 12. Quoted by Tatyana Shchepkina-Kupernik, V2,276.

272

Notes and References

2. SUMMER AT PUSHKINO, *pp.* 18–24
 Turovskaya 23–25.
 1. Baedeker 325. 2. Turovskaya 25. 3. Nemirovich 103. 4. Turovskaya 25. 5. Stanislavsky 300. 6. Nemirovich 147.

3. FIASCO, *pp.* 25–32
 1. *Works 1974–82*, vol. 1 (Works), 558. 2. Nov. 16th, 1884. 3. March 28th, 1886. 4. Nov. 24th, 1887. 5. Oct. 21st, 1895. 6. Dec. 14th, 1896. 7. Nemirovich 64. 8. Komisarjevsky 136. 9. Oct. 13th, 1896. 10. Oct. 22nd, Nov. 1st. 11. Dec. 14th. 12. *Works 1974–82*, vol. 6 (Letters), 547.

4. TRIUMPH, *pp.* 33–42
 Chekhova *Iz dal. proshl.* 185–87; Nemirovich, chs. 10 & 11; Stanislavsky, chs. 31 & 34.
 1. *Works 1974–82*, vol. 6 (Letters), 545. 2. Golubov 743. 3. May 16th, 1898. 4. Stanislavsky 321. 5. Golubov 755. 6. V1,98. 7. V1,47. 8. Oct. 8th, 1898. 9. Oct. 21st. 10. Pitcher & Forsyth 15. 11. Golubov 601. 12. Dec. 26th.

5. THE OTHER WOMEN, *pp.* 43–53
 1. Vinogradov 682. 2. Hingley 2. 3. Golubov 521. 4. Ibid. 339. 5. Bunin, Golubov 772. 6. Quoted by Bunin, Golubov 519. 7. Llewellyn Smith 10. 8. Oct. 26th, 1898. 9. March 23rd,1895. 10. Nov. 10th, 1895. 11. Llewellyn Smith 104. 12. Ibid. 62. 13. Ibid. 119. 14. D2,169–70, 213. 15. Llewellyn Smith 186; translated by her from the manuscript in the Lenin Library, Moscow.

6. DEAR AUTHOR ... DEAR ACTRESS, *pp.* 54–65
 Chekhova *Pis'ma* 91–111, 131–49; D1,51 (June 16th, 1899)–141 (March 26th, 1900).
 1. Feb. 14th, 1900. 2. V1,45. 3. V1,51. 4. D1,53. 5. July 21st, 1899. 6. Baedeker 423. 7. V1,53. 8. D1,72. 9. D1,122. 10. Karlinsky & Heim 360–61. 11. D1,94. 12. D1,107. 13. Oct. 4th, 1899. 14. D1,86. 15. Oct. 30th. 16. D1,98–100. 17. Chekhova *Pis'ma* 145. 18. Feb. 10th, 1900. 19. D1,138.

Notes and References

7. ANTON DELAYS, *pp.* 66–77
   D1,142 (April 24th, 1900)–212 (Oct. 22nd, 1900).
   1. Chekhova *Iz dal. proshl.* 211. 2. D1,144. 3. D1,147. 4. V1,56.
   5. V2,16. 6. D1,148–49. 7. D1,160–61. 8. V2,16. 9. Chekhova
   Iz dal. proshl. 221. 10. V2,15–16. 11. Bragin 190. 12. Nemirovich,
   Izbrannye pis'ma 200. 13. D1,169–70. 14. Nemirovich 203.
   15. Chekhova *Pis'ma* 143. 16. V1,55. 17. D1,155–56. 18. D1,185–
   87. 19. Sept. 14th, 1900. 20. D1,193–94. 21. D1,196–98. 22. Sept.
   9th. 23. Simmons 510.

8. WINTER 1900, *pp.* 78–88
   D1,213 (Dec. 11th, 1900)–376 (March 27th, 1901).
   1. Sept. 28th, 1900 (not in Derman). 2. Dec. 15th, 1902. 3.
   D1,163. 4. D1,188,194. 5. D1,161. 6. Aug. 20th, 1900. 7. Sept.
   28th (not in Derman). 8. Nov. 13th. 9. Dec. 12th. 10. Dec. 28th.
   11. Dec. 21st. 12. Dec. 14th. 13. D1,277. 14. Jan. 2nd, 1901.
   15. D1,269. 16. D1,275. 17. Dec. 26th. 18. D1,287. 19. D1,317–19.
   20. D1,340. 21. Nov. 16th, 1900. 22. Jan. 2nd, 1901. 23. Bragin
   191. 24. D1,297–98. 25. D1,353–54. 26. March 11th, 16th.

9. A QUIET WEDDING, *pp.* 89–102
   D1,376 (April 14th, 1901)–405 (May 20th, 1901).
   1. D1,381. 2. D1,379–81. 3. April 22nd, 1901. 4. Date of this letter
   as given in *Works 1944–51,* vol. 19,440. 5. May 20th. 6. June 12th.
   7. Chekhova *Pis'ma* 182–83. 8. V2,22. 9. Chekhova *Iz dal. proshl.*
   224; Stanislavsky 424. 10. Vinogradov 236. 11. V2,290.

10. MASHA'S REACTIONS, *pp.* 103–108
    1. May 25th, 1901. 2. Chekhova *Pis'ma* 183–84. 3. V2,20–21.
    4. Bragin 191–92; V2,24–25. 5. Vinogradov 236. 6. V2,25–26.
    7. Chekhova *Pis'ma* 186–87. 8. V2,27–28. 9. Bragin 126. 10.
    D2,291. 11. Chekhova *Iz dal. proshl.* 225. 12. V1,380. 13.
    Chekhova *Pis'ma* 187.

11. HOPES AND DISAPPOINTMENTS, *pp.* 109–117
    D1,406 (Aug. 21st, 1901)–D2,433 (April 13th, 1902).
    1. Gitovich, 676. 2. Oct. 29th, 1901. 3. V2,27. 4. D1,408. 5. Aug.
    24th, 1901. 6. D2,114. 7. Chekhova *Pis'ma* 198. 8. Sept. 3rd, 1901.
    9. D2,242. 10. D2,245. 11. Jan. 20th, 1902. 12. D2,381. 13. Oct.

Notes and References

19th, 1901. 14. D2,127–28. 15. D2,149. 16. Golubov 783. 17. March 9th, 1902. Chekhov apparently used two verbs, one of which has been censored by Derman and by the editors of *Works 1944–51*. 18. D2,335–337. 19. March 20th, 1902. 20. D2,421–22.

12. THE LYUBIMOVKA CRISIS, *pp.* 118–127
   D2,433 (June 18th, 1902)–520 (Sept. 21st, 1902).
   1. Golubov 147. 2. V2,132. 3. Simmons 566–67. He makes the point that Masha's first letter to Anton three days after their departure was 'a terse little note which included a single chilly reference to Olga: "Greetings to your spouse and be well". 'In letters to Anton, Masha frequently referred to Olga jocularly as 'your spouse', and her note was hurried because she dashed it off while sitting in the Yalta bookshop (Chekhova *Pis'ma* 213). Of the miscarriage Llewellyn Smith writes: 'Those passages deleted by the editors of Olga's letters to Chekhov which deal with this intimate matter make it clear that Olga had reason to believe she was not pregnant, and that she probably could not have prevented the miscarriage even if she had known.' (206, footnote.) 4. Gitovich 708. 5. V2,39. 6. June 25th, 1902. 7. Golubov 648, 656–57. 8. July 18th, 1902. 9. V2,43. 10. *Works 1944–51*, vol. 19, 331; *Works, 1974 82*, vol. 12–13 (Works), 486–87. 11. Golubov 408–10. 12. V2,43. 13. Aug. 17th, 1902. 14. Chekhova *Pis'ma* 205, 207. 15. Aug. 27th, 1902. 16. Aug. 24th. 17. Aug. 22nd. 18. To Stanislavsky (July 18th) and Gorky (July 29th). 19. Aug. 27th. 20. D2,469–71. 21. Sept. 1st. 22. D2,475–76. 23. April 20th, 1904.

13. ANTON'S LAST APPEARANCE, *pp.* 128–139
   D2,520 (Sept. 22nd, 1902)–V1,346 (Dec. 1st, 1903); Stanislavsky, ch. 44.
   1. V2,359. 2. V1,180–81. 3. Jan. 20th, 1903. 4. Dec. 14th, 1902. See *Works 1944–51*, vol. 19, 391; the paragraph about having children is omitted by Vilenkin. 5. Golubov 674–75. 6. May 24th, 1903. 7. To Suvorin, June 17th, 1903. 8. Vinogradov 698. 9. Chekhova *Pis'ma* 216–17. 10. June 7th, 1903. 11. Oct. 21st. 12. Jan. 3rd. 13. Bragin 131. 14. Golubov 678. 15. V2,49–50. 16. V2,52. 17. March 4th, 1903. 18. Stanislavsky 7,267. 19. Dec. 21st, 1903 and Jan. 13th, 1904. 20. V1,59. 21 Nemirovich 218. 22. Gitovich 787. 23. Stanislavsky 422. 24. Nemirovich 219. 25. V1,60. 26. Vinogradov 255.

Notes and References

14. BADENWEILER, *pp.* 140–149

   Rabeneck; V1,62–68 ('July 2nd'); V1,346 (Feb. 15th, 1904)–378 (April 30th, 1904).

   Olga's first Chekhov memoir was published in Prague in 1922. Her article, 'A Few Words about A. P. Chekhov', formed the introduction to the edition of Chekhov's letters to her published in Berlin in 1924, and was translated into English by Constance Garnett in 1926. It was revised for the first volume of the Chekhov-Knipper correspondence, edited by Derman and published in 1934.

   'July 2nd' (the date of Chekhov's death in the Old Style, which Olga had written at the foot of her manuscript) is an untitled, undated rough draft. At one point it refers to 'the late G. B. Iollos', a Russian newspaper correspondent who was very helpful to the Chekhovs in Berlin. As Iollos died in 1907 (see V1,388), 'July 2nd' was probably written not long afterwards. Perhaps Olga intended to publish it in 1910, the year of Chekhov's fiftieth anniversary, but had second thoughts. The published memoirs make no mention of the sympathetic role played by the German doctor in Badenweiler or of the two requiem services that Olga arranged after Chekhov's death, indirectly confirming that 'July 2nd' was written before the outbreak of war against Germany and before the Bolshevik Revolution made religion a taboo subject.

   Rabeneck's account, 'Chekhov's Last Minutes', was published in 1958. It differs from Olga's in certain small points of detail. In spite of the time lag I have tended to prefer his version, for as he points out, he was a very young man at the time, he had never witnessed a death before, and the events impressed themselves on his memory with exceptional clarity.

   1. March 29th, 1904. 2. April 15th. 3. May 22nd. 4. Chekhova *Pis'ma* 22. 5. V2,54. 6. May 22nd. 7. V1,63. 8. Rabeneck 31. 9. Golubov 489. 10. Bunin 9,217. 11. Rabeneck 30. 12. V1,64. 13. Rabeneck 118. 14. V2,58. 15. V1,65–66. 16. This detail incorporated from Olga's published account (V1,62). 17. Last two sentences from the published account (V1,62).

15. OLGA'S LAST LETTERS, *pp.* 150–161

   Chekhova *Iz dal. proshl.* 251–56; V1,379–84.

   1. Bunin 9,217. 2. Rabeneck 34. 3. Rabeneck 35. 4. V1,67. 5. V1,

68. 6. Gorky, Golubov 506. 7. Vinogradov 618. 8. Nemirovich 221–22. 9. Vinogradov 618–19. 10. Ibid. 619. 11. Aug. 3rd, 1901. 12. Bragin 22. 13. A friend of Chekhov's, 'the mentally unstable, occasionally irritating and intellectually formidable lady mathematician' (Hingley 199).

16. VERDICTS, *pp.* 162–170
   1. Vinogradov 700. 2. Hingley 285. 3. Bunin 9,196–197. 4. Bunin 9,213,215. 5. V2,290. 6. Karlinsky & Heim 388–89. 7.D2,464. 8. V1,181.

17. FIRST REVOLUTION AND FIRST TOUR, *pp.* 171–176
   1. Stanislavsky, 7,298,702. 2. V2,66,364. 3. V2,72–73. 4. V2,73–74. 5. V2,75. 6. Nemirovich 316–18. 7. Bragin 134.

18. KNIPPER THE ACTRESS, *pp.* 177–188
   1. D1,361. 2. See Kyril FitzLyon and Tatiana Browning, *Before the Revolution: A View of Russia under the Last Tsar* (London, 1977). The photograph appears on p. 60. 3. Turovskaya 13. 4. V2,341–42. 5. V2,307. 6. V1,264. 7. V1,279. 8. See Chekhov's letter to Knipper, Jan. 2nd, 1900. 9. Turovskaya 178. 10. V2,314. 11. D1,121. 12. D1,302. 13. V2,309. 14. V2,338–39. 15. V1,91. 16. V1,106. 17. V2,324. 18. V2,318–19. 19. V1,226. 20. V2,86. 21. V2,91–93. 22. Stanislavsky 528. 23. V2,93–94.

19. KNIPPER IN CHEKHOV, *pp.* 189–199
   1. V2,76. 2. V1,298. 3. V2,313. 4. Sept. 30th, 1899. 5. D2,10. 6. D2,155. 7. Turovskaya 81. 8. V2,343. 9. Turovskaya 80. 10. Jan. 20th, 1901. 11. Jan. 21st. 12. April 15th, 1901. 13. V1,310. 14. V2,342. 15. V2,71. 16. Turovskaya 101. 17. Oct. 25th, 1903. 18. Turovskaya 92. 19. V2,344–45. 20. V2,345.

20. DEAR TEMPLE, *pp.* 200–212
   1. Steegmuller 10. 2. Ibid. 360. 3. V2,66. 4. Steegmuller 65,66; Stanislavsky 505. 5. Steegmuller 238. 6. Ibid. 163. 7. V1,72. 8. Steegmuller 83. 9. Ibid.206. 10. Ibid. 13. 11. Stanislavsky 7,433. 12. Steegmuller 330 (quoting correspondence). 13. Ibid. 98. 14. Ibid. 286,287. 15. The story of this intriguing theatrical collaboration has been told in detail by Laurence Senelick (see

Bibliography). 16. Craig 249. 17. V2,104. Wrongly dated February
–March 1911. 18. Previously unpublished letter. 19. Words of a
famous Russian gypsy song. 20. Gogol's *The Inspector General*, in
which Knipper played the Mayor's wife. 21. His son and later
biographer, Edward Craig. 22. Craig 253. 23. Stanislavsky 7,428.
24. Duncan 235–36. 25. Steegmuller 308–09. 26. Stanislavsky 7,
429–30. 27. Ibid. 466. 28. Senelick 101. 29. Ibid. 102. 30. Ibid. 103.
31. Craig 258–59. 32. Stanislavsky 521. 33. Craig 270,271. 34. V2,
126. 35. Clurman 97. 36. V2,252–53.

21. UPHEAVAL, *pp.* 213–218

> V2,117–20. The paucity of published letters, especially
> noticeable when compared to the full coverage of 1905,
> makes it hard to assess Knipper's reactions to the events of
> 1917–19. The letters that are published appear heavily
> edited.

1. Chekhova *Pis'ma* 228. 2. Chekhova (Mariya) and Chekhov
(Michael) 47,48. 3. V2,107. 4. Zernov 216–21. 5. Zernov 246.
6. Stanislavsky 550–56. 7. Bragin 159,219. Wrongly dated Feb.
18th/March 3rd, 1920, instead of 1918. The 'family sorrow'
alluded to is not the death in 1919 of old Mrs Chekhov, to whom
Masha refers three lines below, but that of her nephew Vladimir,
Ivan Chekhov's son, in 1917 (see D1,158). 8. Chekhova *Iz dal.
proshl.* 259. 9. V2,119. 10. V2,118,119. 11. V2,118,120. 12. V2,74.
13. V1,186. 14. V2,119,122.

22. THE YEARS OF WANDERING, *pp.* 219–230

> Bertensson 275–337.

1. V2,120. 2. Like so many of the older generation, Olga's own
mother, Anna Ivanovna, also died in 1919. 3. V2,120. 4. V2,341.
5. V2,121. 6. V2,122. 7. V2,344. 8. V2,126. 9. V2,127. 10.
Bertensson 327. 11. V2,130. 12. 'The second half of April',
according to Bertensson (337), but a letter sent to Olga on April
4th implies that she had already been back in Moscow for several
days (V2,131).

23. THE WHITE HOUSE, *pp.* 231–235

1. Kuleshov 172. 2. Bragin 219. 3. Bragin 75–76. 4. Ibid. 162.
5. Kuleshov 159. 6. Ibid. 144. 7. Paustovsky 218–19. 8. V2,132.
9. V2,148.

Notes and References

24. KNIPPER IN AMERICA, *pp.* 236–250

Bertensson 338–99; *New York Times*, Dec. 5th, 1922–May
13th, 1924; Stanislavsky 8,30–90; V2,131–145.
1. V2,132. 2. Stanislavsky 8,41. 3. Bertensson 351. 4. Edwards
226. 5. NYT Jan. 5th, 1923. 6. Stanislavsky 8,39. 7. Ibid. 43.
8. NYT Jan 28th. 9. April 15th. 10. Jan. 23rd. 11. Jan. 9th, 16th,
28th, March 4th. 12. V2,141. 13. V2,140. 14. V2,139. 15.
Stanislavsky 8,49. 16. NYT March 11th. 17. Stanislavsky 8,48.
18. Ibid. 87,500. 19. V2,143. 20. Stanislavsky 8,89. 21. Ibid. 84.
22. V2,145. Dated April 17th, though from their itinerary
one would have expected a date in February (see Bertensson
394).

25. THE DIFFICULT YEARS, *pp.* 251–262

V2,145–93.
1. V2,146,147. 2. V2,381. 3. Stanislavsky 8,29. 4. V2,149.
5. V2,155–56. 6. Roskin 144. 7. V2,307. 8. Zernov 221. 9. V2,162.
10. V2,176. 11. Slonim 318. 12. Clurman 82,84. 13. Ibid. 89,96.
14. Ibid. 88. 15. V1,83–87. 16. Previously unpublished letter.
17. Rabeneck 121. 18. Symons 17, 197–98; Slonim 329–30.
19. V2,317–18.

26. OLGA'S LAST APPEARANCE, *pp.* 263–271

V2,194–272.
1. Kuleshov 150. 2. Bragin 79–80. 3. Ibid. 171. 4. Kuleshov 151;
Bragin 80. 5. Bragin 171. 6. Vilenkin, *Kachalov* 237. 7. V1,114.
8. V2,223. 9. V2,334. 10. V2,232–33. 11.V2,233–34,253,400.
12. V2,244. 13. V2,256,257,259. 14. V2,401. Llewellyn Smith
writes that 'Masha's story has no happy ending' (165). She draws
attention to a comment that Masha made to Olga in 1948, 'I think
I haven't lived my life in vain, although I devoted it partly to my
dear brother', and detects 'a touching note of uncertainty in that
"although" ' (172). Masha has expressed herself clumsily, but the
context of the letter (long description of a Chekhov celebration
over which Masha has presided) and the whole tenor of her life
seem to make any such reservations unlikely. 15. V2,262. 16. V2,
251–52. 17. Turovskaya 244.

Bibliography of Source Material

Except in the case of the translations into English listed below, all translations from Russian sources are my own.

Baedeker, Karl. *Baedeker's Russia 1914* (first published 1914; reprinted London and Newton Abbot, 1971).

Bertensson, S. *Vokrug iskusstva* (Hollywood, (1957)

Bragin, S. G. (ed.) *Khozyaika chekhovskogo doma: vospominaniya, pis'ma* (second edition, enlarged, Simferopol, 1969).

Bunin, I. A. *O Chekhove: nezakonchennaya rukopis'* (New York, 1955).

—*Polnoye sobraniye sochinenii*, 9 vols (Moscow, 1965–67).

Chekhov, A. P. (Alexander). *Pis'ma A. P. Chekhovu yego brata Aleksandra Chekhova* (Moscow, 1939).

Chekhov, A. P. (Anton). *Polnoye sobraniye sochinenii i pisem*, 20 vols (Moscow, 1944–51).

—*Polnoye sobraniye sochinenii i pisem*, 30 vols (Moscow, 1974–82). Works in eighteen volumes, letters in twelve.

Chekhova, M. P. (Mariya). *Iz dalyokogo proshlogo* (Moscow, 1960).

—*Pis'ma k bratu A. P. Chekhovu* (Moscow, 1954).

Chekhova, M. P. (Mariya) and Chekhov, M. P. (Michael). *Dommuzei A. P. Chekhova v Yalte* (Moscow, 1937).

Clurman, Harold. *All People Are Famous* (New York, 1974).

Craig, Edward. *Gordon Craig: The Story of his Life* (London, 1968).

Derman, A. B. (ed.) *Perepiska A. P. Chekhova i O. L. Knipper*. Vol. 1 (Moscow, 1934); vol. 2 (Moscow, 1936); vol. 3 not published.

Duncan, Isadora. *My Life* (London, 1928).

Edwards, Christine. *The Stanislavsky Heritage: Its Contributions to the American and Russian Theatres* (New York, 1965; London, 1966).

Garnett, Constance. *The Letters of Anton Pavlovich Tchehov to Olga Leonardovna Knipper*. Translated from the Russian by Constance Garnett (London, 1926; reissued New York, 1966).

Gitovich, N. I. *Letopis' zhizni i tvorchestva A. P. Chekhova* (Moscow, 1955).

Bibliography of Source Material

Golubov, S. N. and others (ed.) *A. P. Chekhov v vospominaniyakh sovremennikov* (Moscow, 1960).

Hingley, Ronald. *A New Life of Anton Chekhov* (London, 1976).

Karlinsky, Simon and Heim, M. H. *Letters of Anton Chekhov*. Translated from Russian by M. H. Heim in collaboration with Simon Karlinsky. Selection, commentary and introduction by Simon Karlinsky (New York and London, 1973).

Komisarjevsky, Theodore. *Myself & The Theatre* (London, 1929).

Konshina, Ye. N. (ed.) *Pis'ma A. P. Chekhova k O. L. Knipper-Chekhovoi* (Berlin, 1924).

Kuleshov, V. I. and others (ed.) *Chekhovskiye chteniya v Yalte* (Moscow, 1973).

Llewellyn Smith, Virginia. *Anton Chekhov and the Lady with the Dog* (London, 1973).

Magarshack, David. *Stanislavsky: A Life* (London, 1950).

Nemirovich-Danchenko, Vl. I. *Izbrannye pis'ma* (Moscow, 1954).

—*My Life in the Russian Theatre*. Translated by John Cournos (Boston, 1936; London, 1937).

Paustovsky, Konstantin. *Story of a Life, IV: Years of Hope*. Translated by Manya Harari and Andrew Thomson (New York and London, 1968).

Pitcher, Harvey and Forsyth, James. *Chuckle with Chekhov. A Selection of Comic Stories by Anton Chekhov*, chosen and translated by Harvey Pitcher in collaboration with James Forsyth (Cromer, 1975).

Rabeneck, L. L. 'Posledniye minuty Chekhova', *Vozrozhdeniye*, vol. 84 (Paris, December 1958), pp. 28–35.

—' "Serdtse Chekhova" ', *Vozrozhdeniye*, vol. 92 (Paris, August 1959), pp. 117–22.

Roskin, A. *A. P. Chekhov. Stat'i i ocherki* (Moscow, 1959).

Sayler, Oliver M. *Inside the Moscow Art Theatre* (New York, 1925; reprinted 1970).

Senelick, Laurence. 'The Craig-Stanislavsky *Hamlet* at the Moscow Art Theatre', *Theatre Quarterly*, vol. VI, no. 22 (Summer 1976), pp. 56–122.

Simmons, Ernest J. *Chekhov: A Biography* (Boston, 1962; London, 1963).

Slonim, Marc. *Russian Theater from the Empire to the Soviets* (Cleveland, 1961; London, 1963).

Bibliography of Source Material

Stanislavsky, K. S. *My Life in Art*. Translated by J. J. Robbins (Boston and London, 1924).

—*Polnoye sobraniye sochinenii*, 8 vols (Moscow, 1954–61).

Steegmuller, Francis (ed.) "*Your Isadora*": *The love story of Isadora Duncan & Gordon Craig* (New York and London, 1974).

Symons, James M. *Meyerhold's Theatre of the Grotesque: The Post-Revolutionary Productions, 1920-1932* (Miami, 1971; Cambridge, 1973).

Turovskaya, M. *Ol'ga Leonardovna Knipper-Chekhova 1868–1959* (Moscow, 1959).

Vilenkin, V. Ya. *Kachalov* (Moscow, 1962).

Vilenkin, V. Ya. (ed.) *Ol'ga Leonardovna Knipper-Chekhova* (Moscow, 1972). Vol. 1: *Vospominaniya i stat'i. Perepiska s A. P.Chekhovym (1902–1094)*. vol. 2: *Perepiska O. L. Knipper-Chekhovoi (1896–1959). Vospominaniya ob O. L. Knipper-Chekhovoi.*

Vinogradov, V. V. and others (ed.) *Literaturnoye nasledstvo: Chekhov* (Moscow, 1960).

Zernov, N. M. (ed.) *Na perelome: tri pokoleniya odnoi moskovskoi sem'i* (Paris, 1970).

Index

Academy of Sciences, 63
Adler, Stella, 257
Afinogenov, A. N., 255
Aksyonovo, 103–7, 156
Alexandrinsky Theatre (St Peters-
  burg), 28, 29–30, 40
Al Jolson's Theatre (New York), 239–
  41, 243
Altshuller, I. N., 40, 43, 46, 114, 118,
  128, 130–2, 135, 162–3, 165
America, Moscow Art Theatre tours,
  229, 235, 236–50, 251
American Defense Society, 239
A Month in the Country, 177, 178, 185,
  186–8
Andreyev, Leonid, 177, 178
Antigone, 35
Ariadna, 47
Armoured Train 14–69, 254
Astrov (Uncle Vanya), 47, 192, 261
Avilova, Lydia, 48–9, 84–5, 165

Badenweiler, 142–51, 156, 158, 159,
  194, 213, 229, 256, 259, 270
Bakhchisarai, 57, 58, 116
Baklanova, Sofia, 266
Barrymore, John, 240, 245
Batum, 68, 150
Bear, The, 28
Beerbohm, Max, 200
Belgrade, 228
Berlin, 142, 145, 152, 174–6, 190, 200,
  201, 224, 228, 229, 230, 237, 244
Bertensson, Sergei, 219–20, 227, 229,
  237, 238, 244, 278
Bishop, The, 217
Blue Bird, The, 177, 228
Boleslavsky, Richard, 228
Bolshevik Revolution, 215–18
Book Topsy, 206
Borzhom, 150, 224
Boston, 247, 249
Bratislava, 229

Brook, Peter, 212, 269
Brooklyn, 249
Brothers Karamazov, The, 177, 208,
  248
Bulgakov, M. A., 257
Bunin, Ivan, 44, 46, 66, 89, 107, 134,
  143, 150, 162–5

'Cabbage Parties', 178
Charlotte Ivanovna (The Cherry
  Orchard), 121, 140, 195–6
Chebutykin (Three Sisters), 80–1
Chekhonte ('Antosha Chekhonte'),
  25–7, 39, 48, 50, 58, 85, 92, 107,
  110, 128, 136, 147, 152, 153
Chekhov, Alexander Pavlovich
  (brother), 28, 50, 140, 154
Chekhov, Anton Pavlovich, 1–3, 24,
  Chs. 3–16 passim, 171, 172, 177–84,
  Ch. 19 passim, 200, 204, 213, 217–
  18, 219, 226, 228, 231–3, 234–5,
  243, 244, 245, 247, 250, 252–3, 254,
  256, 260, 261–2, 263–4, 266, 267–8,
  269, 270–1; first meeting with Olga
  Knipper, 24, 27, 35; physical
  appearance, 43, 118; fictional
  women, 47, 96–7; attitude to
  Masha, 50–3, 93–4, 96, 103–8,
  132–3; first letter to Olga, 56; becomes Olga's lover, 68; wedding,
  94–5; death, 148; will, 154
Chekhov, Georgii (cousin), 150
Chekhov, Ivan Pavlovich (brother),
  39, 50, 64, 95, 113, 142, 150, 153,
  156, 158, 224, 231, 233, 278
Chekhov, Michael Alexandrovich
  (nephew), 214
Chekhov, Michael Pavlovich (brother),
  47, 50, 153
Chekhov, Nicholas Pavlovich
  (brother), 43, 50
Chekhov, Paul Yegorovich (father), 25,
  37, 95, 153

283

Index

Chekhov, Vladimir Ivanovich (nephew), 216, 278

Chekhova, Mariya Pavlovna (sister), 1, 2, 28, 31, 40, 41, 49, 50-2, 55, 56, 58, 63-5, 66-72, 75, 76, 81, 84, 85-6, 87, Chs. 9 & 10 *passim*, 109, 111, 118, 119, 124, 131-4, 142, 143, 145, 150-1, 153, 154-5, 159, 160, 162-3, 164, 172, 173, 191, 197, 213-14, 216, 219, 221, 224-5, 226, Ch. 23 *passim*, 236, 253, 261, 267-9, 279; fears before *Seagull*, 38-9; rejection of marriage proposal, 52-3; reactions to Anton's marriage, 93-4, 103-8; relations with Olga after marriage, 112-13, 121-2, 155-6; life from 1920-22, 231-5; life from 1941-44, 263-4; death, 269

Chekhova, Yelyena (cousin), 154

Chekhova, Yevgeniya Yakovlevna (mother), 56, 74, 86, 87, 96, 103, 104, 105, 108, 110, 118, 122, 140, 142, 151, 153, 154, 172, 173, 216, 219, 233, 278

Cherry Orchard, The, 47, 121, 134-9, 140, 163, 173, 177, 195-8, 201, 203, 214, 215, 220, 225, 226, 237, 240, 241-3, 246, 247, 254, 265, 270

Chicago, 247, 249, 250

Clurman, Harold, 257

Colony Club, 245

Coolidge, President, 249

Copenhagen, 228, 229

Corbin, John, 240, 244

Craig, Edward, 203, 205, 210, 278

Craig, Gordon, 200-12, 228

Crawford, Cheryl, 198, 257

Death of Ivan the Terrible, The, 61, 67

Denikin, General, 220, 221

Derman, A. B., 79

Detroit, 249

Diaghilev, S. P., 201

Dostoyevsky, F. M., 177, 178, 181, 183, 233, 254

Dragonfly, The, 25

Drama of Life, The, 177

Dreary Story, A, 44

Dresden, 175, 229

Dresden Hotel, 81, 82

Duncan, Isadora, 200-8

Duse, Eleonora, 202, 203, 248-9, 250

Edwards, Christine, 239

Efros, N.Ye., 136

Enemies, 257, 258, 259

Enemy of the People, An, 175

Era, 174-6, 238, 244

Ewald, Professor, 142-3

Fear, 255

Fedotik (*Three Sisters*), 270-1

Fedotova, G., 17

Florence, 202, 204, 205

Freiburg, 144, 151

Gayev (*The Cherry Orchard*), 136, 138, 198, 241, 244, 261

Georgia, 222-6

Germanova, Maria, 226, 230

Gest, Morris, 237, 238-9, 244, 247, 249

Ghosts, 178

Glassby, Lily, 121, 195

Gogol, N. V., 177

Gold, 19

Goncharov, Dmitri, 11-12, 55

Gorky, M. M., 10, 67, 81, 119, 129, 152-3, 165, 174, 177, 181, 256-7, 258

Griboyedov, A. S., 177

Griboyedov Prize, 33

Grigorovich, D. V., 26

Group Theatre (New York), 198, 257

Gurzuf cottage, 63, 68, 108, 132, 154, 190, 217, 221, 225, 235, 266, 267-8

Hamlet, 203, 206, 207, 208-12, 228, 269-70

Hamsun, Knut, 177, 178, 227

Hannele, 38

Hartford, 249

Hauptmann, G., 38, 57, 263

Hedda Gabler, 177

Hermitage Theatre (Moscow), 20, 24, 36

Hingley, Ronald, 43, 163

Ibsen, H., 137, 175, 177, 178, 202, 248

Ideal Husband, The, 265

Innkeeper's Wife, The, 16

Inspector General, The, 177, 178, 205, 278

In the Claws of Life, 177, 227

Iollos, G. B., 155, 276

Index

Irina (*Three Sisters*), 226, 267, 270
Irving, Henry, 200
Ivanov, 27–8, 29–30, 158, 159, 171, 198–9, 249
Ivanov, Vsevolod, 254

Julius Caesar, 135, 137

Kachalov, V. I., 109, 115, 158, 199, 209, 210, 214, 219, 225, 226, 227, 228, 229, 240, 243, 259–60, 265
Kachalov Group, 219–30, 235, 236, 269
Kachalov's son (V. V. Shverubovich), 115, 179, 181–2, 194, 196, 198, 199, 222, 227
Karlinsky, Professor S., 165–6
Keller, General, 152
Kharkov, 219–21, 228, 230
Khrushchev, N. S., 3, 269
Kislovodsk, 181, 208
Klara (*Fear*), 255
Knebel', Maria, 261
Knipper, Anna Ivanovna, *née* Zal'tsa (mother), 7–10, 12–13, 64, 67–8, 72, 95, 119, 278
Knipper, Konstantin Leonardovich (brother Kostya), 7, 9, 56, 167, 135–6, 139, 157, 158
Knipper, Leonard (father), 7–9, 12
Knipper, Olga Leonardovna, first meeting with Chekhov, 24, 27, 35; physical appearance, 54–5; becomes Chekhov's mistress, 68; wedding, 94–5; qualities that appealed to Chekhov, 96–8; relations with Masha after marriage, 112–13, 121–2, 155–6; giving up the theatre, 114–15, 130, 161; miscarriage, 117; reflections on Chekhov's character, 126–7; reactions to 1905 Revolution, 171–4; exchange of letters with Stanislavsky, 185–9; reactions to 1917 Revolution, 216–18, 278; leaving for the West, 224–6; Chekhov memoir, 228–9, 276; 'dropped' after dress rehearsal, 255.
Anna (*Lonely Lives*), 57; Anna Andreyevna (*The Inspector General*), 178; Arkadina (*The Seagull*), 29, 41, 42, 49, 55, 63, 71, 97, 179, 181, 191, 192, 196, 198, 226; Countess Char-

skaya (*Resurrection*), 255; Gertrude (*Hamlet*), 208–9, 212, 228; Irina (*Tsar Fyodor*), 36, 37, 97, 244; Lady Markby (*The Ideal Husband*), 265; Lona Hessel (*The Pillars of the Community*), 137, 178; Masha (*Three Sisters*), 3, 78–9, 80, 84, 109, 181, 191, 192–5, 199, 216, 227, 228, 245, 252, 261, 267, 270–1; Maya (*When We Dead Awaken*), 178; Moskaleva (*Uncle's Dream*), 255; Nastya (*The Lower Depths*), 129, 178, 179, 244; Natalya Petrovna (*A Month in the Country*), 178, 185–9; Ranyevskaya (*The Cherry Orchard*), 3, 47, 138, 173, 191, 195–8, 199, 244, 247, 254, 261, 265; Rebecca West (*Rosmersholm*), 178; Regina (*Ghosts*), 178; Sarah (*Ivanov*), 171, 198–9, 249; Yelyena (*Uncle Vanya*), 47, 62, 84, 191–2, 261
Knipper, Vladimir Leonardovich (brother Volodya), 7, 9, 95, 171, 172, 173, 184, 190, 201
Koni, A. F., 32
Konshina, Liza, 247, 252
Korolenko, V. G., 118
Korsh's Theatre (Moscow), 27
Kostya (*The Seagull*), 29, 251
Kokkoz Valley, 57–8
Kuchukoi, 132
Kulygin (*Three Sisters*), 78
Kundasova, Olga, 157, 277
Kuprin, A. I., 67

La Dame aux Camélias, 49, 191
Lady from the Provinces, A, 244
Lady from the Sea, The, 248
Lady with a Little Dog, 58–9
Lavrenev, Boris, 268
Leipzig, 229
Lensky, Alexander, 13, 16, 28, 34
Levitan, I. I., 55
Levkeyeva, Ye.I., 30
Lilina, M. P., 180, 181, 188–9, 208–9, 214, 256, 263
Literary Heritage, 96
Llewellyn Smith, Virginia, 47, 49, 50, 275, 279
London, 176, 269–70
Lonely Lives, 57, 63

Index

Lopakhin (*The Cherry Orchard*), 196, 198

Lower Depths, The, 67, 129, 135, 137, 175, 177, 179, 228, 240, 244

Lunacharsky, Anatole, 11, 253, 254

Luzhsky, V. V., 158, 250

Lyubimovka, 22, 23, 120–7, 133, 135, 166, 195

Maeterlinck, Maurice, 177

Maklakov, V. A., 207, 224

Mal'tsev, Father, 151–2

Maly Theatre (Moscow), 12, 16, 20, 24, 28, 33

Maly Theatre drama school, 12–13, 16

Marriage Proposal, The, 250

Massalitinov, N. O., 269

Meierhold, Vsevolod, 16, 20, 180, 251–2, 257, 260–1

Melikhovo, 28–9, 30, 31, 37, 46, 51, 52, 55–6, 57, 133, 154

Merchant of Venice, The, 38

Mizinova, Lydia (Lika), 49–50, 56, 63, 97

Molière, 257

Morozov, Savva, 119

Moscow, 1, Ch. 1 *passim*, 21, 24, 25, 27, 28, 30, 31, 36, 40, 48, 49, Chs. 6–9 *passim*, 106, 107, Chs. 11–13 *passim*, 140, 141, 142, 152–4, 155, 162, 163, 166, 172–3, 177, 193, Ch. 20 *passim*, 215, 216–17, 219, 220, 221, 224, 225, 227–8, 229, 230, 231, 233, 235, 236, 240, 246, 248, Chs. 25 & 26 *passim*

Moscow Art Theatre, 1, 3, 18–24, 29, 35–42, 50, 60, 61–3, 78, 81, 84, 97, 109, 111, 119, 128, 134–9, 152, 158, 163, 165, 167, 172, Chs. 18 & 19 *passim*, 202, 203–4, 206, 209–12, 214–16, 219, 221, 223, 225–6, 228, 229, 230, 233, 251–2, Ch. 25 *passim*, 263, 265–6, 267, 269–71, 272; guiding principles, 18–20, 180; Crimean tour (1900), 64–7; St Petersburg tours, 84–5, 116–17, 135, 141, 192, 206; European tour (1906), 173–6, 190, 235, 237, 238; American tours (1923–24), 229, 235–50; Paris tour (1937), 258–60

Moskvin, I. M., 23, 37, 38, 182, 185, 240, 264

Mother, 258

Musical Studio, 228, 240, 254

My Life in Art, 182, 201, 248

Natasha (*Three Sisters*), 47, 79, 105, 107

Nemirovich-Danchenko, Vladimir Ivanovich, 2–3, 21–4, 31, 32, 37, 38, 66, 70–1, 72, 111, 113, 117, 120, 136, 137, 138, 152, 158, 163, 165, 171, 176, 178, 180, 187, 195, 203, 208, 211, 212, 216, 225, 228, 229, 230, 232, 237, 240, 243, 249, 251, 254, 257, 261, 263; teaching at Philharmonic, 14–17, 20; conference with Stanislavsky, 18–20, 33; involvement with *The Seagull*, 33–6, 38–42; attitude to acting, 182–4

Newark, 249

New Haven, 249

New York, 237–50

New York Times, 237–50

Nice, 82

Nikolai Stavrogin, 177

Nina (*The Seagull*), 29, 32, 35, 42, 47, 48, 50, 188

Novodevichy Convent, 153, 157, 158, 159

Novorossisk, 57, 221, 222, 223

Odessa, 221

Orator, The, 153

Oreanda, 59

Ostroumov, Professor, 131–2, 133

Ostrovsky, A. N., 177

Paris, 165, 176, 224, 237, 239, 246, 248, 256, 258–60

Paskhalova, A. A., 180

Paustovsky, Konstantin, 233–5

Peer Gynt, 177

Pension Russe, 82–3

Perm, 119–20, 121, 123, 127

Philadelphia, 247, 249

Philharmonic School, 13–16, 20, 23, 24, 34, 178, 182, 251

Pillars of the Community, 137, 178

Pittsburgh, 249, 250

Podgorny, N. A., 221, 228, 229

Potapenko, I. N., 45, 46, 50

Poti, 223

Prague, 176, 224, 228, 229, 237

286

Index

Prague Group, 230, 269
Prozorov, Andrei (*Three Sisters*), 78
Pushkin, A. S., 11, 194, 270–1
Pushkino, 21–3, 34, 182
Pushkin Prize, 26

Rabeneck, Leo, 143–4, 147–9, 150–1, 158, 259–60, 276
Rachmaninov, S. V., 67
Raikh, Zinaida, 260
Reinhardt, Max, 249
Resurrection, 255, 265
Revolution (1905), 171–4, 217
Richter, Svyatoslav, 266
Rigoletto, 260
Roksanova, M., 23, 42
Romeo and Juliet, 257
Rosmersholm, 178, 202, 203
Rostov, 221–2
Russian Thought, 140, 153
Russo-Japanese war, 141, 143, 152, 158, 171

St Petersburg, 13, 28, 29, 30, 31, 39, 45, 49, 56, 72, 88, 118, 139, 152, 157, 201, 206–8; see also Moscow Art Theatre, St Petersburg tours
Sakhalin, 44
Savitskaya, Margarita, 15, 20, 21, 181, 208–9
Schwörer, Doctor, 143, 146–8, 151, 159, 256
Scofield, Paul, 269
Seagull, The, 24, 27, 29–32, 33–42, 48, 49, 55, 61, 62, 63, 81, 129, 138, 172, 181, 191, 195, 261
Senelick, Laurence, 209, 277
Sergeyenko, P. A., 48
Sevastopol, 66, 67, 68, 72, 89, 117, 221, 233
Shalyapin, F. I., 141, 152–3, 233, 235
Shaw, Martin, 206
Shverubovich, V. V., *see* Kachalov's son
Simferopol, 116, 232
Simmons, E. J., 275
Skobelev March, 227
Sofia, 224, 227–8
Sparrow Hills, 73
Stalin, J. V., 257
Stalinist Terror, 3, 258

Stanislavsky (Alekseyev), Konstantin Sergeyevich, 16–17, 20–4, 34, 36–42, 66, 67, 69, 71, 72, 81, 83, 117, 118, 119, 120, 121, 134, 136, 137–9, 141, 143, 171, 173, 178, 179, 180–4, 201, 202, 206–11, 214–16, 225, 226, 228, 251–2, 254, 255, 256, 257, 260; conference with Nemirovich-Danchenko, 18–20, 33; exchange of letters with Olga Knipper, 185–9; system of acting, 181, 182, 186–7, 188, 251; in America, 237–50.
  Astrov (*Uncle Vanya*), 192, 261; Dr Stockmann (*An Enemy of the People*), 175; Gayev (*The Cherry Orchard*), 138, 198, 241–3, 244, 261; Trigorin (*The Seagull*), 41, 42; Vershinin (*Three Sisters*), 109, 193, 194, 252, 255, 261
Stanislavsky Heritage, The, 239
Steegmuller, Francis, 202
Steppe, The, 26
Student, The, 250
Sulerzhitsky, L. A., 207
Sumbatov-Yuzhin, A. I., 33, 34
Suvorin, Alexander, 31–2, 36, 40, 46, 48, 52, 85, 165

Taganrog, 25, 35, 45, 97, 135, 154
Tarasova, Alla, 261
Taube, Dr, 142
Teacher of Literature, A, 47
Terry, Ellen, 200, 211
This Happy Day, 31
Thomas, A. E., 243
Three Sisters, 75, 78–86, 109, 117, 174, 177, 181, 190, 191, 192–5, 214, 216, 227, 228, 240, 244, 245, 246, 247, 252, 254, 261–2, 270–1
Tiflis, 68, 223–5
Tikhonov, A. N., 120
Tolstoy, A. K., 61
Tolstoy, L. N., 8, 27, 44, 186–7, 255, 265
Trigorin (*The Seagull*), 27, 29, 41, 42, 48, 50, 226, 261
Trofimov (*The Cherry Orchard*), 121, 196
Tsar Fyodor, 23, 36–9, 174, 175, 177, 228, 239–40, 244
Tsar Nicholas II, 117
Turgenev, I. S., 33, 177, 178, 185, 244

Index

Turovskaya, M., 180, 192, 196, 197, 255, 266, 270–1
Tuzenbach (*Three Sisters*), 173, 251, 261, 267

Uncle's Dream, 254, 255
Uncle Vanya, 28, 40, 47, 61–2, 66, 67, 81, 135, 174, 177, 192, 203, 244

Van'ka, 232
Vershinin (*Three Sisters*), 78, 79, 109, 166, 193–4, 227, 252, 255, 261
Vienna, 82, 228, 229
Vilenkin, V.Ya., 2, 255, 265
Vishnevsky, Alexander, 23, 35, 55, 66, 73, 119, 120, 131, 133, 135, 173, 263
Volunteer Army, 220, 221, 222

Warfield, David, 240
Warsaw, 176
Washington, 249
When We Dead Awaken, 178
White House (Yalta), 61, 66, 132–3, 154, 159–60, 213, 221, 226, 231–5, 253, 263–4, 266, 267

Wilde, Oscar, 265
Wood Demon, The, 28, 29
Worth of Life, The, 33
Writers' Union, 257

Yakunchikova, Mme, 133
Yalta, 1, 36, 40, 42, 43, 53, Chs. 6–11 *passim*, 118, 119, 121–2, 123, 127, 129–37, 140, 141, 142, 143, 144, 150, 153, 154, 155, 156, 157, 159–60, 162, 163, 165, 166, 193, 216, 219, 268, 269; see also White House (Yalta)
Yavorskaya, Lydia, 49, 84, 97
Yekaterinodar, 222
Yepikhodov (*The Cherry Orchard*), 121

Zagreb, 228, 237
Zal'tsa, Alexander Ivanovich (Uncle Sasha), 10–11, 62–3, 80–1, 95, 141, 158, 160
Zal'tsa, Karl Ivanovich (Uncle Karl), 10, 62, 141
Zernov, Dr, 214, 215
Zernova, Sonya, 214, 215, 256, 258–9